13.99

TUDOR BRIT
1485–1603

Roger Lockyer and
Dan O'Sullivan

Contents

Contents

Contents

Editorial introduction

This aim of this book is to give you as clear a picture as possible of the events and developments in the period you are studying. You may well be using this book to prepare for an examination and the book has several special features, listed below, to help you in this. Most of all, we hope it will help you to develop a critical awareness about, and a continuing interest in, the past.

FOCUS: Each chapter has a main focus, listed in the contents. These are the main issues and 'concepts', like cause and consequence, the evaluation of evidence, the role of the individual, key themes, historical controversies or interpretations and so on. All of these are important in studying and understanding history. Identifying a focus does not mean that the chapter only looks at the past in one way; rather that you are encouraged to find out about topics from a different slant.

TIME CHARTS: Most chapters begin with a time chart. It helps you follow the chronology. Some time charts develop a basic point which is not in the main text. You should also find that the charts provide you with a handy reference point.

KEY TERMS: There are some words or phrases which it is important to know in order to understand a wider topic. These have been highlighted in the text so that you can easily look up what they mean. Sometimes quite simple ideas appear in unfamiliar form or in jargon. Decoding these should help you to make sense of the wider ideas to which the terms relate. Towards the end of the book you will find a separate index of the key terms.

PROFILES: There is not space in a book like this to provide full biographies of the people you will meet. The profiles give you the information you need to understand why an individual is important and what his or her main achievements were. Like the time charts, you might want to use these for reference. As with 'key terms', there is a separate index of people who are the subject of profiles.

TASKS and ACTIVITIES: Nearly all the chapters end with some suggestions for follow-up work and further study. These include:

- guidance on how, and why, to take notes
- suggestions for class discussion and debate

- help on how to use historical evidence of different types
- tips on answering source questions
- hints on planning and writing essays
- specimen examination questions so that you can prepare for assessment.

These tasks are listed in the contents.

FURTHER READING: You will find that you need more help on certain topics than can be provided in a book like this. The further reading guides you to some more detailed or specialist texts. The reading is listed with the most immediately obvious supporting texts placed first, followed by others – some of which may be considerably more detailed – and ending with articles and other shorter pieces, where these are appropriate.

INDEX: Many individuals, issues and themes are mentioned in more than one chapter. The index is designed to help you find what you are looking for quickly and easily by showing you how to collect together information which is spread about. Get practice in using an index; it will save you a lot of time.

The historian's job is to recreate the past. On one level, this is obviously an impossible task. There is far too much of it to put into one book while at the same time much of the information we need has been long since lost. Most of it can never be recovered. It is because there is so much of it that the historian has to impose his or her priorities by selecting. It is because so much more has been lost that he or she has to try to fill in the gaps and supply answers which other people can challenge. The processes of **Selection** and **Interpretation** are the key tasks of the historian and they help to make the subject endlessly fascinating. Every time a historian makes a decision about what to put in and what to leave out that decision implies a judgement which others might challenge. Historians try to get as close to the truth as they can, in the knowledge that others may disagree with what they say. Don't be surprised, then, to find a number of personal views or 'interpretations'. Some of these will make comparisons between the present and the period you are studying. These personal views have not been included in order to persuade you to agree with them. We aim to make you *think* about what you are reading and not always to accept everything at face value. If this book helps you to tell the difference between fact and opinion while keeping up your interest in the past, it will have served its purpose.

Christopher Culpin
Eric Evans
Series Editors

Part One   **1485–1558**

1 England in 1485

When Henry VII defeated Richard III at the Battle of Bosworth and thereby inaugurated the rule of a new, Tudor dynasty, England was not – in economic, cultural or military terms – one of the leading nations of Europe. Scotland was a separate and often hostile kingdom; English rule in Ireland was confined to the area around Dublin known as the Pale; Wales, and in particular the Welsh borderlands, were in a state of perpetual disorder; and the English crown had long since lost all its lands in France, with the exception of Calais. English armies, over-influenced by memories of Agincourt and Crecy, still relied on the bow, whereas other nations were moving over to firearms. Moreover, the culture of the Renaissance, which had permeated Italy as well as England's near-neighbour, Burgundy, had not yet made its impact felt. As for the English language, it was not among those which a cultivated foreigner might feel the need to acquire.

Population and the economy

Before the mid fourteenth century the population of England and Wales was between four and five million, possibly even higher, but the Black Death of 1348–9, and successive outbreaks of plague reduced it to as low as two million by 1450. After this, very gradually the figure started to creep up again, although it was not until well into the seventeenth century that the population got back to its pre-Black Death level. The Tudor period still suffered outbreaks of plague and other epidemics, but with certain exceptions (see chapter 13) these tended to be local.

The stagnant rate of population growth during the fifteenth century led to conditions of comparative prosperity for many. Food prices were low and so were rents, whereas money wages had risen to reflect the smaller labour force available after the Black Death. Another result of the scarcity of labour was that it became possible for **villeins** to commute these services into rent, so that villeinage was on the way out by 1500. Generally, the fifteenth century was a good age for labourers and the poor, but the following century, with its rising population and its unprecedented inflation, was to change all that.

Ninety per cent of the population lived in the countryside and earned their living from the land, although methods of farming varied widely. England was not a single economic unit but rather a collection of regional

KEY TERM:

Villeins

Those peasants who were tied to the land and under obligation to do personal labour for their lord.

economies, each of which was largely self-supporting. There was a broad division between the highland zone, north and west of a line drawn between Weymouth and Teesside, and the more densely populated lowlands south and east of that line. On the moorlands and hills to the north and west pastoral farming predominated, whereas the lowland zone tended to support mixed animal and arable husbandry under the open-field system (see chapter 29). In many areas throughout the country the accent was on the production of wool, which was far and away England's biggest export. Wool merchants, banded together as the Merchants of the Staple, exported their wares to the rest of Europe via Calais, their staple town. However, by the early sixteenth century the production and export of woollen cloth, under the control of the Merchant Adventurers, was beginning to take over from the trade in raw wool (see chapter 30). Within England, consumer demand was for a restricted range of products – woollen textiles, leather goods, building materials, household implements – and these, along with raw materials and food, were the main items in domestic trade.

The remaining ten per cent of the population lived in towns, of which there were several hundred, ranging in size from London, which had perhaps 50,000 inhabitants, to many with less than 1,000. Outside London, the largest towns were Norwich, Bristol, Coventry, Exeter and Salisbury, though none had over 12,000 inhabitants. Some previously prosperous towns had declined owing to changes in trade patterns. York, for instance, had been the second city in the kingdom in the fourteenth century but had been hit badly by the closing of the Baltic trade to English merchants, and was now down to ninth place, going by taxable wealth. On the other hand, Southampton and Exeter had recently risen in the pecking order. Although towns, especially London, had a higher death rate than the countryside, due to insanitary conditions and epidemics, they attracted migrants from rural areas and were swelling in size. This was in spite of the fact that municipal authorities did their best to keep out strangers, especially the 'vagabonds and beggars' who were a strain on the public purse (see chapter 28).

The king's government

The office of monarch was a very exacting one, and the king's personal qualities were a crucial factor in the efficiency of government. To be king required physical energy, constant application, and talent. Unfortunately, there was no guarantee that every monarch would possess such qualities. In Henry VI, for instance, they were conspicuously lacking, and it was during his long but ineffective reign (1422–61) that the so-called Wars of the Roses – a term unknown at the time, and probably invented by

Sir Walter Scott in the nineteenth century – commenced. After several rounds of civil war Henry was deposed and killed by his more forceful Yorkist rival, who succeeded him as Edward IV. It was Edward's brother and successor, Richard III, who was defeated and killed at the Battle of Bosworth in 1485, leaving a vacant throne for Henry Tudor to claim.

With the benefit of hindsight, we can see that Bosworth signalled the end of the Wars of the Roses, but this was not obvious to contemporaries. The Yorkists were far from reconciled, and in 1487 Henry had to fight another battle – at Stoke, near Newark (see chapter 2) – to keep his hold on the throne. Even after that he could not afford to relax his guard. Although he had two sons to succeed him, the death of the eldest, Prince Arthur, in 1502, left the future of the Tudor dynasty in doubt. Arthur's younger brother, Prince Henry, was the nominal heir, but a peaceful transfer of power from the first to the second Tudor was far from certain. One of Henry VII's officials told him of a conversation at Calais in which there was a discussion of what would happen when the King died:

> *'Some of them spake of my lord of Buckingham, saying that he was a noble man and would be a royal ruler. Other there were that spake ... in like wise of your traitor, Edmund de la Pole, but none of them ... spake of my lord prince [Henry].'*

The first Tudor, when he seized the throne, acquired the major departments of state which had come into existence during the Middle Ages – principally the Exchequer and Chancery. He also followed tradition by appointing a royal council to advise him. But this did not mean that Henry could leave the government of his kingdom to run on 'auto pilot'. Everything depended on the king, for he was the source of energy which made the machine function. The fate of the Tudor dynasty would have been very different if Henry VII had been a less effective ruler. By paying constant attention to every aspect of government and insisting on obedience to his will from all his subjects, high and low, Henry VII restored the royal authority and established the foundations on which his heirs could build.

Henry was, of course, a Catholic – as were his subjects – and there was no suggestion during his reign of any breach between the crown and the papacy. As a new ruler who needed to win prestige both at home and abroad, Henry valued the support of the Pope. He also valued the services provided to the royal government (at minimum cost) by the leading English churchmen. Chief among the royal councillors was John Morton, whom the Pope, at Henry's request, appointed Archbishop of Canterbury

Figure 1.1 *Henry VII's chapel at Westminster Abbey, London*

in 1486. The following year Henry put Morton in charge of the whole royal administration by making him Lord Chancellor. Another senior cleric and administrator was Richard Fox, whom Henry chose as his secretary, rewarding him with the bishopric of Exeter.

In religion, then, Henry was conventional and conservative. Likewise, in government, he generally followed the paths that had been laid out by his predecessors. Bosworth was a break with the recent past, but the Wars of the Roses had been untypical. Generally speaking, medieval England had been a peaceful and well-ordered state, and Henry VII aimed to restore his kingdom to this happy condition. He took over the established systems in church and state and made them work to maximum advantage.

2 Was Henry VII an innovator?

Time chart

1422: Death of Henry V; Henry VI succeeds as a minor

1461: Henry VI deposed by Edward, Duke of York, who defeats Lancastrians at Towton and seizes throne as Edward IV

1469: Edward briefly imprisoned by Nevilles

1470: Warwick 'the kingmaker' drives Edward into exile and restores Henry VI

1471: Edward returns from France and defeats Warwick. Henry Tudor goes into exile in Brittany

1474: Edward IV invades France

1481: Brief war against Scotland

1483: Death of Edward IV. His brother assumes the crown as Richard III

1485: Henry defeats and kills Richard at Bosworth

1487: Lambert Simnel defeated at Stoke

1489: Treaty of Medina del Campo between England and Spain

1496: Henry joins Holy League. Brief war against Scotland

1497: Perkin Warbeck lands in Cornwall and is captured

1509: Death of Henry VII

On 22 August 1485 the forces of Henry Tudor, amounting to some 5,000 men, took on those of Richard III which outnumbered them by two to one. The ensuing battle has been described as one of the most sordid ever fought on English soil, because Henry's success was largely due to the calculated treachery of certain commanders. The Earl of Northumberland, commanding Richard's right wing, refused to fight, and the Stanley brothers, powerful landowners in North Wales and Cheshire, kept their forces on the sidelines for most of the battle but joined in on Henry's side at the crucial moment. Sordid or not, Bosworth has been seen as a landmark in English history, enshrined in textbooks and exam syllabuses as the dividing line between medieval and modern. Certainly it was this victory and not his hereditary claim to the throne – which was weak – that ensured Henry the throne. He dated the official start of his reign from the day before the Battle of Bosworth, so that he could declare

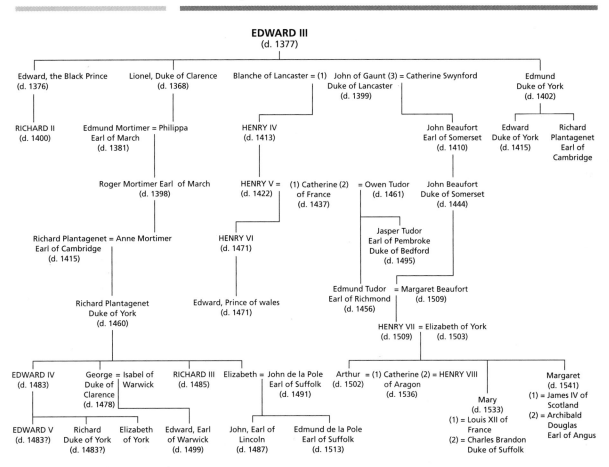

EDWARD III
(d. 1377)

Edward, the Black Prince (d. 1376)

Lionel, Duke of Clarence (d. 1368)

Blanche of Lancaster = (1) John of Gaunt (3) = Catherine Swynford
Duke of Lancaster
(d. 1399)

Edmund Duke of York (d. 1402)

RICHARD II (d. 1400)

Edmund Mortimer = Philippa
Earl of March
(d. 1381)

HENRY IV (d. 1413)

John Beaufort Earl of Somerset (d. 1410)

Edward Duke of York (d. 1415)

Richard Plantagenet Earl of Cambridge

Roger Mortimer Earl of March (d. 1398)

HENRY V = (1) Catherine (2) = Owen Tudor
(d. 1422)   of France   (d. 1461)
            (d. 1437)

John Beaufort Duke of Somerset (d. 1444)

Richard Plantagenet = Anne Mortimer
Earl of Cambridge
(d. 1415)

HENRY VI (d. 1471)

Jasper Tudor Earl of Pembroke Duke of Bedford (d. 1495)

Richard Plantagenet Duke of York (d. 1460)

Edward, Prince of wales (d. 1471)

Edmund Tudor = Margaret Beaufort
Earl of Richmond (d. 1509)
(d. 1456)

HENRY VII = Elizabeth of York
(d. 1509)   (d. 1503)

EDWARD IV (d. 1483)

George = Isabel of
Duke of | Warwick
Clarence
(d. 1478)

RICHARD III (d. 1485)

Elizabeth = John de la Pole
Earl of Suffolk
(d. 1491)

Arthur = (1) Catherine (2) = HENRY VIII
(d. 1502) of Aragon   (d. 1536)

Mary (d. 1533)
(1) = Louis XII of France
(2) = Charles Brandon Duke of Suffolk

Margaret (d. 1541)
(1) = James IV of Scotland
(2) = Archibald Douglas Earl of Angus

EDWARD V (d. 1483?)

Richard Duke of York (d. 1483?)

Elizabeth of York

Edward, Earl of Warwick (d. 1499)

John, Earl of Lincoln (d. 1487)

Edmund de la Pole Earl of Suffolk (d. 1513)

Figure 2.1 Lancastrians, Yorkists and Tudors

Richard's supporters to be traitors and confiscate their lands. And he arranged his coronation just before the first meeting of Parliament so that it could never be said that Parliament had made him king. The following January he strengthened his position still further by marrying Edward IV's daughter, Elizabeth of York, thus uniting the Houses of York and Lancaster (see Figure 2.1).

This chapter is about change and continuity in the field of political history. In it we ask: how far is it justifiable to see Bosworth as a crucial landmark in English history? Or, to put it another way, was Henry VII an innovator, or was he mainly carrying on with methods which had been initiated by previous monarchs?

Twenty-four years before Bosworth another claimant to the English throne had won another battle and become king. In 1461 Edward, Duke of York, defeated his Lancastrian enemies at Towton, near York, and seized the throne. Edward IV's reign lasted 21 years, nearly as long as Henry's, although he was temporarily ousted between 1469 and 1471. He, too, was to die unchallenged, with a full treasury and a realm at

Figure 2.2 A portrait of Edward IV

Figure 2.3 A portrait of Henry VII painted in 1505

peace. So was Henry merely an Edward IV mark II, or did his reign contain original features?

An older generation of historians took the latter view, seeing Bosworth as the opening of a 'new monarchy'. A powerful influence behind this view has always been the work of Francis Bacon whose *History of King Henry VII* was produced in 1622. Bacon made Henry out to be a reserved, cold and somewhat unloved character, but nevertheless a fountain of wisdom and especially a great legislator, 'the best law-giver in the nation after King Edward I'. However, Bacon was writing over a century after Henry's death, and furthermore he was trying hard to regain the favour of his own monarch, James I, who was of course Henry's descendant.

In recent years historians have inclined towards a more modest view of Henry VII, arguing that he followed policies that had been initiated by his predecessors, Richard III and Edward IV. But perhaps this 'revisionist' interpretation has itself gone too far and requires modification? It is impossible to cover the whole of Henry's reign in a short chapter so we shall consider here three key areas, chosen in order to see just how innovatory he was: finance; relations with the nobles; and foreign policy.

Finance

Money was a subject which lay close to Henry VII's heart, probably owing to the insecurity created by his years of exile in France and Brittany. A full treasury was a way of insuring against ever again having to go on his travels. It is also clear that Henry possessed a flair for finance; both contemporaries and historians have emphasised his success in this field.

The Exchequer, which had always been the main department for receiving and paying out government money, was bureaucratic, slow and over-specialised. So Edward IV had developed a new, more flexible, system which he could personally keep his eye on, as it was based on the Chamber, part of the royal household (see chapter 4). This system originated from the way the great nobles administered their estates and it involved officials known as receivers and auditors, responsible for getting in, and checking, the rents. Immediately after Bosworth, when Henry's mind was no doubt on other things, Exchequer officials had reintroduced the old methods. But within a few years Henry, like Edward before him, was using the Chamber to process the bulk of his revenue. We know this because the account books of about forty of the royal receivers have survived, as have the books recording payments out of the Chamber between 1495 and 1509, drawn up by John Heron, treasurer of the Chamber (see Figure 2.4). These sources prove how much Henry had in

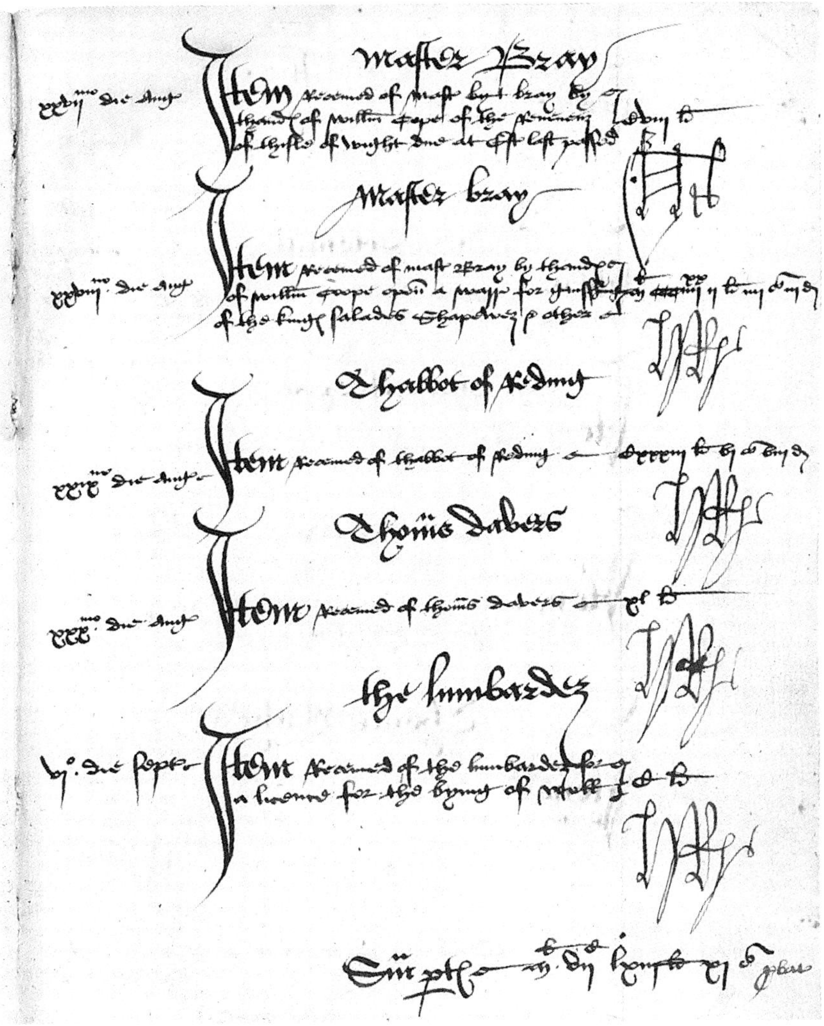

Figure 2.4 A page from the Book of Receipts of the Treasurer of the King's Chamber. Each item has been checked by Henry VII. A comparison of the first two items shows how, in August 1492, the king altered his 'sign manual' so that he could write more quickly.

common with his Yorkist predecessors in what has been called 'the great land revenue experiment' of 1461 to 1509.

However, the evidence also shows that Henry was much more successful than Edward when it came to maximising his revenues. This is especially true of the largest source of income, the crown lands, which were yielding £15,000 or less per year in Edward's reign, but about £42,000 by the end of Henry's. This is partly because Henry supervised his accounts more closely than Edward and drove his receivers harder, but mainly because Edward gave away many of his estates to prominent supporters or close relatives. Henry, of course, was lucky that he did not have many close relatives. He had no brother; his only uncle, Jasper, died in 1495; and he was careful not to give away much to his wife's relatives, the Woodville connection, to whom Edward had been over-generous.

Recognizances

Recognizances, or bonds, were a source of income which Henry developed to a fine art. They were principally a way of ensuring that Henry's more important subjects obeyed the law and lived in peace. Nobles and gentlemen who offended the king, or whose conduct was a threat to public order, were obliged to accept recognizances committing them to pay a specified sum of money if they broke the conditions laid down (see the profile of Lord Burgavenny on page 12). It has been reckoned that out of 62 peers in existence between 1485 and 1509, 46 were under recognizance at one time or another. And there were probably thousands of gentlemen similarly bound. It was Henry's method of holding the upper classes to ransom for their good behaviour. But although effective from the king's point of view, it was deeply resented by the English landowners, on whose loyalty and cooperation the Tudor monarchy ultimately depended.

Council Learned

Under Henry VII various tribunals or committees of councillors were set up for specialist tasks and of these the most important was the **Council Learned**, composed mainly of lawyers. It was responsible for collecting the King's debts and prosecuting defaulters. It also played a key role in drawing up bonds and recognizances. Although it significantly increased the King's income it was accused of acting in a high-handed manner. Two of its leading members, Richard Empson and Edmund Dudley, were executed by the young Henry VIII in a bid for popularity at the outset of his reign.

Other sources of revenue which Henry exploited with much more zeal than Edward included feudal dues and **recognizances**. As their feudal lord Henry could claim certain 'incidents' from leading landowners, his tenants-in-chief. For instance, if the holder of an estate died without heirs then the land 'escheated', or reverted, to the crown. If the heir was a minor, then the 'wardship' (*i.e.* the right to look after both heir and land) went to the king. In the case of a young heiress the king had the (very profitable) right to dispose of her in marriage. Similarly, all tenants-in-chief had to contribute an 'aid' on special occasions, specifically the knighting of Henry's son Arthur and the marriage of his daughter Margaret. All these feudal obligations were quite legal but Henry pursued them with particular energy. In fact, there was a special tribunal of councillors known as the **Council Learned** which specialised in such cases.

Edward IV inherited a considerable debt when he succeeded to the throne, but he died solvent. Henry VII not only became solvent quite early in his reign but secured a surplus in his later years. Some of this he spent on an ambitious building programme, which included a new palace at Richmond in Surrey and an elaborate chapel at the east end of Westminster Abbey, where he planned to be buried. He, like Edward, maintained a Renaissance court which featured 'impressive ceremonial, lavish displays of costly clothing, decorations, jewels and plate, festivity on appropriate occasions, pageantry, banqueting, jousting, music, dancing, disguisings, revels, play-acting …' Furthermore, he was able to leave to his son perhaps £200,000 in jewels and plate (the contemporary form of investment).

Was the reputation for greed and avarice which Henry undoubtedly acquired in his later years justified? The discovery in 1971 of a previously unknown document in a private archive belonging to the Marquis of Anglesey seems to show that it was. This document is a confession by Edmund Dudley of 84 cases of unjust exactions for which he thought compensation was due. Dudley wrote this confession after Henry VII's death and when he was himself a prisoner in the Tower of London awaiting execution, so he had no reason to lie. It seems that Henry was able to 'live of his own', as the contemporary phrase had it, but only at the price of considerable ruthlessness and unpopularity.

Relations with the nobility

It was chiefly over the nobility that Henry VII had to assert himself if he wanted to uphold his authority as a monarch. During the Wars of the Roses, nobles had taken advantage of factional strife to increase their own power. Edward IV was a strong king who had done something to

PROFILE: *Earl of Surrey*

Thomas Howard, Earl of Surrey (1443–1524), had supported Richard III at Bosworth alongside his father, John, Duke of Norfolk, who was killed in the battle. Thomas was imprisoned in the Tower by Henry and convicted of treason, thus losing all his estates. Gradually, he recovered his high position owing to his value as a councillor and a general. Released from prison in 1489 his attainder (conviction) was reversed, the earldom restored and he was sent up north to control the unruly Scottish border region after the death of the Earl of Northumberland. Later that year he was given back the original Howard family estates but not the lands acquired by his father under the Yorkists. His military achievements against the Scots secured him further favours and in 1501 he was appointed treasurer of the Exchequer. However, Henry never let him become as powerful as his father had been, and it was not until the next reign, after he had won the Battle of Flodden (1513), that he regained the ancestral dukedom of Norfolk.

reverse this trend, but Henry had a more dominating relationship to the nobility than his predecessor did. In the first place, while Edward made nine new earls, Henry made only two – his stepfather Lord Stanley, who became Earl of Derby, and Edward Courtenay, Earl of Devon. Secondly, as Alexander Grant has pointed out, there were no 'super-nobles' in Henry's reign. Edward had allowed magnates such as his mother's brother, Earl Rivers, to become still more powerful by showering land on them and authorising them to act as virtually independent trouble-shooters in their particular areas of the country. Henry could not do away with strong regional nobles altogether, nor would he have wished to – he was not 'anti-noble'. Thus, Lord Stanley controlled Lancashire and Cheshire, and Henry's uncle Jasper dominated Wales until his death in 1495. Other peers – such as John de Vere, Earl of Oxford – were prominent members of Henry's council. But they were all carefully watched and their power closely balanced against their loyalty. Henry was cautious about rewarding too generously even those nobles who were most useful to him, such as the **Earl of Surrey**.

One major problem connected with the nobility was **retaining**. Both Edward and Henry passed acts concerned with retaining, and it used to be argued that they were trying to end it altogether. However, we know that retaining continued throughout the sixteenth century, and it seems unlikely that Henry would have promoted a series of acts which he could not enforce. The truth is that he recognised a noble's right to his retinue;

KEY TERM:

Retaining

A great lord could retain servants or followers to serve him in war or peace. They would wear his livery, meaning his uniform or badge, and he would 'maintain' them (*i.e.* look after their interests). But this 'good lordship' could easily be abused; for instance, the lord might use his influence to pervert justice and get his man off the hook in a criminal case. Both Edward IV and Henry VII promoted legislation to restrict **retaining**, but they never had any intention of trying to abolish it altogether.

these ties of loyalty between lords and their followers were important for the smooth functioning of society. And in time of war royal armies were mostly made up from noble and knightly retinues. For instance, when Henry led an army into Yorkshire in 1489 to avenge the Earl of Northumberland, who had been murdered when collecting royal taxes, his army contained the armed retinues of 31 peers as well as those of numerous knights and gentlemen.

Henry's aim, which was the same as Edward's, was to end the lawlessness and corruption which could result from unchecked retaining. In their various Acts a distinction was made between retaining for 'lawful service' – which meant enlisting those who already had a legal relationship with the lord, such as domestic servants or officials – and retaining merely to swell a lord's private army. Henry's Act of 1504 brought in an additional rule: that the lord had to obtain a licence for his retinue from the king by furnishing him with a list of named retainers.

The difference between Edward and Henry on this issue was that Henry enforced his laws in a more determined way. A story told by Francis Bacon sums up Henry's attitude. Apparently, when Henry visited the Earl of Oxford the men of Oxford's retinue, dressed in his livery, were lining the route of the king's entry to the castle. In spite of his status as a guest, Henry turned on the Earl and questioned him closely about whether they were all legitimate servants. According to Bacon, Oxford was subsequently fined £10,000 for breaking the law. Another peer who fell foul of the regulations was the notorious **Lord Burgavenny**. But Burgavenny's case was exceptional and most retinues were never challenged. What it

---

PROFILE: *Lord Burgavenny*

George Neville (?1469–1535) succeeded his father as **Lord Burgavenny** in 1492 and was believed to be the wealthiest man in England. He owned land in many counties, but his chief residence and richest estates were in Kent, where he built up a numerous retinue of followers whom he seems to have been unwilling or unable to control. For nine years his retainers were a threat to law and order, organising riots and fighting the retainers of other Kentish gentlemen. Juries often failed to convict them because of bribery or threats. Finally, Henry's patience gave way. It is likely that the 1504 Act against retaining was largely directed at Burgavenny and in 1506 he was fined the enormous sum of £70,000, which was £5 per month per retainer. Although he did not in the end have to pay all this, Lord Burgavenny did have to enter into a recognizance to stay out of Kent for the rest of Henry's reign.

came down to, from the king's point of view, was whether a particular retinue was a threat, and this depended more on the relationship between king and magnate than on the size of the retinue. It seems that Henry, in the words of one historian, 'tamed the retinue by rooting out its worst abuses and managed to adapt an institution which had proved a severe problem to his predecessors into an instrument which on the whole served its purpose well'.

In these ways Henry avoided the strife of noble factions which had bedevilled Edward's reign and was to re-emerge under Henry VIII. By keeping the nobles at a distance and imposing heavy penalties on those who were unable or unwilling to conform to his pattern of behaviour, Henry ensured that the factions never threatened his rule.

Foreign policy and security

At first sight there seems considerable similarity between the foreign policies of Henry VII and Edward IV. Both had token claims to the French throne, both led invasions of France, and both achieved treaties by which the French king agreed to pay them annual pensions. Again, as regards England's other near-neighbour, Scotland, both kings concluded long truces which were eventually broken by open war, focusing in both cases on the disputed border town of Berwick.

However, the differences between their foreign policies are even clearer. This was the age of the Renaissance prince, who sought glory and prestige on the field of battle. In this respect Edward was typical. His well-prepared invasion of France in 1475 was a serious attempt to defeat Louis XI and regain some of the French territory which England had possessed before her expulsion from all French soil except Calais towards the end of the 100-years-war (1337–1453). Edward's attack on Scotland in 1482 was another deliberate attempt to gain territory and even to overthrow the Scottish king. Edward's aims regarding both France and Scotland were aggressive, unrealistic and unsuccessful.

Henry, on the other hand, was far from being a typical Renaissance prince. As the contemporary historian Polydore Vergil put it, he was 'more inclined to peace than war'. Perhaps this was owing to his cautious nature, but additionally there were important differences between his situation and Edward's a quarter-century earlier. One was the rise of Spain. In 1479 Spain, under Ferdinand and Isabella, had become a united nation for the first time. This completely altered the balance of power in Europe. Now there were two major states, France and Spain, and the main arena for their competition was Italy. England, a weaker power, was on the sidelines – a country which might be brought into the struggle by joining an alliance (as Henry joined Ferdinand's so-called Holy League in 1496) but whose real interests were not directly affected by these Mediterranean squabbles. Nevertheless, Henry added to his security and prestige by concluding a treaty of friendship with Spain at Medina del Campo in 1489, which opened the way to a marriage between Catherine of Aragon, the daughter of Ferdinand and Isabella, and Henry's eldest son, Prince Arthur.

The second factor which helps to explain the differences between Henry's and Edward's foreign policies is Henry's insecurity. His major concern was to secure his throne and his succession against a series of claimants – in particular Lambert Simnel (1486–7) and Perkin Warbeck (1491–9), each of whom received support from foreign powers. In other words, dynastic threats dominated Henry's dealings with foreign rulers. As well as his diplomatic skill, he used any other instruments at hand to prevent support for the pretenders. In the case of Burgundy a three-year trade boycott led to a useful trade agreement (the *Magnus Intercursus*, 1496) and a promise by Philip and Margaret, the rulers of Burgundy, to cease helping Warbeck. Earlier, Henry's invasion of France achieved a similar promise by Charles VIII as part of the Treaty of Etaples (1492).

There is no doubt, too, that Henry was obsessed by the problem of internal security throughout his reign, because his original claim to the throne had been so weak. He relied on a network of agents and informers, and here again there is a contrast with Edward who, being rather careless about security, was taken completely by surprise by rebellions in 1469 and 1470. Two examples of Henry's obsessive caution are: first, his execution of the young Edward, Earl of Warwick, in 1499, although he had been a prisoner in the Tower of London for the previous ten years and his only crime was to be the nephew of Edward IV; second, the way Henry treated his surviving son Henry after the death of his elder brother Arthur. A lot depended on Prince Henry, so he was kept under the closest supervision – 'like a girl', according to the Spanish ambassador – with no one allowed near him except chosen companions and tutors. It has been suggested that this might help explain something about his subsequent behaviour as an adult.

Such cautious policies, while not as glamorous as those of Edward IV (or, later, those of the warlike Henry VIII), were basically successful. By the end of his reign Henry VII had eliminated a series of dangerous pretenders, had been recognised by other major rulers, and had strengthened his dynasty by marrying his daughter Margaret to James IV of Scotland and arranging that Catherine of Aragon, following the death of Prince Arthur, should marry the future Henry VIII.

A new monarchy?

What answer can we give to the question of Henry's originality? In many areas the apparent similarities with Edward IV evaporate on closer inspection. Henry took more trouble over his finances than Edward, he kept his nobility under firmer control, he tried harder to reach accommodation with neighbouring powers and he was more security-conscious. Whether these differences can be put down to his character, to the long years he spent in exile before the Battle of Bosworth, or to the nature of the problems with which he was faced, is impossible to say.

KEY TERMS:

Despotism

Cruel and unfair government by a tyrant (an unelected ruler) who has a lot of power.

Magnates

These are rich people who have gained a lot of money, and with it power and possibly authority. Originally, this wealth often came from inheritance and landowning. Gradually, the term **magnate** has become associated more with money earned from a particular business or industry.

If we take a longer perspective, Henry's reign, along with those of the Yorkist kings Edward and Richard, can be seen as leading to important changes in the nature and status of the English monarchy. Both Edward and Henry helped to develop what has been called the 'New Monarchy', although this phrase has to be used with caution. An older generation of historians took it to mean that the Yorkists and early Tudors created a **despotism** and that the rights and liberties of Englishmen were eroded during their reigns. This was not the case, but if one takes the whole period from the 1470s to the 1530s there is no doubt that the monarchy became stronger, the king's government more efficient and centralised, and the forces which might have threatened such a development, especially the great **magnates**, weaker. This was a process which was going on not just in England but in Europe, under monarchs such as Louis XI of France and Ferdinand and Isabella of Spain.

Many of Henry's actions which have been mentioned here contributed to this process; the growth in the Crown's revenues and the limitations on retaining are cases in point. However, other things that Henry VII did were reversed by his son. Examples here are the development of specialist tribunals of councillors and the abuse of recognizances. But overall, Henry's cautious and systematic style of government certainly did make a major contribution to the development of the 'New Monarchy'.

Another point which should be made is that contemporaries would not have approved of, or even recognised, this phrase. At that time people generally did not believe, as perhaps they do today, in progress. As Anthony Goodman puts it, 'the concept of novelty was itself unattractive to subjects'. In the case of the monarchy people were right to think like this. The Yorkists were restoring the monarchy after its collapse into poverty and ineffectiveness during the reign of the pious but incapable Lancastrian Henry VI. So when Henry VII made innovations he was always careful to represent what he was doing as a restoration, a return to how it used to be in the 'good old days'. There is a parallel here with

Henry VIII claiming to be cleansing the Church from medieval corruption and returning to the days of early Christianity when he took the revolutionary step of making himself head of the English Church (see chapter 7). But the past can never be fully restored, and with the advantage of hindsight we can see that while Henry built on medieval and Yorkist foundations, the monarchy which he created was significantly different from that which the first Lancastrian, Henry IV, had seized a century earlier.

Task: note-taking

This is an important skill that you need to acquire early in your A-Level course. (See also suggestions at the end of chapter 19.)

Why make notes?

Taking notes helps you to make sense of a topic and to get your ideas in order. They give you a chance to make your own selection of what is important from a mass of detail. Also, good notes will be much easier to revise from when the time comes.

What makes good notes?

Notes are for *you*. So devise your own personal system. However, here are some suggestions:

1 You don't practise how to write essays in notes, so don't worry about complete sentences, or even about spelling (although it is always best to take care over the spelling of proper names). Don't be afraid to use abbreviations – so long as you are sure you will remember later what they mean!

2 Notes will be much shorter than the books you have read, and probably shorter than class handouts. The art is knowing what to leave out and what to include.

3 The way this book is organised should help you with your notes. It is probably a good idea to incorporate the headings and subheadings of different topics in your notes. The specific factual information in the time chart at the beginning of a chapter is also intended to be used.

4 It is sometimes a good idea to incorporate relevant quotations in your notes. If you do, be sure to make them accurate, and give the source of the quote.

5 Some people find it a good idea to use numbering or lettering (a, b, c) as much as possible as an aid to help sort out a topic. Another technique is to underline key words or names that have to be remembered.

An example of note-taking

Look at the following example of notes on this chapter. The aim has been to shorten, to simplify, and yet to include sufficient information to make sure that when you come back to the topic – perhaps just before an examination – you will remember what it was about.

Henry VII an innovator?

Older historians, e.g. Fr. Bacon, say yes – 'the best law-giver in the nation after Ed. I'
Revisionists say H = like Yorkists, Rchd III & Ed IV

Finance

Like Ed. H. used Chamber for revenue – but more successful because

(a) H. increased Crown lands rev. (Ed. over-generous to relatives, etc.)
(b) H. exploited feudal dues via Council Learned
(c) "   "   recognizances (= bonds for good behaviour)
But both H. & Ed. maintained expensive Renaissance court.
Both died solvent.

Nobility

H. made fewer peers than Ed. – not v. generous (e.g. to general, E. of Surrey)
Both H. & Ed. allowed, but tried to limit, retaining (Act of 1504 – licence needed).
H. = more determined to control nobles (case of Burgavenny). H. 'tamed the retinue'.

For. Pol.

H. & Ed. similar? (both invade France, get Fr. pension)
But differences: Ed's invasion of France, 1475 = serious. So was his invasion of Scotland.

H. 'more inclined to peace than war' (Polydore Vergil) because
(a) Eng. now more on sidelines in Fr–Span. rivalry
(b) H. threatens war to make profitable treaties (Medina del Campo 1489, Etaples 1492)
(c) H. obsessed by security (threat of pretenders).

Conclusion

1   H. & Ed. not too alike.
2   However, both = 'new monarchs' – like Louis XI, F. & Isabella (but careful over use of term!)

Further reading

Michael van Cleave Alexander, *The First of the Tudors: A Study of Henry VII and his Reign* (Croom Helm, 1981) – readable and well researched.

Anthony Goodman, *The New Monarchy: England 1471–1534*, Historical Association Studies (Blackwell, 1988).

Roger Lockyer and Andrew Thrush, *Henry VII*, Seminar Studies in History (Addison Wesley Longman, 3rd edn, 1997) – covers all recent work in the field and has a comprehensive bibliography.

Caroline Rogers, *Henry VII*, Access to History (Hodder and Stoughton, 1991) – a very good introduction.

3 The Pre-Reformation Church

It is important not to see the Pre-Reformation Church in England only through the eyes of the Reformers. During the fifteenth and early sixteenth centuries the church was probably not in greater need of reform than in any other age, and it seems to have fulfilled its functions relatively well. Certainly there were failures and abuses. Most of the monasteries, for instance, were no longer the spiritual powerhouses they might once have been. The level of education of the parish clergy left a lot to be desired, especially by the standards of the new humanist learning that were beginning to percolate through from Italy. Sections of the laity, on the other hand, were becoming more literate and were profiting from the invention of printing, as can be seen from the increasing sale of devotional books. Hence the clergy no longer retained a monopoly of learning, and the laity were becoming more critical of their standards.

Anti-clericalism is a term that has been overworked by earlier historians writing about this period. It certainly existed, but was usually directed against particular priests who were falling down on their duties, rather than against the clergy as a whole. One has to remember, too, that many of the documents which have come down to us about the Church give evidence only of what went wrong. For instance, the records of church courts and of bishops' visitations reveal only the complaints made by parishioners about their ministers, or about each other – they do not list the good points. Most clergy, however, were hard-working, dedicated men. Even today a great deal of architectural evidence remains as proof that parishioners loved their churches and spent large sums of money on enlarging and beautifying them. The commonest cause of disputes was tithes, a tax which parishioners had to pay to their vicar, consisting of the tenth part of their produce or income for the year. This gave rise to arguments about how much one was liable to pay, and to whom. The tithe had originated as a rural tax and therefore disputes were particularly prevalent in urban areas where it was often difficult to estimate commercial or industrial wealth. Nevertheless, although no one liked paying it, there was little disagreement about the principle of the tax and overall remarkably few disputes compared with the number of parishes. For instance, in the large diocese of Norwich, with its 1,148 parishes, there were only some ten cases a year in the early 1520s.

Another issue which undoubtedly raised many hackles was **'benefit of**

'Benefit of clergy'

If a prisoner under trial for felony could demonstrate his literacy by reading out aloud in court a particular verse from the Psalms (known as a 'neck verse' because it might save him from the gallows), he could 'plead his clergy'. He would then be transferred to the church's jurisdiction instead of that of the common law. This did not mean he went scot-free; what usually happened was that he spent some months, possibly years, in an ecclesiastical prison before being allowed to proceed to compurgation, meaning that he would be released if he could find a certain number of clergy to swear to his innocence of the original crime.

Lollards

Originally followers of John Wycliffe (c. 1329–84), a theologian who translated part of the Bible into English. Their ideas were a mixture of commonsense rationalism (*e.g.* denying miracles) and Biblical fundamentalism (*e.g.* attacking the sacraments and the powers of the priesthood). By the late fifteenth century the movement was in decline. There were small groups of **Lollards** in certain small, well-defined areas, such as parts of Essex and south Buckinghamshire, but under repeated persecution these groups were weak and fragmented. Historians have debated how far the existence of Lollardy helped the later spread of Protestantism, but the links seem fairly tenuous.

clergy'. Apart from this issue and tithe disputes, pluralism (the holding of more than one living) and non-residence, the most common criticism of the clergy involved sexual misconduct. Human nature being what it is, not all priests maintained the total celibacy that was expected of them. Some lived with their housekeepers in 'concubinage', although few so notoriously as the Lincolnshire vicar who was said to ride round the parish collecting his tithes with his mistress riding pillion in front of him.

The church courts came under powerful attack during the Henrician Reformation, especially in the Commons' *Supplication against the Ordinaries* of 1532 (see chapter 7), but the evidence suggests that they were not unpopular in the country as a whole. They dealt with a whole range of behaviour, including sexual and commercial misconduct. Their main function was as a mechanism of social control, to express and enforce socially accepted standards in such matters as adultery, prostitution, blasphemy, witchcraft, not attending church, Sunday trading, and breach of promise. Such cases were usually initiated by laymen, and the records suggest that the clerical judges on the whole showed tolerance and humanity in dealing with them. The courts could sentence offenders to prison, but a more common punishment was to do penance in church during the Sunday service, wearing only a shift or smock, carrying a candle, and making a public confession of one's guilt.

The Pope was, of course, the head of the Pre-Reformation Church, though his hand did not lie particularly heavily on England. Few challenged papal authority as a whole, although **Lollards** did. They argued that 'there never was any pope after the death of Peter', and that, 'the true pope is that person who is the holiest on earth' (statements taken from the confession of a fifteenth-century Lollard). But most people never came into contact with the Pope or his officials. Those who did were usually seeking a dispensation; for example, permission to marry a relative, to have one's own private chapel, or, for a priest, to hold more than one benefice. Such requests were almost invariably granted – for a consideration – which is why it came as such a shock to Henry VIII when Pope Clement VII refused his request to have his marriage with Catherine annulled.

In practice the monarch had more control over the English Church than did the Pope. He received more taxation from the Church than went to Rome, and he had the major say in the appointment of bishops. There had been a long history of struggle between English kings and popes, one of the results of this struggle being the Statute of Praemunire (1353), which prohibited appeals to Rome in any matter that might affect royal jurisdiction. However, by the beginning of the sixteenth century relations between crown and papacy were harmonious and this statute was rarely

Mass

The Roman Catholic Eucharist service (usually called Holy Communion by the Church of England). It is the most important act of devotion that can be offered to God. The proceedings were in Latin.

invoked. One could argue that the Church was better off when the king was capable and strong. Under the devout but weak Henry VI church discipline had been eroded and some bishops had taken sides in the Wars of the Roses. But Edward IV and Henry VII re-imposed royal control. They themselves were conventionally pious and they picked bishops who were hard working and conscientious.

Masses for the dead

The ceremony of the **mass** was central to the Pre-Reformation Church. The mass was also a sacrament which reached its climax when the priest used his special powers to consecrate the bread and the wine so that they changed their nature or substance and became the body and blood of Christ – an event known to the theologians as transubstantiation. It was not necessary for the congregation to participate in the service, or even to understand what was going on and it is hardly surprising that the mass had acquired in the popular mind an almost magical significance. There were masses for every conceivable occasion: for the sick, for women in labour, for good weather, for safe journeys, against the plague and other epidemics – above all, for the dead.

Figure 3.1 A pre-Reformation service

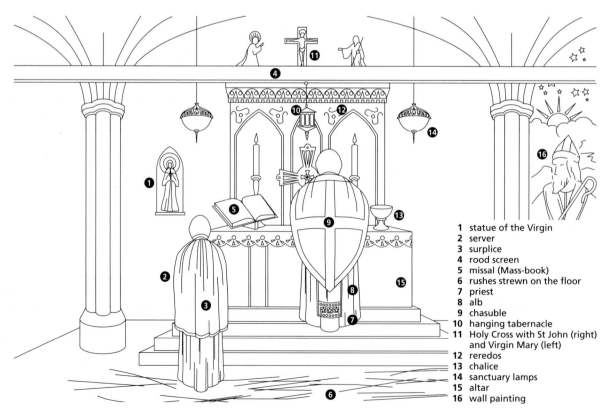

1 statue of the Virgin
2 server
3 surplice
4 rood screen
5 missal (Mass-book)
6 rushes strewn on the floor
7 priest
8 alb
9 chasuble
10 hanging tabernacle
11 Holy Cross with St John (right) and Virgin Mary (left)
12 reredos
13 chalice
14 sanctuary lamps
15 altar
16 wall painting

KEY TERMS:

Purgatory

Those who died in mortal sin went straight to hell, where they were beyond help, whereas those who died without sin went to heaven. But most people carried beyond the grave a heavy burden of venial (minor) sins which had to be purged in the flames of **purgatory** before they were worthy of heaven. The great medieval theologian, St Thomas Aquinas, had said that the mildest pain suffered in purgatory was worse than the severest pain on earth. But the prayers of the living could reduce the time a soul spent in purgatory. So could an indulgence, which was a certificate issued by the Pope or a bishop allowing a certain period – often 40 days – in purgatory to be remitted in return for certain specified good works such as contributing towards rebuilding a church, or defence against the Turks. The whole idea of purgatory, indulgences and prayers for the dead was to be strongly condemned by the Reformers, starting with Luther.

Chantry

An institution staffed by one or more priests whose main duty was to perform a specified number of prayers at fixed times. **Chantries** could be for a term of years, or perpetual, and there were thousands of them up and down the country, the majority attached to parish churches. London alone, by the Reformation, had over 300 in less than a hundred parishes. Chantry priests were usually not very well paid, but luckily there was a surplus of priests without livings, and this clerical proletariat was always available to perform the required duties.

Was there in fact a difference between the powers of the priest in the mass, and the incantations of a magician or a witch? The Reformers of the second half of the sixteenth century did not think so. 'If a man will take a view of all Popery', wrote the Calvinist theologian William Perkins, 'he shall easily see that a great part of it is mere magic' – and he would certainly have included the mass in this category. Round this service there had grown up many popular beliefs, some sanctioned by the Church, others not. It was the Church that insisted that the host (the consecrated bread) should be kept locked in a special container on the altar so that it could be an object of devotion. It was the people who held that if a communicant were not to swallow the bread but to take it away from church in their mouth undetected, he or she would possess a source of magical power. He or she could use it to cure the sick, carry it round as a guard against danger, or even crumble it and sprinkle it over the garden as protection against caterpillars! Of course the theologians did not sanction such notions; they made a clear distinction between religion (what the church taught) and superstition (what it did not). But it seems unlikely that such distinctions were appreciated by the average church-goer.

We present here some documents concerned with pre-Reformation views about life after death, and especially about masses for the dead. From a modern point of view this is a revealing topic because it gives an insight into a mentality significantly different from our own. It also reveals something about both the good and the bad sides of contemporary religion: the good being the extent of lay piety and commitment to the doctrine of the church; and the bad the tendency of popular devotion to degenerate into what we, in our scientific age, might categorise as magical or superstitious beliefs.

The saying of prayers for the dead had developed into an industry by the fifteenth century, special emphasis being placed on the sheer quantity of prayers. A rich man might arrange for thousands of masses and other prayers to be said for the health of his soul after his death. The idea was to reduce the time his soul had to spend in **purgatory** before (hopefully) being admitted to heaven.

The rich man might endow a **chantry**. Lay persons who were not sufficiently well off to endow a chantry could join a (con)fraternity. Even relatively poor people who could not afford to join a **confraternity** did their best to have as many prayers said for their souls as possible, and left a good proportion of whatever wealth they had for this purpose. The desperate desire to save one's soul from the pangs of purgatory was common to all classes. Henry VII left funds for 10,000 masses to be said for him within a month of his death. This multiplication of masses was

KEY TERM:

Confraternity

This was a kind of assurance society with the object of organising masses for the souls of its deceased members. Some were of a high status and as difficult to get into as a good golf club today; the most prestigious organised impressive processions on the day of the saint to whom the **confraternity** was dedicated. Others were exclusively for the members of a particular craft or profession. Like the chantries (see key term, page 21), the confraternities often performed useful social functions, such as helping the poor, in addition to their main role.

due to lay initiative. It was a response to consumer demand, not a plot by profit-hungry priests. The evidence of wills shows that right up to the Reformation and beyond there was no sign that belief in purgatory and in masses for the dead was flagging.

Document 1

Simon Fish, *A Supplication for the Beggars*, c. 1528.

'*Neither have they [i.e. the clergy] any other colour to gather these yearly exactions into their hands, but that they say they pray for us to God, to deliver our souls out of the pains of purgatory; without whose prayer, they say, or at least without the pope's pardon, we could never be delivered thence; which, if it be true, then is it good reason that we give them all these things, all were it C. [i.e. 100] times as much. But there be many men of great literature and judgement that, for the love they have unto the truth and unto the common wealth, have not feared to put themselves into the greatest infamy that may be, in abjection of all the world, yea, in peril of death, to declare their opinion in this matter, which is, that there is no purgatory, but that it is a thing invented by the covetousness of the spirituality, only to translate all kingdoms from other princes unto them, and that there is not one word spoken of it in all holy scripture. They say also that if there were a purgatory, and also if that the pope with his pardons for money may deliver one soul thence, he may deliver him as well without money: if he may deliver one, he may deliver a thousand: if he may deliver a thousand, he may deliver them all, and so destroy purgatory. And then he is a cruel tyrant without all charity, if he keep them there in prison and pain, till men will give him money.*'

From *English Historical Documents*, C. H. Williams (ed.), 1971.

Document 2

Regulations of a trade fraternity: the carpenters of York, 1482.

'*... it is ordained and established by the said mayor, aldermen and all the whole council of the said ... city, that the said fraternity and brotherhood shall be hereafter upheld and continued for ever, as it has been in past times, and that every brother thereof shall pay 6d [2½ p] annually for its support (that is to say, 3d at every half year), providing always that every man of the said craft within the said city shall not be compelled nor obliged to be of the said fraternity ...*

'*Also, it is ordained and established ... that all the said brethren of the said fraternity shall come together twice in the year ... at each of which days each one of the said brethren shall pay 1d to the use of the said brotherhood, and also the said brotherhood shall cause a trental [i.e. 30] of masses to be performed at each of the said days by the Austin friars of this city, to the worship of God and all saints, for the souls of all the brothers and sisters previously deceased of the said fraternity and brotherhood, and that every brother who is then absent ... shall pay a pound of wax to the use of the said fraternity, and 6d to the use of the chamber of this ... city, unless he has a reasonable excuse ...*

'Also it is ordained that if anyone of the said fraternity shall die, the said brotherhood shall give 5s [25p] for a trental of masses to be performed for his soul by the said Austin friars ...

'Also, it is ordained that if any of the said fraternity shall fall into poverty, so that they may not work, or happen to be blinded, or to lose their possessions by misfortune of this world, then the aforesaid brotherhood shall give them 4d every week, as long as they live, as alms, provided that he who is so treated shall have truly fulfilled the ordinances above written.'

From York Memorandum Book, part II (1388–1493), M. Sellers (ed.), 1914.

Document 3

The will of Joan Brytten, a widow, 1 October 1540.

'I, Joan Brytten of the parish of Saint Michael's in Woodstreet, sick in my body, bequeath my soul unto Almighty God and unto Our Blessed Lady and unto all the holy company in heaven, and my body to be buried within the parish church of Saint Gregory's by Pauls under a stone there prepared all ready for me. I bequeath unto the high altar of Saint Michael's for my tithes negligently forgotten 8d I will have at the time of my burial half a trental of masses [i.e. 15 masses] 5s 4d ... Also I will that at my death an inventory of my plate and of all the rest of my goods be made and so priced and sold, and then when the charges of my burying and my bequests paid, the rest of my goods I will that a priest shall sing for my soul, my master Milard's soul, his wife's soul and all Christian souls within the church of Saint Gregory's in London for one half year, and in the church of Saint Michael's in Woodstreet for the space of one quarter of a year, or more if the goods will extend.'

From *London Consistory Court Wills 1492–1547*, Ida Darlington (ed.), 1967.

Task: source evaluation

Hints on answering source questions:

■ Always read the documents slowly and carefully first. You may find the language unfamiliar but don't give up because you can't understand particular words or phrases. Remember that part of your training as a student of history involves 'getting inside' the period you are studying, and that with practice you will get better at understanding the language.

■ Look carefully at the information given about the origins of a source – its provenance, to give it its technical name.

■ In examinations each sub-question will carry a maximum mark. The number of marks available is always a clue as to how much you are expected to write. Arrange your time so as to spend longest on the questions that carry the most marks.

■ Make sure you take in the wording of each question. It is particularly important to notice whether the question specifies that you use only the information contained in the documents, or whether you may bring in your own knowledge as well.

1 Study document 1.
Find three arguments which the lawyer and pamphleteer Simon Fish uses here against the doctrine of purgatory. *3 marks*

2 Study documents 2 and 3.
  a How can the attitudes of these authors towards the doctrine of purgatory be worked out from these extracts? *4 marks*
  b How might one argue from this evidence that those making provision for the dead could also serve the living, and play a useful social role? *4 marks*

3 Read all three documents.
'A great part of it is mere magic', said the puritan writer William Perkins, in reference to pre-Reformation belief. With reference to the documents, as well as your own knowledge, explain whether you agree with this statement. *9 marks*

Total: 20 marks

Further reading

Eamon Duffy, *The Stripping of the Altars: Traditional Religion in England 1400–1580* (Yale University Press, 1992) – readable, revisionist and controversial.

Christopher Harper-Bill, *The Pre-Reformation Church in England 1400–1530*, Seminar Studies in History (Addison Wesley Longman, 2nd edn, 1996) – has a very useful bibliographical update.

J. J. Scarisbrick, 'How the English Reformation Happened', *History Review* No. 13, 1992.

4 The Tudor Court 1: the royal household

The royal court

The court as an institution with its own special values and behaviour only appeared during the fifteenth century. Before that there had merely been the royal household which originated many centuries earlier, chiefly as accompaniment to the king when he went to war. In the mid fifteenth century this function of the household was again needed, as kings had to play their parts as war-lords, this time in civil conflict. The terms 'court' and 'courtier' only became current towards the end of the century when influences from abroad, particularly from Burgundy, started to transform the household into something more civilised and more elaborate, a Renaissance court. An example of the new usage occurs in 1479 when the London Mercers admitted a young man to their company as a shop-keeper on condition 'that he sadly [*i.e.* soberly] dispose him and mannerly both in his array and also in cutting of his hair, and not to go like a gallant or a man of court.'

It was the rise in the power and prestige of the monarchy under the Yorkists and early Tudors that produced the court. Since Edward IV's accession the monarch was no longer merely first among equals but had raised himself to a pinnacle above all others. Similarly, the great nobles started to decline in status, and noble households ceased to be important sources of patronage. One reason for this (discussed in chapter 2) is the restrictions on retaining that Edward IV and Henry VII were able to impose. The great magnates of Edward's reign still had their own princely households, but under Henry magnates tended to yield place to office-holders, men whose wealth and status was derived from the king rather than from their own hereditary power in the country – in other words, courtiers. This centralisation meant that the royal court became the main centre of patronage. It was the place to be for any young gentleman of ambition. It has been calculated that in 1509 there were about 120 posts available at court which were worth a gentleman's having; by the end of Henry VIII's reign the number had gone up to 200.

But how to define the court? One definition is that it consisted of all those persons who, on any given day, were in attendance upon the monarch. But this might include all kinds of temporary visitors, from messengers to foreign ambassadors, so a more restricted definition is: all those who had *bouge of court*, meaning those on the payroll, or entitled to receive free food. There were hundreds of these and no doubt the system was extremely wasteful and extravagant, but that was hardly the point. The point was, rather, to give an impression of style and magnificence in order to enhance the status of the monarch.

Geographically, the court was highly mobile. Henry VIII owned over 30 houses, mostly within 20 miles of London, and he travelled round them regularly in all seasons, as well as often lodging in houses belonging to nobles or gentry, according to whim or convenience. When the courtiers had eaten all the available food and clogged up the primitive plumbing, they tended to move on. Among the palaces most visited were Greenwich, Richmond, Windsor and, in London, Westminster – until the disastrous fire of 1512, after which it was abandoned to the 'men in black', the judges, administrators and members of parliament. Henry also acquired from Wolsey Hampton Court and, just next door to West-minster, York Place, which became his favourite palace after it was rebuilt and renamed Whitehall.

The structure of the court derived from the upstairs/downstairs division of a medieval nobleman's household. Originally, the great hall had been the key area in a noble house. The king's great hall was where the entire royal household feasted, the king and his personal followers on a dais at one end, his other followers and servants in the body of the hall (see Figure 4.1). Adjoining the great hall were the kitchens and the numerous other domestic offices. All this area was under the charge of the Lord Steward and his staff of domestics. However, above the great hall was the royal chamber, a large room which was in effect the royal bed-sit, for sleeping, ceremonies and leisure activities. This came under the charge of the Lord Chamberlain, whose staff included ushers, pages, and others with titles such as 'knights of the body' and 'grooms of the chamber'. The division of authority between Steward and Chamberlain went back to the early middle ages; the Steward's staff were more numerous, but the Chamberlain's had a higher proportion of gentlemen among them.

During the fourteenth and fifteenth centuries the single-room chamber had been replaced by a suite of three specialised apartments: the Great or Guard chamber, the Presence chamber and the Privy or Secret chamber. The first two were semi-public reception rooms, and the Privy Chamber was where the king actually lived. Later on, the growing desire for more comfort and privacy that affected the monarch along with the rest of the upper class led to the building of additional 'privy' rooms such as bed-rooms, libraries and closets behind the Privy Chamber. Another develop-ment was that the great hall went out of fashion, and its functions were taken over by the specialised chambers. By the early sixteenth century

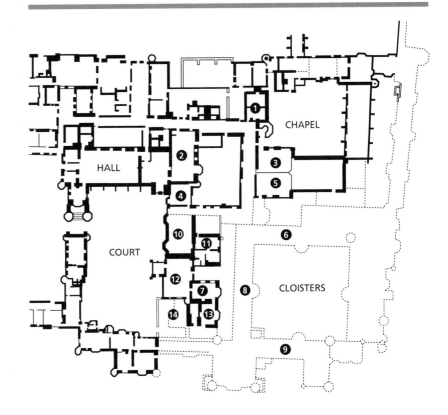

1 Council Chamber 1529
2 King's Watching Chamber
3 King's Holyday Closet
4 Chamber of Estate
5 Queen's Holyday Closet
6 Queen's Watching Chamber
7 Bed Chamber 1529
8 King's Long Gallery
9 King's New Lodgings
10 King's Presence Chamber
11 Closet
12 Privy Chamber
13 Study 1529
14 Bathroom

Figure 4.1 A plan of part of Hampton Court to show the Presence and Privy chambers opening into one another

the Steward, whose department was responsible for all domestic arrangements including food, fuel and transport, was in charge of about 220 people, while the Chamberlain controlled another 170, together with about 50 choristers and musicians from the royal chapel. Together with guards, and the staff of another important official, the Master of Horse, the entire household numbered some 500.

The Privy Chamber

Such was the structure of the court by the time of Henry VII, and it applied to all the royal palaces, although numbers had to be reduced when the king was visiting some of the smaller houses. Thus Henry inherited the arrangement whereby the Chamberlain was responsible both for the king's private quarters and the more public rooms. However, in 1495 he decided to make an alteration which had major implications. This was the year in which both Henry's Lord Chamberlain, Sir William Stanley, and his Lord Steward, Lord Fitzwalter, were implicated in treasonable correspondence with Perkin Warbeck. So Henry took the logical step of splitting the Chamberlain's department into two – ceremonial and personal – so as to correspond with the existing geography of the royal palaces. The Privy Chamber was now to be served by a small staff led by

KEY TERM:

Groom of the Stool

The origins of this office go back to when the 'close-stool' (*i.e.* a pewter chamber pot enclosed in a stool) succeeded the 'draught'. The latter was the usual form of sanitation in medieval castles and consisted of an open shaft cut into the castle wall and venting directly onto the moat. The servant (or 'groom') in charge of the stool had to stand by while the monarch relieved himself. Later this official was given other responsibilities, and in Henry VII's reign became head of the hived-off Privy Chamber and keeper of the Privy Purse, the monarch's private treasury. Under Henry VIII, Sir William Compton was particularly influential in this office. The post lingered on until the beginning of Victoria's reign when it was abolished by the House of Commons 'amidst laughter'.

an official called the **Groom of the Stool** who would provide an intimate and continuous service, while the rest of the court were forbidden entry into the privy apartments. These intimate servants were to be humble creatures, of no special standing socially, who could be expected to give totally loyal service. The Chamberlain would no longer have any jurisdiction over the Privy Chamber; from now on the court would be divided into three separate departments, not two.

At Henry VIII's accession there was an immediate change in the style of the court. The new young king was highly gregarious, and he loved to hunt and to participate in tournaments. His skill at tilting was so notorious that the Duke of Buckingham once wrote that he would rather make a pilgrimage to Rome than have to run against the king. Henry kept his father's arrangements regarding the Privy Chamber but within a few years he had transformed its membership, which was now made up of his contemporaries and intimates, continually on hand to sport, gamble or make music with him (see Figure 4.2). The new favourites were collectively known as the king's minions (*i.e.* pretty young men). The minions were high-spirited and talented, and inevitably they wielded great influence over the king, with whom they spent so much time, so that Henry's private apartments became as important politically as the

Figure 4.2 *Henry VIII dining in the Privy Chamber*

Figure 4.3 *The Renaissance prince: Henry VIII painted c. 1511*

Council chamber. In 1518 it became necessary to give them official status and a title, 'Gentlemen of the Privy Chamber'.

These new-style courtiers very much fulfilled the specifications given by the Italian writer, Castiglione, whose bestseller, *The Book of the Courtier*, was at this time popular throughout Europe. Castiglione was writing a manual of advice for the aspiring courtier to an Italian Renaissance prince; his ideal was the all-rounder, the gentleman who could compose a sonnet, or dance with the ladies, as easily as lead soldiers into battle. All these talents were to be directed towards pleasing one's prince, and serving only him – Henry's minions did just that. This was the politics of intimacy, of manipulation, and Henry, although self-willed and opinionated, was eminently manipulable.

Faction

According to David Starkey, the gentlemen of the Privy Chamber aroused the intense jealousy of Cardinal Wolsey, who made two attempts to reduce their power. Starkey says that in 1519 Wolsey used his influence with the king to have most of the minions expelled from the court, accusing them of unbecoming conduct such as treating the king with undue familiarity and encouraging him to gamble. However, within a few months they were back, regaining all their old ascendancy. Then in January 1526 Wolsey published the *Ordinances of Eltham* with the ostensible intention of reforming the household in order to save money by abolishing superfluous posts. However, Starkey sees this measure as primarily a faction-inspired attempt to get rid of Wolsey's enemies at court, in particular Sir William Compton.

Peter Gwyn, Wolsey's biographer, disagrees with this interpretation. He feels that the *Ordinances* were a genuinely cost-effective exercise and he argues that Wolsey was never, either in 1519 or in 1526, inspired by faction, and that his relations with the minions were generally excellent. Sir William Compton, according to Gwyn, was quite pleased to be able, in 1526, to exchange his position as Groom of the Stool for the post of Under-Treasurer of the Exchequer. Gwyn feels that Starkey generally exaggerates the influence that the Gentlemen of the Privy Chamber exerted; these, he says, were young men's posts: the Privy Chamber was where you started your career, not where you hoped to end it.

In any case, the reduced Privy Chamber continued to be one of the two main political arenas, the other being the Privy Council (see chapter 10). The 1530s saw a saga of factional in-fighting between Thomas Cromwell and his opponents. Cromwell's first success was to form an alliance with the 'Aragonese' faction (the supporters of Catherine of Aragon), led by Nicholas Carew and the Marquis of Exeter, in order to bring down Anne Boleyn and her supporters. Cromwell accomplished this coup in the spring of 1536, and thereafter he was able to pack the Privy Chamber with his supporters, such as Sir Anthony Denny and Sir Thomas Heneage, who became Groom of the Stool. According to Starkey, the difference between Wolsey and Cromwell in this sphere was that where Wolsey neutralised the court, Cromwell packed it.

After Cromwell's fall from power in 1540 the factional struggle went on, but now between a conservative Privy Council (dominated by those such as Gardiner and Norfolk, who had engineered Cromwell's fall) and a Privy Chamber where the reformers picked by Cromwell, and now led by Denny, continued to hold sway.

When Henry VIII was dying, the question of which faction was in control was crucial because they controlled the use of the dry stamp. This left an un-inked impression of the royal signature which was then gone over in ink by a clerk, producing a near-perfect facsimile. Sir Anthony Denny used the dry stamp to authenticate both the attainder of his opponent, the Duke of Norfolk, and a version of Henry's will that gave Edward Seymour the power to rule the country after the king's death.

Under Somerset the Privy Chamber went into eclipse, because he succeeded in so dominating Edward VI that the young king and his personal servants virtually became a sub-department of the Protector's household. However, it revived under Northumberland, who, as Edward approached his majority, found it worthwhile to pack the royal household with his own supporters in order to influence the adolescent king. After 1553, under a female ruler, the Privy Chamber ceased to have any political importance. Naturally, Mary chose exclusively women to staff her private apartments, and the ones she chose had no interest in politics. However, she did give special trust to a small group of household officials, including Sir Edward Hastings, her Master of the Horse, and Sir Henry Jerningham, her Vice-chamberlain. These officials, working in alliance with Mary's chief minister, Stephen Gardiner, fulfilled to some extent the previous role of the Henrician Privy Chamber. Elizabeth, too, refused to allow her ladies of the bedchamber a political role, and chose to rule exclusively through her Council and her Secretaries, especially Sir William Cecil.

Conclusion

To sum up: recent research, and especially the work of David Starkey, has established that the early Tudor court was central to the politics of the day. It is not merely that the Privy Chamber became an alternative source of patronage and political power to the Council (though it did). Even more, the Council was in a sense part of the court. Most leading ministers were also, or had been, court officials. Thomas Cromwell himself was once a collector for the privy purse, and ended his career as Lord Great Chamberlain. The geography of the royal palaces is another indication. At Whitehall the Council chamber was just across the corridor from the royal bedchamber. It is misleading to make too much of a distinction between courtiers and councillors, or between a personal court and a bureaucratic government – there was a continuous overlap.

The way the royal court operated largely depended on the personality – and the age and sex – of the monarch. Henry VII's politics of distance gave way to the politics of intimacy under the youthful Henry VIII. Wolsey and Cromwell had different strategies for dealing with the court, as did Somerset and Northumberland during Edward's minority. Neither Mary nor Elizabeth allowed male politicians into their personal apartments, but they had their favourites and gave them key court positions (both Hastings, under Mary, and Leicester and Essex, under Elizabeth, were appointed Master of the Horse). In a personal monarchy there inevitably has to be change as well as continuity.

Tasks: finding out more

1 Read some of Castiglione's *The Book of the Courtier* (Penguin). This was first published in 1528, although not translated into English until 1561. What were the qualities and accomplishments which, according to Castiglione, a young courtier should cultivate? How far are they typical of Henry VIII's courtiers?

2 Find out about the meaning of the word 'faction'. Why have historians found this term so useful in describing politics under the early Tudors? Give some examples of factional struggles that took place between 1509 and 1558.

3 Find out something about the workings of another contemporary European monarch's court – for instance, that of Francis I of France. How close are the parallels with Henry VIII's court?

Further reading

David Loades, *The Tudor Court* (Batsford, 1987) and *The Tudor Court,* New Appreciations in History No. 18 (Historical Association, 1989).

David Starkey, *The Reign of Henry VIII: Personalities and Politics* (George Philip, 1985) – a lively and colourful account.

David Starkey (ed.), *The English Court from the Wars of the Roses to the Civil War* (Addison Wesley Longman, 1987) – a pioneering study, full of insights.

Simon Thurley, *The Royal Palaces of Tudor England: Architecture and Court Life 1460–1547* (Yale University Press, 1993).

5 The Humanists

Humanists

Humanism was the name given to the intensive study of the classical past – particularly its authors – which characterised the Renaissance period in Italy, from where it spread over western Europe. **Humanists** put much emphasis on writing and teaching the purer classical Latin of Cicero and Virgil, as opposed to the 'barbarous' Latin of the Middle Ages. They also studied Greek, a language which had long been forgotten in medieval Europe, but which had been that of Plato and Aristotle as well as of the New Testament. These linguistic studies led the Humanists to a stress on the value of education and to a more critical attitude to the secular and religious issues of their day. They wanted to reform both the church and society.

During Henry VII's reign a small group of pioneers was seeking to spread the new scholarship derived from Renaissance Italy. These **Humanists** were young graduates from the universities of Oxford or Cambridge who had mostly gone on to study in Italy, before returning to England to teach and to write. They included William Grocyn, who initiated the teaching of Greek at Oxford, and John Colet, whose course of lectures on St Paul's Epistles broke new ground, and who went on to found the first humanist grammar school, St Paul's, in 1504 (see chapter 31). Another member of the group was the brilliant young lawyer and scholar, Thomas More.

Through the international medium of Latin, this group was in touch with scholars from abroad, and especially with the most famous humanist of all, Desiderius Erasmus, who visited England several times in the early sixteenth century and who dedicated his bestselling satire, *In Praise of Folly*, to his friend, Thomas More. Henry VII's mother, Lady Margaret Beaufort, was an important patron for these scholars, and Henry entrusted the education of his own children to them, so that much was expected of Prince Henry, who had shown aptitude for scholarship, when he succeeded to the throne in 1509. The young king did not entirely fulfil humanist expectations (for example, Erasmus did not receive from him a permanent source of income, as he hoped), but he showed himself to be personally interested in the new learning. The same was true of his first queen, Catherine of Aragon, who employed the well-known Spanish scholar, Juan Luis de Vives, to educate her daughter, Mary.

By this time humanist studies were taking root in the universities as well as at Court. New lectureships in Greek and Latin had been established, and the statutes of two new colleges, Corpus Christi, Oxford, and St John's, Cambridge, emphasised the different approach to learning. A third college to do so was Wolsey's foundation at Oxford – Cardinal College, which became Christ Church after his fall from power. One project that Humanists supported was to spread knowledge of the Bible to the educated laity; a key event for them was Erasmus's publication of a Greek text and Latin translation of the New Testament in 1516. This gave a boost to Greek studies and even inspired the king himself to start learning Greek.

It would, nevertheless, be a mistake to overemphasise the impact of Humanism at this time. There were still very few who could aspire to the

Figure 5.1 *Sir Thomas More and his family at their home in Chelsesa, London – painted by Rowland Lockey in 1593 (nearly 60 years after More's death)*

level of scholarship of a More or an Erasmus. At the universities there were many old-fashioned teachers determined to resist the new ideas. For example, a major controversy erupted at Oxford between the 'Greeks' and the 'Trojans', who rejected Greek and wanted to stick with the old scholastic curricula. Only Henry VIII's intervention on the side of the Greeks in 1518 ended the quarrel. It remains true, however, that Henry's attitude to Humanists was always somewhat schizophrenic. Although he enjoyed patronising scholars, fundamentally he had little sympathy with their pacifist and enlightened ideas, being himself keener on personal glory won on the battlefield.

Scholars always had a fairly low status in society. They usually depended on a royal or noble patron for their livelihood, and even those with an international reputation often had much to complain about in their living conditions, as this extract from a letter by Vives, then living in London, shows:

33

> '*My room is a tiny box, very narrow, where there is no table and scarcely a seat, and which is surrounded by other rooms full of noise and clamour, so that I cannot collect my thoughts without all my will and effort. Also I live quite far from the Court, and so as not to lose the whole day in going and coming, once I have left the house in the morning I do not return until night. If I dine here, I cannot walk about in this narrow space (indeed, how could I?), so I curl up as though in a hole, and cannot devote myself entirely to my work. For I have to take care of my health, especially here where, if I fell ill, I would be thrown into some sewer and thought of only as a vile, sick dog.*'

The crucial question facing the Humanists – something which has worried intellectuals in every age – was whether or not to participate in public affairs. Here, the ancient philosophers gave contrary opinions. Plato argued that an active public life could easily corrupt a scholar, who ought therefore to stick to his books and avoid politics. Aristotle, however, held that it was the duty of a wise and virtuous man to play his part in society, because otherwise the state would be dominated by those of lesser virtue. Erasmus tended to take the Platonic view, but Thomas More disagreed. In his famous early work, *Utopia* (1516), he inserts a discussion between the traveller, Hythloday, and himself. Hythloday argues that, as governments will always be corrupt, wise men should 'refrain to meddle with the commonwealth'. 'More' replies:

> '*I must needs believe that you, if you be disposed, and can find in your heart to follow some prince's court, shall with your good counsel greatly help and further the commonwealth. Wherefore there is nothing more appertaining to your duty, that is to say, to the duty of a good man.*'

This issue suddenly became real when Luther burst onto the European scene in 1519. Humanists were expected to take sides, although their instinct was to steer a *via media* (middle way) between the papacy and the Lutherans. Erasmus managed to delay pronouncement on the question until 1524, when he finally had to come out against Luther. However, Henry VIII produced his own condemnation of Luther, *In Defence of the Seven Sacraments*, in 1521, and most English Humanists were expected to follow his lead. Their dilemma is clearly shown by the case of Cuthbert Tunstal, originally one of the Colet–More group, who had become Bishop of London. He found himself having to perform some un-humanistic actions, such as burning prohibited Lutheran books and punishing people who were found with a copy of the Bible in English.

KEY TERM:

Papal legatine court

The court set up in England under the papal legate [*i.e.* the Pope's official representative], Cardinal Campeggio.

It was when Henry VIII's 'Great Matter' was broached (see chapter 7) that Humanists discovered that their options really were narrowing. In 1529 the **papal legatine court** refused to pronounce in favour of the annulment of Henry's marriage with Catherine, and the king started to look for an alternative solution. Academic opinion became polarised when English and foreign universities were canvassed for their opinions about the validity of the marriage. Scholars suddenly found that their views could become a matter, not only of wealth and employment versus neglect and poverty, but also of life versus death.

The majority of English scholars somewhat naturally sided with the government, and a collection of historical texts was put together, the *Collectanea satis copiosa*, giving Henry the academic backing he required. Humanist opposition was suppressed; in the case of More and Fisher, it was punished by execution. So the issue of the king's marriage, and subsequently of the headship of the English church, swept away the Erasmian Humanism of the early part of the reign. It was no longer possible to be neutral, as Plato had advised, and Humanists, who had previously held the somewhat naïve hope that they could keep out of religious conflict, now found themselves swept up in it. For the next decade it was the radical humanists, those who fully supported the Henrician changes, who made the running, under the patronage first of Anne Boleyn, and then of Thomas Cromwell. One or two, such as Hugh Latimer, became bishops; other, younger scholars, like John Cheke and Thomas Smith, were sent abroad to study at royal expense.

A decade of reform

Provided one was prepared to go along with Henry's headship of the church, the period of Thomas Cromwell's ascendancy (1532–40) was a golden age for those who wanted to change society, as did most Humanists. A whole generation of intellectuals who had been disappointed by Wolsey (because he represented in himself much of what was wrong with church and state) now looked to the new minister. Cromwell had enormous energy and he was always keen to find scholars who could help him with plans for reform or with propaganda. **Thomas Starkey** is a prime example of a Cromwellian recruit: a humanist with a fertile range of ideas, who worked closely with Cromwell, even if, in the end, few of his schemes saw the light of day.

The range of subjects to which Cromwell turned his attention is impressive. Many of them are discussed in other chapters (especially chapters 7 and 10). They included education – Cromwell produced schemes of reform for both Oxford and Cambridge universities along humanist lines, and

Thomas Starkey (?1499–1538) was an Oxford scholar who introduced himself to Cromwell as a virtual stranger, in 1535. He asked if he could help towards the 'restitution of the common weal'. Before that he had spent ten years on the continent studying, mainly attached to the household of the future archbishop of Canterbury, Reginald Pole, in Venice and Padua. Unlike Pole, who remained a devoutly Catholic Humanist, Starkey was very anti-papal, and an effective writer. Cromwell employed him, first, to correspond with his ex-patron, Pole, in order to persuade him to support Henry over the divorce. This failed, but Starkey's employment as a propagandist continued. His best-known work was a fictional dialogue between Pole and another Humanist, Lupset, into whose mouths he put his own ideas about reform. He set out what the historian G. R. Elton called a primitive Keynesian philosophy, proposing that the king's wealth, and especially the wealth from the monasteries, be used to create employment.

assisted in the setting up of several grammar schools. He was responsible for the printing and dissemination of a government-sponsored version of the Bible in English, the 'Great Bible'. He also tackled numerous social and economic issues, including vagrancy, enclosures, the cloth trade and the law of inheritance. Among his papers there are yet other plans – often proposed by humanist advisers – which never reached the statute book. Much of what Cromwell and his supporters wanted did not happen because of the short time at his disposal and the constraints he was working under. For instance, there was powerful opposition from land-owners in Parliament to his attempts to limit the amount of pasture land any one farmer might own. Or, to take another example, he probably would have liked to abolish the system of church courts, but Henry, who was very conservative once he had gained what he wanted, stopped him.

Nevertheless, much was achieved. Cromwell's decade represents the high-water mark of humanist-directed reform. The less capable leaders who succeeded him did not have his voracious appetite for change. During the early 1540s the conservatives in the Council, led by Gardiner and Wriothesley, would have nothing to do with political and social theorists whom they suspected of Protestantism. Therefore the impact of would-be reformers on government was much less than in Cromwell's day. In the following reign the religious pendulum swung the other way, but it is now recognised that Somerset's commitment to reform was really very slight, his main preoccupation being to retain power (see chapter 11).

One area in which a humanist atmosphere did continue to flourish was in the education of future monarchs. The young Prince Edward was brought up in a household supervised by Henry's last queen, Catherine Parr, a patron of learning, and staffed by humanist scholars. Their leader was Roger Ascham, who went on to be responsible also for the education of Princess Elizabeth. Both Edward and Elizabeth were taught according to the most advanced methods of the day, and Elizabeth in particular imbibed a love of the classics, a sound knowledge of modern languages and a personal, undogmatic and moderate form of Protestantism.

Conclusion

One might argue that although the period of Cromwellian reform enthused many Humanists, the real heyday of Humanism – that is, of the broad-minded Erasmian brand – ended earlier, perhaps in 1529, when Humanists were forced to take sides over the royal divorce. An earlier generation of scholars had tried to avoid religious and political confrontation by promoting a generalised commitment to reform and scholarship. However, in G. R. Elton's words, 'they were playing with ideas too strong for them'. In England, as on the continent, the age of Erasmus was overtaken by the more brutal, but perhaps more realistic, age of Luther and Calvin. Nevertheless, the legacy of the early Humanists, their concern for the 'commonweal' and their moderation where religion was concerned, was to influence greatly the nature of the Elizabethan state.

Task

This chapter is about the rise and decline of Humanism in England during Henry VIII's reign. Humanism arrived in England from Italy early in the sixteenth century, but international developments – the appearance of Luther; the Henrician divorce issue – divided the Humanists, causing them to abandon their tolerant attitudes. Thomas More, the most brilliant of the early English Humanists, was among those forced to take sides, and the choices he made ultimately led to his death.

This task gives you the chance to find out about the life of Thomas More, to show how it illustrates the theme of this chapter. You will need to do some research first. The books in the 'Further reading' section below will be a help. Use the main index to locate specific references to More. You could also look up Thomas More in an encyclopedia (book or CD-ROM format). When you have done this work, and discussed your findings with others in your group, you will be able to answer some of the following questions.

a In what sense can the young More be described as a Humanist?

b How far did he abandon his humanist position as he grew older?

c What was the choice he faced which ultimately caused his imprisonment and execution (on this, see also chapter 7)?

When you have assembled your material, write it up as an essay with the title:

'How does the career of Thomas More illustrate the difficulties and dilemmas faced by Humanists in early sixteenth-century England?'

Further reading

Maria Dowling, *Humanism in the Age of Henry VIII* (Croom Helm, 1986) – useful on English Humanism generally.

G. R. Elton, *Reform and Renewal: Thomas Cromwell and the Common Weal* (Cambridge University Press, 1973).

Richard Marius, *Thomas More* (Yale University Press, 1985) – the most accessible life of More.

Alistair Fox and John Guy, *Reassessing the Henrician Age: Humanism, Politics and Reform 1500–50* (Blackwell, 1986).

John Guy, *The Political Career of Sir Thomas More* (Harvester Press, 1980).

6 Thomas Wolsey: rapacity or reform?

Time Chart

1472: Born at Ipswich, son of butcher and innkeeper

1497: Elected fellow of Magdalen College, Oxford, where he had been undergraduate

1498: Ordained priest

1502–7: Chaplain successively to Archbishop of Canterbury and Governor of Calais

1507: Chaplain to King. Sent on diplomatic missions

1509: Death of Henry VII. Wolsey is appointed Dean of Lincoln by Henry VII, and royal almoner by Henry VIII

1510: Appointed to royal council

1513: Organises Henry's successful campaign in France; rewarded with bishopric of Tournai

1514: Appointed Bishop of Lincoln and subsequently Archbishop of York. Negotiates peace treaty with France

1515: Accession of Francis I to French throne. Wolsey is created cardinal by Pope Leo X and appointed Lord Chancellor by Henry VIII

1516: Accession of Charles I to throne of Spain

1517: Luther publishes his 95 theses

1518: Wolsey brings European powers together in Peace of London

1519: Charles I of Spain elected Emperor as Charles V

1520: Francis I and Henry VIII meet at Field of Cloth of Gold

1521: Henry VIII publishes attack on Luther and is rewarded by Pope with title 'Defender of the Faith'. Charles V and Wolsey sign Treaty of Bruges directed against France

1522: English expedition under Suffolk strikes towards Paris

1523: Wolsey's demands for money arouse opposition in Parliament

1525: Francis I is defeated at Battle of Pavia and sent prisoner to Spain. Wolsey's attempt to levy 'amicable grant' fails

1527: Wolsey negotiates treaty of alliance with France. Imperial troops sack Rome

1528: Pope issues commission to Cardinals Campeggio and Wolsey to decide on validity of Henry VIII's marriage

1529: Legatine court held at Blackfriars, London. French defeated by imperial troops at Battle of Landriano. Pope comes to terms with Emperor and recalls Henry's divorce case to Rome. Francis I and Charles V conclude peace at Cambrai. Parliament summoned in England. Wolsey falls from power

1530: **November** Death of Wolsey

Wolsey was a man who aroused controversy among his contemporaries and, subsequently, among historians. Was he a genuine reformer or did he simply seek power in order to glorify himself? In this chapter we shall look at Wolsey as both statesman and churchman, considering what he did as well as what he failed to do.

The King's chief minister

Although, as you can see from the time chart, Wolsey had already made his mark under Henry VII, real power only came his way after the accession of Henry VIII in 1509. The new King, not yet 18, was described by George Cavendish, one of Wolsey's gentlemen-ushers, as 'young and lusty, disposed all to mirth and pleasure and to follow his desire and appetite, not caring to toil in the busy affairs of this realm'.

Wolsey, who had enormous energy and an exceptional capacity for hard work, therefore took over the routine business of government, which included supplying men, money and munitions for the campaigns against France in which Henry hoped to win glory on the battlefield. In 1513 Henry defeated the French at the Battle of the Spurs and captured the town of Tournai. He returned home highly pleased with both himself and Wolsey, the organiser of victory, whom he appointed (with the Pope's agreement) Bishop of Lincoln, and subsequently Lord Chancellor.

For the next 15 years Wolsey was Henry's chief minister, responsible for maintaining law and order. As Lord Chancellor he regularly presided over the **Court of Chancery**, dealing with more than 500 cases a year, but his principal weapon in the fight against disorder was the Court of Star Chamber (see chapter 21). Since the most important men in the kingdom sat in this court, Wolsey had no hesitation in summoning before it all those, no matter how high their station in life, who had ignored or perverted the normal processes of law. The poet John Skelton, a bitter critic of Wolsey, recorded how:

KEY TERM:

Court of Chancery

Medieval Chancellors were usually churchmen and were regarded as 'keepers of the king's conscience'. Among their most important duties was that of ensuring that the king and the officials he appointed did not act unjustly. Subjects who felt they had been treated unfairly could appeal for justice to the Chancellor, and by the time Henry VII came to the throne a **court of Chancery** had developed to deal with such cases. Chancery could override decisions of the ordinary law courts in the interests of equity or fair play.

In the Star Chamber he nods and becks,
And beareth him there so stout [i.e. proud]
That no man dare rout [i.e. riot],
Duke, earl, baron, nor lord
But to his sentence must accord.

Figure 6.1 *Cardinal Thomas Wolsey, by an unknown artist*

Wolsey enjoyed sitting in judgement, especially when those who came before him were from the upper sections of society. Skelton gave voice to the sense of outrage felt by men who were more accustomed to issuing orders than obeying them:

For all their noble blood
    He plucks them by the hood
And shakes them by the ear
    And brings them in such fear ...
And maketh them to bow the knee
    Before his majesty.

This was not simply an instance of inverted snobbery – the butcher's boy enjoying riding roughshod over the ancient nobility. Within living memory feuding among the great nobles had brought English government close to collapse, and Wolsey was determined to carry forward the restoration of royal authority set on foot by the first Tudor, Henry VII. His enemies accused him of arrogance, and it is true that he lived in great state with a household numbering some 500 persons. But the display of power was one way of compelling obedience, and even if Wolsey used his position to pay off some private scores, it was the King who was the real beneficiary.

Parliament and finance

Henry VII had restored the royal finances, but they would not provide the large sums Henry VIII needed to force his way on to the European stage as a major player. Wolsey, with his accustomed energy, determined to bring the tax system up to date. He therefore introduced the subsidy, which in due course became the standard parliamentary tax in Tudor and Stuart England (see chapter 18). Taxpayers were now required to give details of their property and income to local officials who would determine how much they should pay. The subsidy produced sums far greater than under the old system, but even so, Henry was still short of money for his projected campaign against France in 1523 and Parliament was therefore summoned. Things went badly wrong, for Wolsey's demand for a subsidy of four shillings in the pound provoked deep resentment. Sir Thomas More's son-in-law and biographer later described how:

> '... the Cardinal, fearing it would not pass the Commons House, determined for the furtherance thereof to be present himself ... Where, after he had in a solemn oration by many reasons proved how necessary it was the demands there moved to be granted, and further said that less would not serve the King's purpose; he seeing the company still silent ... and contrary to his expectation showing in themselves towards his requests no towardness of inclination, said unto them: "Masters, ye have many wise and learned men among you, and seeing I am from the King's own person sent hither unto you for the preservation of yourselves and all the realm, I think it meet you give me a reasonable answer." Whereat, every man holding his peace, [Wolsey commented] "Here is without doubt a marvellous obstinate silence" ... Whereupon the Cardinal ... suddenly arose and departed.'

Subsidies were eventually voted, though not at the rate Wolsey had demanded. But the King was still short of money, and in 1525 Wolsey sent out commissioners to demand a non-parliamentary tax which he called an 'amicable grant'. This aroused widespread opposition which in some places flared into open rebellion. Henry was forced to intervene and cancel the grant, declaring he had known nothing about it. This is extremely unlikely, for Wolsey was always careful to consult with the King, and it was Henry's insistence on renewing the war against France which had made the demand for money necessary in the first place. In this instance, as in so many others, Wolsey acted as a lightning conductor, diverting public anger away from Henry.

Wolsey and the Church

Wolsey recognised the need to root out abuses from the Church, yet as Archbishop of York he was only second in the ecclesiastical hierarchy, and as long as William Warham lived there was no chance of his succeeding to the key post of Archbishop of Canterbury. But the papacy had the right to despatch envoys or legates to any part of Christendom to exercise its supreme authority. These legates *a latere* – so called because they were sent 'from the side of' the Pope – usually had a limited and specific mission, but Wolsey and Henry now called for the Cardinal to be given indefinite legatine powers so that he could undertake a thorough

Figure 6.2 *Two illustrations from the biography of Wolsey by his servant, George Cavendish: (above) Wolsey riding in procession, preceded by his great crosses as archbishop and legate, and his cardinal's hat; (below) Wolsey's fall. He is summoned to justice by his enemies, the Dukes of Norfolk and Suffolk.*

reform of the Church in England. The Pope was reluctant to make such a concession, but he had no wish to offend Henry, and by 1524 Wolsey was legate *a latere* for life.

One of the major needs was to improve educational standards among the clergy, and Wolsey planned to do this by founding a new college at Oxford and grammar schools throughout the country. Cardinal College, as Wolsey's new foundation was called, was conceived on a princely scale. It occupied the site of a former priory which Wolsey dissolved, transferring its revenues to the college as well as those of some 20 other monasteries which he likewise suppressed. The scheme for feeder schools was slow in getting off the ground. In fact, only one actually came into being – at Ipswich, Wolsey's home town. It had a short life, for no sooner had it started functioning than Wolsey fell from power and the King closed it down. Cardinal College suffered a similar fate, but Henry eventually refounded it and it survives to this day as Christ Church College.

The very name of Cardinal College was designed to glorify its founder rather than God or one of the saints, and Wolsey's coat of arms was prominently displayed. The same ostentation was visible at Wolsey's private residences, particularly Hampton Court palace on the Thames near London. It would be easy to dismiss such extravagance as vain and worldly, but Wolsey was the last in a long line of archbishops who took it for granted that they should live in a manner suitable for princes of the Church. As Henry's chief minister and the principal papal representative in England, Wolsey was at the centre of an administrative machine which needed staffing on a big scale. His palaces, then, were partly offices. Moreover, the King was a frequent visitor, and expected to be accommodated in appropriate state.

Wolsey's lifestyle needed great sums of money to sustain it, and he used his legatine authority to intervene in the administration of the dioceses, claiming fees and other perquisites ('perks') that had previously gone to the bishops. Moreover, although he claimed to be a reformer he embodied many of the principal abuses in the Church. By holding one other bishopric as well as the archbishopric of York he introduced episcopal pluralism into England. He appointed non-resident Italians to a number of English sees, paying them a stipend while he pocketed the surplus, and he set an example of non-residence himself by never even visiting his sees during his tenure of power. Although he was not a monk, he had himself elected abbot of the rich monastery of St Albans; and although vowed to celibacy he fathered a daughter, whom he placed in a nunnery, and a son on whom he showered lucrative church livings.

It is tempting simply to dismiss Wolsey as a hypocrite, but this would be only a half-truth. Wolsey appreciated the need to reform the Church and genuinely meant to do something about it. The principle of dissolving small or corrupt monasteries in order to transfer their funds into education was one which reformers had long advocated, and shortly before his fall Wolsey was considering a plan to convert a number of major abbeys into cathedrals in order to create new dioceses, which were badly needed. Had he lived longer he might have achieved more, but Henry was a demanding master, and Wolsey was constantly distracted from spiritual matters by the demands of politics.

Wolsey and foreign affairs

After organising Henry VIII's successful foray into France in 1513, Wolsey negotiated the treaty which ended hostilities. But the European situation was transformed by the accession of two young rulers to the crowns of France and Spain. Francis I, who became King of France in 1515, was determined to reassert a French presence in Italy, but this would inevitably bring him up against Charles I, King of Spain from 1516, who had similar aims. The Pope, fearing the outbreak of war among the Christian rulers at a time when they should be uniting against the Ottoman Turks, proposed a peace conference. Wolsey took over this papal initiative and in 1518 successfully concluded the Treaty of London, which bound all the major European powers together in a non-aggression pact.

There is no reason to doubt Wolsey's genuine commitment to peace – even if Henry was lukewarm – but treaties were not sufficient by themselves. Following the election of Charles I of Spain as the Emperor Charles V in June 1519, Francis I felt encircled by Habsburg power and determined to break out into Italy. He sought the friendship, or at least the neutrality, of England, and in appearance he obtained it. In June 1520 Henry and Francis came together, in a setting of calculated splendour which Wolsey had masterminded, at the Field of Cloth of Gold (see Figure 6.3).

A year later, however, Wolsey went to Bruges, where he negotiated a treaty with Charles V committing England to offensive operations against France. A. F. Pollard, in his classic biography of Wolsey which was first published in 1929, attributed this change of course to a special induce-

Figure 6.3 The Field of Cloth of Gold, setting for the meeting of Francis I and Henry VIII in 1520

ment, for Charles undertook at Bruges to secure Wolsey's election as pope, whenever a vacancy occurred. Pollard was convinced that:

> '... the papal throne was the natural and, indeed, a proper, aim for Wolsey's vast ability and ambition. It is hard to believe that the idea was planted in Wolsey's mature breast by the fostering care of his youthful sovereign and only suffered to grow through Wolsey's devotion to his master's interests.'

However, J. J. Scarisbrick, in his equally classic biography of Henry VIII, published in 1968, takes a different view:

> 'It may have been Charles who first planted the idea that Wolsey might become the second English pope ... Whatever the agency, it seems that it was sown in Henry's, rather than Wolsey's, mind and that it now became the King's ambition to have his chancellor become pope; a plan to which Wolsey acceded but which he did not initiate.'

Scarisbrick goes on to say that Wolsey was not guilty of deception when he allied with Charles. Since he now saw Francis as a threat to the peace established by the Treaty of London, it made sense to join with the Emperor in an attempt to restrain him. Wolsey fought to preserve what he had built, and failed; but he failed because others never seriously intended that he should succeed, not because he did not try.

In 1523 an English invasion of France was launched, and the Duke of Suffolk came within striking distance of Paris. But with the onset of winter, Suffolk had to return to base, and Parliament's refusal to vote money on the scale Wolsey demanded meant that plans for future offensive operations had to be curtailed. As Charles lost patience with his English ally, Wolsey turned towards France. By the beginning of 1525 he was ready to enter an anti-Habsburg league, but in February of that year Francis I was crushingly defeated by the Emperor's troops at the Battle of Pavia, south of Milan, and sent prisoner to Spain.

Henry hastily congratulated Charles on his victory and proposed that they should partition France between them. Charles, who felt bitter about English betrayal, dismissed the idea. Wolsey therefore reverted to his pro-French policy and in 1526 played a major part in constructing the League of Cognac, which linked England in an anti-Habsburg coalition with France and the Papacy. However, this strategy backfired when

Charles sent his troops into Rome, where they sacked the city and compelled the Pope to take refuge in the castle of San Angelo in May 1527. Two years later, in June 1529, he put the seal on his victory by routing the French army at Landriano. The Pope now came to terms with the Emperor, announcing that he had resolved 'to become an imperialist and to live and die as such'.

Events in Italy were of crucial importance to Wolsey, for just at this moment he was confronted with the King's 'great matter' (see chapter 7). If the papacy had been truly independent, or if Charles V had valued English friendship, the problem of Henry's marriage might have been resolved by agreement. The fact that neither of these two key factors was present led directly to Wolsey's downfall.

Wolsey's reputation

Wolsey's servant, George Cavendish, wrote a biography of his master's life. He summed Wolsey up as follows:

> 'Whatsoever any man conceived about him when he lived or since his death, thus much I dare be bold to say ... that in my judgement I never saw this realm in better order, quietness, and obedience than it was in the time of his authority and rule, nor justice better administered.'

Not everybody shared Cavendish's opinion, however. Wolsey, in the course of his meteoric career, made many enemies, among them Henry VIII's first queen, Catherine of Aragon. The speech that Shakespeare puts into her mouth summarises the views of those who feared and hated the great Cardinal:

> He was a man of an unbounded stomach [i.e. pride], ever ranking himself with princes ... His own opinion was his law. In the presence [of the King] he would say untruths and be ever double both in his words and meaning ... His promises were, as he then was, mighty; but his performance, as he is now, nothing.

Historians have been similarly divided in their judgement of Wolsey. Here, first of all, is Pollard's verdict:

> '[Wolsey's] egotism exceeded even Tudor arrogance, and it was exhibited in more than Tudor ostentation. The papal legate became the richest man in England save the King ... It had all come to him by exploiting the favour of Henry VIII and the opportunities afforded him by the discharge of his official duties: he pillaged as papal legate the goods of every bishop he succeeded, made as foreign minister a financial profit out of every treaty he concluded, and took as chancellor a commission for every favour he conferred.'

Scarisbrick does not deny that Wolsey had many defects, but emphasises the positive features of his personality:

> '[There was] something lofty and great about him – as a judge, as a patron of education, as a builder, as an international figure. For all his faults, he had deserved more generous treatment from his King, and has, perhaps, deserved more generous treatment from some historians.'

Scarisbrick has no time for the claim that Wolsey, by abusing his legatine authority, alienated the Church in England from its papal head and left it so divided and weak that it fell easy prey to Henry VIII. Nor does he accept that Wolsey, by uniting high spiritual and temporal authority in his own person, opened the way to Henry's royal supremacy. The church, in Scarisbrick's view, put up a strong fight against Henry, and the course of events after 1529 was determined primarily by the conditions prevailing then, and not by anything that Wolsey had done or left undone.

Conclusion

If Wolsey's contemporaries and subsequent historians are so divided in their views, what are we to think? There is no simple answer. History is the study of human beings, and human beings are complex characters. Wolsey cannot be simply categorised as good or bad. He achieved much but could have achieved more. He served two masters faithfully, the King and the Pope, but at the same time he served himself. In some ways he was a victim of his own success. He was quick to identify problems and work out solutions, but the press of business meant that he rarely had time to pursue them to the end. Fifteen years in office was a long time, but from Wolsey's point of view it was not long enough.

Task: class discussion

Divide into groups to debate the character of Thomas Wolsey. Here are some phrases which might be applied to Wolsey. You will see that some of them conflict with others:

- deceitful diplomatist
- true servant of the king
- extravagant spendthrift
- energetic reformer
- peace-loving statesman
- greedy egoist
- impartial dispenser of justice

1 Find some evidence, in this chapter or elsewhere, to support each of these descriptions.

2 Pick two or more of them which you strongly agree with, and justify your choice to the rest of the group.

3 Discuss your findings with those who have taken a different view of Wolsey.

Further reading

A. F. Pollard, *Wolsey* (1929), reissued with introduction by G. R. Elton (Fontana, 1965) – for many years the standard account.

J. J. Scarisbrick, *Henry VIII* (Methuen, 1983).

J. A. Guy, *The Cardinal's Court. The Impact of Thomas Wolsey in Star Chamber* (Harvester Press, 1977).

G. W. Bernard, *War, Taxation and Rebellion in Early Tudor England: Henry VIII, Wolsey, and the Amicable Grant of 1525* (Harvester Press, 1986).

Peter Gwyn, *The King's Cardinal: The rise and fall of Thomas Wolsey* (Barrie and Jenkins, 1990) – the most recent full-length life. A good read but too indulgent towards Wolsey.

S. J. Gunn and P. G. Lindley (eds), *Cardinal Wolsey: Church, state and art* (Cambridge University Press, 1991).

7 The King's 'great matter'

KEY TERM:

Praemunire

Various statutes of **praemunire** were passed during the second half of the fourteenth century. They made it illegal to introduce into England foreign (*i.e.* papal) jurisdiction. These statutes were rarely applied until Henry VIII decided to use them as a weapon against the Church. The underlying theory, which was advanced by a contemporary writer, Christopher St Germain, was that canon, or church, law must always be subordinate to the common law. The term praemunire can be applied either to the statute or to the offence against the statute.

Time chart

1501: Catherine marries Prince Arthur

1502: Death of Arthur

1509: Catherine marries the newly ascended Henry after dispensation from Pope Julius II

1521: Henry publishes *Assertio Septem Sacramentorum* (In Defence of the Seven Sacraments) against Luther, and is granted the title *Fidei Defensor* (Defender of the Faith) by Pope Leo X

1527: Sack of Rome by Imperial army

1529: Fall of Wolsey. Thomas More becomes Lord Chancellor

1531: **Praemunire** charge against the clergy. Fine of £100,000 imposed

1532: Act withdrawing annates from the Pope (not to be enforced for a year)
Supplication of the Commons against the Ordinaries (*i.e.* the bishops and their deputies)
Submission of the Clergy (to Henry's headship of the church)

1533: Anne marries Henry (January)
Cranmer becomes Archbishop of Canterbury (March)
Act of Appeals (forbidding appeals to Rome)

1534: Execution of Elizabeth Barton, the 'Holy Maid of Kent'
Act of Succession (incorporating oath of succession)
Act of Supremacy
Treason Act

1535: Executions of Fisher, More and others

1536: Execution of Anne Boleyn

1538: Royal Injunctions issued which include the order to make an English Bible freely available in every parish

In 1521, after Pope Leo X had been presented with a bound copy of Henry VIII's anti-Lutheran tract, *In Defence of the Seven Sacraments*, he granted Henry and his successors a new title, *Fidei Defensor* (Defender of the Faith). Yet, 13 years later Henry was to declare that the Pope's power was usurped, and that he himself was the head of the English church.

This chapter is about causation. It looks at how and why this momentous change came about. It really was momentous. In the short term the Henrician Reformation vastly increased the status and wealth of the monarchy, and in the long term the process of change initiated by Henry was to affect British history for centuries. It still does today.

On his accession to the throne in 1509 Henry, aged 18, married Catherine of Aragon, who was five years older. Catherine, the daughter of Ferdinand and Isabella of Spain, had been married to Henry's elder brother, Arthur, who died in 1502. Therefore permission had to be obtained from the pope of the day, Julius II, to allow Henry to marry his deceased brother's wife. To start with, the relationship between the young couple was happy, but after about 15 years Henry was beginning to get restive. Not only was he taking a succession of mistresses from the women available at court – this was to be expected of a man in his position – but the real problem was the lack of a male heir. Catherine produced three infants who were either still-born or who died at birth, two others (a boy and a girl) who died within weeks, and one surviving child, Mary. Henry shared the contemporary patriarchal view that women were unfit by nature to rule. Also, without a male heir England might well be precipitated into another round of the Wars of the Roses on Henry's death. There still survived at this time a Yorkist claimant to the throne, Richard de la Pole, known as the White Rose.

Henry, it seems, became convinced that his failure to produce a son was evidence that God looked unfavourably on his marriage. It was against God's law for a man to marry his brother's widow, and no pope – so Henry now believed – had the right to sanction such a union. Did not the Bible specifically forbid what Henry had done?

> *And if a man shall take his brother's wife, it is an unclean thing: he hath uncovered his brother's nakedness; they shall remain childless.*
>
> Leviticus 20: 21

By 1527 Wolsey was spending much time and energy trying to get Henry's marriage annulled. He wanted the pope, Clement VII, either to agree that the marriage had never been valid because of the previous marriage to Arthur, or at least to say that the case could be tried in England, preferably by Wolsey himself. Normally, the Pope would have been only too pleased to favour someone as important as Henry. Annulments were not uncommon among the rich and powerful. Louis XII of France had obtained one, and so had Henry's sister Margaret, so that she could divorce the Earl of Angus. But in this case there was a major snag.

PROFILE: *Anne Boleyn*

Anne (1507–36), Thomas Boleyn's younger daughter, was sent to France when she was about 12 to enter the household of Queen Claude, wife of Francis I. She stayed in France until 1522 and then came home and joined the royal court. At about this time her older sister, Mary, became Henry's mistress. Anne was not a remarkable beauty, although vivacious and intelligent. By 1525–6 Henry was determined to make her his mistress but she, unlike her sister, insisted on marriage or nothing. She became pregnant at the end of 1532 and was secretly married to Henry in January 1533. Over the next three years she stamped her personality on the court and government, using her powers of patronage to promote her own family and supporters, as well as evangelical (*i.e.* reforming) churchmen, such as Hugh Latimer. However, she failed in her main task of giving Henry a male heir, and in 1536 he sanctioned her execution, on the grounds of adultery and of incest with her own brother. Henry was now free to marry Jane Seymour, who gave him the son he so much wanted.

In May 1527 an Imperial army had sacked Rome, and after this the Pope came under the domination of the Emperor Charles V, who happened to be Catherine of Aragon's nephew. Clement did not want to offend Henry but still less could he afford to offend Charles by allowing Henry to humiliate Charles's aunt. The result was stalemate – a long period of prevarication during which the unfortunate Pope tried to keep in with both sides and avoid committing himself to a final decision.

In 1528 Wolsey managed to persuade Clement to send a papal legate, Cardinal Campeggio, to England to try the case. However, Campeggio had secret instructions to delay as long as possible. Then, in the summer of 1529, came the news that Catherine herself had appealed to Rome (on the grounds that she could not expect a fair hearing in England), and that the Pope had accepted her appeal. This made Campeggio's mission irrelevant, and it also meant the fall of Wolsey, who had failed to get what Henry most wanted.

Over the next few years, and without Wolsey, Henry pursued various policies in a thoroughly inconclusive way. He appealed to the universities to support his case, and throughout Europe scholars and theologians had a field day arguing about degrees of affinity and the powers of the papacy. The trouble was that, as so often with the Bible, there was another text which seemed to say exactly the opposite to the one in Leviticus quoted on page 51. This was a verse in the book of Deuteronomy which stated that if a brother died it was the surviving brother's duty to marry his widow. But it could be argued (and was, by Henry's supporters) that the Deuteronomy text only applied if the original marriage had not been consummated. If it had been, then Leviticus applied, and a second marriage was against divine law. Catherine, of course, swore that her marriage with Arthur never had been consummated. For those who would like to investigate these complex issues further, the best account is in chapter 7 of J. J. Scarisbrick's *Henry VIII*.

Another policy attempted by Henry was to put pressure on the Pope, either directly, by threatening his income from the Church in England, or indirectly, by attacking the powers of the Church itself. In 1531 the English clergy as a whole were accused of praemunire in that by acknowledging Wolsey's authority as papal legate they had made the Pope rather than the King the final arbiter in judicial matters. Henry only agreed to pardon their offence after they 'voluntarily' offered him a grant of £100,000.

The following year there was a more serious attack, probably orchestrated by Thomas Cromwell. It started with the Commons presenting to Henry a list of grievances against the Church, known as the Supplication against the Ordinaries. Complaints included excessive costs and delays in the church courts, especially over the issues of tithe and probate. The crisis ended with the clergy having to make a submission which gave the king control over the church courts and their canon laws. At the same time, an Act was passed which put direct pressure on Pope Clement by forbidding the payment of annates (a tax paid by bishops to the Pope); this was not to come into force for a year. None of these measures, however, had the intended effect and Clement's only response was to threaten Henry's **excommunication**.

A new kingship

KEY TERM:

Excommunication

This was a sentence barring the offender from the services of the Church, including burial. Since excommunicates were not allowed to swear oaths or make contracts, they were technically excluded from office holding and commercial transactions.

While he was on the attack against the Church Henry was also developing something of greater long-term significance, a new theory of kingship. This was the idea that a king ought to have no rivals within his own realm. A nation like England was an 'empire', meaning that it had both a spiritual and a temporal aspect, and its king was in charge of both (see chapter 10). He was God's representative, vicar of Christ and holder of the 'imperial' crown. The people's duty was to obey him, and him only; he was their majesty (a word which now came into fashion borrowed from the ancient Roman empire). All this was put very clearly in the famous opening to the Act of Appeals, which stopped legal appeals to Rome, and which was probably drafted by Thomas Cromwell.

> *Where by divers sundry old authentic histories and chronicles, it is*
> *manifestly declared and expressed, that this realm of England is an*
> *empire, and so hath been accepted in the world, governed by one Supreme*
> *Head and King, having the dignity and royal estate of the imperial Crown*
> *of the same, unto whom a body politic, compact of all sorts and degrees of*
> *people, divided in terms, and by names of spirituality and temporality, be*
> *bounden and owe to bear, next to God, a natural and humble obedience*

24 Henry VIII, c.12

The idea that church and state were merely two departments of a unified realm under the king was, of course, not new. It had been put forward by the fourteenth-century writer, Marsilius of Padua, whose work was translated into English through the patronage of Cromwell, and it was brought to Henry's attention by the scholars who had been assembled to support his cause in the divorce issue.

One kind of evidence relied on for this view of kingship was the 'old authentic histories' mentioned in the extract above. Chroniclers such as Geoffrey of Monmouth favoured a version of British history that had Christianity first brought to England by Joseph of Aramathea in Biblical times, and the kings of England as being descended, via Arthur, from Helena, the mother of the Roman Emperor Constantine. The point of all this was that it left out the role of the papacy. In fact, the pope had no place at all in the new theory. Henry had come to believe that the Christian world had started as, and still should be, a federation of autonomous, local churches, each ruled over by a prince appointed by God. The superior power of the Bishop of Rome was clearly usurped, and must be rejected.

Another source for the new kingship, and one which seemed more securely based than the old chronicles (whose authenticity was being undermined by Renaissance scholarship), was the Old Testament. Henry was impressed when he read of kings such as David and Solomon who had ruled over the priests, as well as the people, of Israel. One Old Testament king who was a particularly good role-model was Josiah, who, in the twelfth year of his reign, 'began to purge Judah and Jerusalem from the high places, and the groves, and the carved images, and the molten images' (2 Chronicles 34: 3). Josiah also discovered 'the book of the law of the Lord', which he then caused all the people to read and obey.

Henry was to do the same. Once he had taken over the English Church, he had an official version of the Bible printed and distributed to every parish. He did this not because he was a proto-Protestant wanting to challenge the old doctrines, but because he saw the Bible as inculcating his own view of kingship and the supreme virtue of obedience. One part of the Bible that Henry especially liked, and expected his people to follow, was Paul's Epistle to the Romans, chapter 13, which starts:

> *Let every soul be subject unto the higher powers. For there is no power but of God: the powers that be are ordained of God. Whosoever therefore resisteth the power, resisteth the ordinance of God: and they that resist shall receive to themselves damnation.*
>
> Romans 13: 1–2

The frontispiece to the new English Bible (Figure 7.3) reflects this philosophy. It shows Henry enthroned, handing out copies of the Bible to his bishops, who in turn hand them on to the clergy and people. They then salute Henry with the cry '*Vivat rex*' ('Long live the king').

The supremacy

The years between 1529 and 1534 are a time of twists and turns; it is clear that Henry did not have a premeditated plan, and only reached his solution to the divorce problem by stages. Historians disagree as to exactly when the irrevocable decision to take over the Church was arrived at. It may have been in 1532, when the clergy abandoned their legislative independence to Henry. Thomas More certainly thought so, because within a few days of the Submission he resigned as Lord Chancellor (see profile on page 58).

Perhaps the deciding event was the public announcement of Anne's pregnancy in January 1533. After this, events speeded up. Henry married Anne secretly, Thomas Cranmer was picked to be Archbishop of Canterbury (his predecessor, Warham, who opposed the divorce, having conveniently died the previous summer), and the Act of Appeals was passed. The latter enabled Cranmer to hold his court at Dunstable and pronounce Henry's marriage to Catherine invalid without the fear of an appeal to Rome. Anne was then crowned queen and, in 1534, a number of Acts ensured the succession to the throne, swept away papal authority, and made Henry Head of the Church in England. The most important of these was the Act of Succession which declared Catherine's marriage

Figure 7.2 *Thomas Cranmer, painted by Gerlach Flicke in 1546*

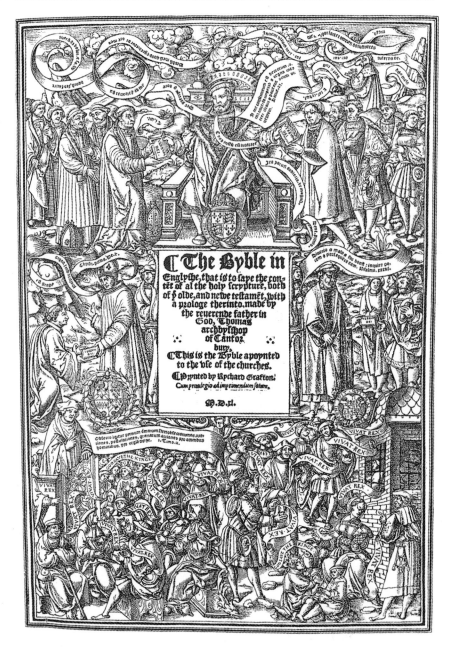

Figure 7.3 Woodcut on the title page of Thomas Cranmer's 'Great Bible' of 1540, showing Henry VIII as Supreme Head of the Church, handing out Bibles to his bishops, who in turn pass them on to the people

contrary to God's law, confirmed the Boleyn marriage, fixed the succession on Anne's and Henry's children, and set out an oath which all leading citizens had to take.

It has often been pointed out that the Henrician Reformation was accomplished by statute, and therefore had the effect of enhancing the status of Parliament. Perhaps Henry might have tried to make the changes by proclamation, using his royal prerogative, but he did not. By using

Parliament to alter the control of the church Henry was setting an important precedent. When, in future reigns, it became necessary once again to deal with these issues, it had to be done once more through Parliament. Even Elizabeth, who had strong views about her prerogative when it came to religious affairs, did not hesitate to make her religious settlement by statute. Nevertheless, one also has to remember that the point of the whole exercise so far as Henry was concerned was to make the monarchy stronger. The new laws were made by Parliament, but they were the laws the king wanted; Parliament was only the tool.

Opposition

One surprising thing about Henry's measures is the weakness of opposition to them. The papacy was not unpopular in England, as the number of applications for papal indulgences and dispensations shows. England's later hostility to 'popery' was the result, not the cause, of the Reformation. Furthermore, there is plenty of evidence that Catherine of Aragon was popular and that there was much muttering against Anne. 'I will take none for queen but Queen Katherine; who the devil made Nan Boleyn, that whore, queen, for I will never take her for queen', declared a Lancashire priest, and he was not unique. Thomas Cromwell was informed by his agents of dozens of such comments, and it was his task to discriminate between serious cases of opposition and those that were mere bravado or loose talk.

One would expect any serious opposition to be orchestrated in the first place by the bishops. At this time the English bishops were an impressive lot, far superior in morals and learning to their French or German counterparts. But of them all it was only John Fisher who refused the oath of succession and was martyred for his stand. The problem facing the bishops was the length and uncertainty of the process which led to the takeover. It was not easy to find the right moment at which to stand and fight, and many deluded themselves that in the end Henry might change his mind and return to the papal fold. In 1539, when it was all over, John Stokesley, Bishop of London and an outstanding Humanist, said, 'Oh that I had holden still with my brother Fisher and not left him when time was.' Another result of the long period between Wolsey's fall and the Act of Succession was that several new bishops appeared on the scene, and inevitably care was taken to appoint radicals, such as Hugh Latimer, who became Bishop of Worcester.

It was also true that potential opponents received very little help from Rome. Pope Clement was always trying to placate Henry – short of actually granting him what he wanted. One example is his agreeing to the appointment of Cranmer as archbishop, which harmed Rome's cause and gave Cranmer unnecessary status. And when Clement did act decisively, giving a cardinal's red hat to the imprisoned Fisher, it was too late and may only have provoked Henry into executing him sooner.

The 'Holy Maid of Kent'

One of Henry's most dangerous opponents was a woman of no particular social status, Elizabeth Barton, the charismatic 'Holy Maid of Kent'. She took a strong line against the divorce and claimed to have had a vision that if Henry put away Catherine he would cease to be king within six months. She attracted attention and had to be arrested and made to confess (under torture) that her visions were fraudulent. The authorities then used her to entrap other opponents. Fisher was caught in this way – he had corresponded with her – but **Thomas More** had been too cautious and for him other means were needed.

PROFILE: *Thomas More*

Having trained as a lawyer, and with a reputation as the leading Humanist in England, **Thomas More** was eminently qualified for his appointment as Lord Chancellor after the fall of Wolsey. But there was a problem – his opinion on the royal divorce did not coincide with Henry's. He was promised that as Chancellor he need not concern himself with the affair, and could keep his opinions to himself, but in 1534 Henry broke his word and demanded that More take the oath of succession. He refused and was sent to the Tower, but since he never openly opposed the oath, no treason could be proved against him. However, in 1535, perjured evidence was produced that he had spoken against the divorce, and he was condemned to death under the Treason Act. Before he was executed he did speak out and utter his real opinion (according to his biographer, Nicholas Harpsfield):

❝And for proof thereof, like as among divers other reasons and authorities he declared that this realm, being but one member and small part of the Church, might not make a particular law disagreeable with the general law of Christ's universal Catholic Church, no more than the city of London, being but one poor member in respect of the whole realm, might make a law against an Act of Parliament to bind the whole realm.❞

More, Fisher and three Carthusian priors were among those executed under the 1535 Treason Act which made it treasonable to deny the royal supremacy, even in words. Altogether, between 1534 and 1540 there were over 500 executions for treason, although nearly half were of those who took part in the Pilgrimage of Grace (see chapter 9). Cromwell's network of informers and his severity were enough to keep most people quiet even if they disapproved of what was happening.

Conclusion

So Henry became a new Josiah, and 'the only supreme head in earth of the Church of England'. This had a major impact on the structure and organisation of the church. Although the church courts retained their role, their prestige and effectiveness declined. The same was true of the bishops, who now had to toe the royal line. Another result of great significance was the disappearance of the monasteries (the subject of the next chapter). However, as far as doctrine was concerned, there was not much change. Henry was essentially conservative in his personal faith, and so long as he had what he wanted – namely, power, status and revenue – he aimed to keep things much as they were. It is true that for a few years, under Cromwell, the Church moved in an evangelical direction, with an English Bible and a critical attitude towards Catholic superstition. But after Cromwell's fall, and for the remainder of the reign (1540–47), orthodoxy prevailed. Denial of transubstantiation (see page 20) was treated as heresy, and Lutherans such as Robert Barnes were burnt. The Protestant Reformation had to wait until after Henry's death.

Task

Few major historical events have only one cause. Usually, there is a whole range of causes – from long-term background factors through to seemingly trivial events which may act as a 'trigger'.

This exercise should help you realise that 'causes' are not always simple. The event we will look at is Henry VIII's assumption of the headship of the English Church. Here is a list of ten points connected with this event and taken from the chapter:

- Catherine's failure to produce a son
- The sack of Rome
- The belief that the pope's power was usurped
- The death of Archbishop Warham
- Henry's need for increased revenue
- The lack of opposition from the bishops
- The Biblical text forbidding a man to take his brother's wife
- The new theory of 'empire'
- Resentment at the Church's heavy taxation of the laity
- The attractions of Anne Boleyn

1 Note down briefly how each of these points might help to explain why Henry took over the headship of the Church.

2 List the points in what you consider to be their order of importance as causes of this event.

3 Justify the order you have chosen to another member of the class, and listen to the order they have chosen.

4 Discuss your findings and see if you and your partner can agree on an order you are both happy with.

Further reading

Christopher Haigh, *English Reformations: Religion, Politics and Society under the Tudors* (Macmillan, 1993).

Richard Rex, *Henry VIII and the English Reformation* (Macmillan, 1993) – good on the new theory of kingship.

J. J. Scarisbrick, *Henry VIII* (Methuen, 1983).

John Guy, 'Henry VIII and his ministers', *History Review* No. 23, 1995.

Diarmaid MacCulloch (ed.), *The Reign of Henry VIII: Politics, Policy and Piety* (Macmillan, 1995) – an excellent survey of all the major topics.

8 The Dissolution of the Monasteries

KEY TERM:

Monasteries

Although there were many different orders of monks, canons, friars and nuns, they can be known collectively as monks, or 'religious', to distinguish them from the ordinary, or 'secular' clergy.

Christian monasticism in the West really started in the sixth century AD with the Italian, St Benedict, who composed a Rule based on a daily round of prayer and manual work under which communities of monks could dedicate their lives to God. The great age of the monasteries in England was the twelfth century, when the new, reformed order of Cistercians arrived from France, choosing some of the most remote areas to found their houses. They were followed in the thirteenth century by the Friars, who taught and worked among the laity, as opposed to the enclosed orders of monks. By the sixteenth century English monasticism was in decline, and this is reflected in the reduced number of monks. Although there were over 800 religious houses in England and Wales, about one to every 10 parish churches, yet many had less than six, or even four, inmates. Altogether there may have been fewer than 10,000 monks out of a population not far off 3 million.

The dissolution of the **monasteries** was accomplished between 1536 and 1540. It had great social and economic, as well as religious and human, significance. In this chapter we look at its causes as well as its results, taking on board the subsidiary questions of the state of the monasteries before the dissolution, and why there was so little opposition to it.

On the whole the monks were well off, and led a comfortable and pampered existence cocooned by lay administrators and domestic servants. Their income derived mainly from monastic lands which were rented out to **tenant farmers**, though there was also the directly farmed **demesne land**. Another source of income was 'spiritual', consisting of tithes from those parishes 'appropriated' to the monastery. Butley Priory in Suffolk, for instance, was an average-sized house, with an income of £210 from rents, £32 from the demesne and £108 from 'spiritualities'. At the dissolution Butley had 84 lay officials and servants to farm the demesne land and look after the 12 canons (*i.e.* monks).

Heads of monasteries (called abbots or priors) were particularly well off, and usually maintained a separate household, and a standard of life considerably above the rest, as the example of **Prior More** shows.

A very few monasteries, such as the Carthusian houses and the Bridgettine nuns at Syon, near Richmond, managed to maintain high standards, but these were exceptional. Monks and nuns tended to assume that the monastic life need not deprive them of the pleasures enjoyed by lay persons.

What were the services that the monasteries provided which might justify, in the eyes of laymen, their existence and their wealth? The main ones were prayer, hospitality, alms and learning, and for the average citizen, prayer probably had always come top of the list. A monastery was supposed to be a spiritual powerhouse, in which the daily round of intercession to God for all Christian souls, both living and dead, never ceased. The belief that prayer could reduce a deceased soul's time in purgatory (see chapter 3) was clearly tied up with the existence of monasteries, and when they were dissolved that doctrine came under attack at the same time. As Bishop Hugh Latimer said, 'the founding of monasteries argueth purgatory to be, so the putting down of them argueth it not to be'.

KEY TERMS:

Tenant farmers

Tenant farmers did not own their own land. They rented it from landowners and were responsible for keeping it productive. The tenant farmer would pay an agreed sum for a lease from the landlord which gave him the right to farm the land.

Demesne land

Land belonging to a lord and used by himself, and not by a subordinate tenant. It was often land surrounding the lord's mansion, and might include parks, farms and hunting land.

Ordinary folk may have continued to believe, but an Erasmian scepticism about this function of prayer, and hence about the role of the monks, was becoming widespread among the educated.

Hospitality and alms were still important. Every monastery had a guest house where travellers could stay, at a standard far removed from the horrors of a medieval inn.

> *'The cooking and accommodation was far superior to those that could be got in inns, the bread was whiter, the beer of better quality, the feather beds in the guest chambers softer, the sanitary arrangements far in advance of the time.'*
>
> Geoffrey Baskerville, *English Monks and the Suppression of the Monasteries* (1940).

It was important for a monastery to attract wealthy and influential guests, who might be feasted and entertained, sometimes for long periods, in the hope they would use their influence in the monastery's favour. We know from the chronicle of Butley Priory that Mary Tudor, Henry VIII's sister, and her second husband, the Duke of Suffolk, made several prolonged visits. They went hunting in the neighbourhood and had picnics in the priory grounds, but there is no evidence that all this free hospitality helped Butley when the time of dissolution arrived. Nevertheless, the disappearance of the monasteries caused great inconvenience to travellers, especially in the wilder parts of the kingdom.

Almsgiving to the poor was supposed to be a monastic duty, and in some cases it was even a legal obligation, originally laid down by the founder of the house. Butley, for instance, had to distribute money to the poor on certain feast days during the year. Monasteries also had a general obligation to give away any food not eaten by the monks. However, the total amount of charity dispensed was not really significant; it has been calculated that it comprised only about 3 per cent of monastic income. The dissolution was not one of the major causes of the mid-century vagrancy problem (see chapter 28).

In earlier centuries the monasteries had been renowned for their learning, and especially for their copying of manuscripts. However, the invention of printing had rendered this function increasingly obsolete, while the growth of lay education presented a challenge to which the monasteries were slow to respond. On the whole, the new, humanist scholarship had not penetrated the cloister; there were still large monastic libraries of mainly manuscript books, but they tended to remain

---

PROFILE: *Prior More*

William More was prior of the wealthy Benedictine monastery of Worcester from 1518 to 1536. His life, which we know quite a lot about because he kept a journal of his expenses, was much more like that of a wealthy country gentleman than a monk. He received a large, regular income, equivalent to about a quarter of the entire revenue of the priory. He rarely stayed for long at the priory, but travelled about the countryside, accompanied by a large retinue of servants and attendants, moving from one to another of the larger manor houses on estates owned by the priory. Every year, there was a shopping trip to London, lasting several weeks.

Prior More did not have to supervise the farming of the estates – this was done by the tenants – so he spent most of his time and energy furnishing and maintaining his favourite manors: glazing the windows, hanging the walls of living rooms with painted cloth, draining and restocking the fish ponds. He also played a role in local affairs, acting as a **Justice of the Peace**, and dispensing hospitality to the landed gentry of Worcestershire.

When the moment came, he and his monks all took the oath of succession, but when Cromwell's agents visited the priory in 1535 they received various complaints against More, particularly from one ex-monk who had been caught stealing years before. With this ammunition, the visitors were able to pressurise the prior into resigning. He was treated generously because he had cooperated, received a substantial pension as well as the freehold of one of the manors, and died peacefully in 1552 at the age of 82.

---

uncopied and unread. When Prior More wanted a new copy of the Rule of St Benedict, he sent to a London bookshop, and for the 'lymning gylding and drawing of certen of my masse bookes' he employed a craftsman who was not a monk.

Causes of the dissolution

The general verdict must be that, from a lay point of view, monasteries were no longer pulling their weight. However, this was not the reason why Henry VIII decided to abolish them. As a young man Henry may have read Erasmus's criticisms of monks, as had most educated people, but his priorities were quite different from those of a reformer; his motivation was financial, not religious. All governments at this time were

Valor Ecclesiasticus (1535)

Under the Act of First Fruits and Tenths (1534), which imposed royal taxes on the Church, commissioners were appointed to survey ecclesiastical wealth, including the monasteries. Very likely, before the survey the government did not even know for sure how many monasteries there were. The commissioners, who were local gentry, did their work quickly and thoroughly, and their conclusions have been largely verified by modern historians, although they may have underestimated the value of demesne lands (see key term, page 62).

The *Valor* (see Figure 8.1) records the net income of every monastery from all different sources, after allowances have been made for fees and legal obligations such as dispensing charity. The total net income of all the monasteries came to over £136,000 a year, or more than three times Henry's existing income from the crown lands.

short of cash, suffering from increasing debts and soaring rates of interest, and Henry was an extravagant ruler. Also, the break with Rome had brought the threat of invasion from Catholic powers, so that he needed to look to the coastal defences and the navy. The Geraldine rebellion in Ireland and the Pilgrimage of Grace (see next chapter) were to be additional heavy items of expenditure.

Calling on Parliament for funds might well provoke criticism and opposition. An easier option was the church, and especially the monasteries, which were disliked by the secular clergy, regarded with indifference by the laity, and cut off from Rome by the Dispensations Act of 1534. Moreover, Thomas Cromwell had gained experience under Wolsey of dissolving monasteries, and his own philosophy made him hostile towards them. As the king's vicar-general he had the authority to undertake the new policy, and his first step was to conduct a survey of their wealth, the *Valor Ecclesiasticus* (Figure 8.1).

Cromwell could hardly broadcast that his real motive for dissolving the monasteries was to raise money. He had to produce another reason, and what better than the laxity and immorality of the monks? Under the Act of Supremacy the king had acquired the power to 'visit, repress, redeem [and] reform' the Church. Cromwell now used that power, appointing deputies to visit monastic houses up and down the country. His visitors were usually clerical lawyers with a bias against monks, such as Richard Leyton and Thomas Legh. They readily accepted any local gossip available about loose behaviour, and they produced the *Comperta*, or Black Book, a report highly unfavourable to the majority of religious houses.

Armed with this, the government proceeded to pass the Act of 1536 against the lesser monasteries. The Act was crudely drafted and may not have been Cromwell's handiwork. It contained inconsistencies, the most obvious being that the preamble to the Act condemned houses with 'under the number of 12 persons', whereas the Act itself provided for the dissolution of all houses whose lands were not 'above the yearly value of two hundred pounds'. The £200 limit covered 304 houses, although about a quarter of these managed to buy themselves temporary exemption from closure.

At this stage there was probably no plan to dissolve all monasteries – as is evident from the fact that the 1536 Act offered the religious in the smaller houses the alternative of quitting the monastic life or of moving to one of the 'great and honourable monasteries'. In the summer of that year another set of commissioners descended on the monasteries due for closure, to survey them and carry out inventories of their property. In most places there was no opposition, especially in the south,

Figure 8.1 *A page from the Valor Ecclesiasticus, referring to Whitby Abbey*

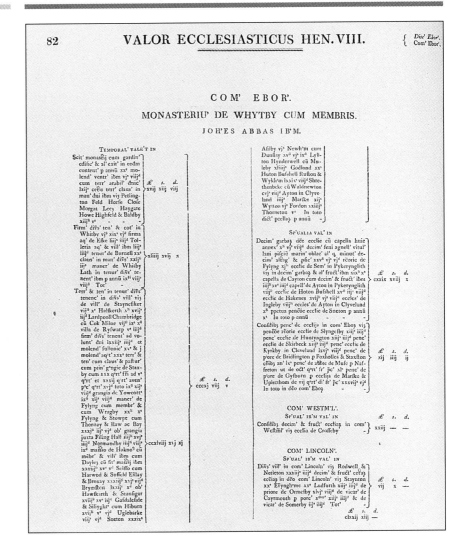

but in the north the anger aroused by the Dissolution was a contributory cause of the Pilgrimage of Grace (see next chapter).

The defeat of this challenge, in which a number of Lincolnshire and Yorkshire houses were implicated, opened the way to the total destruction of English monasticism. Between 1536 and 1539 there occurred a piecemeal surrender of monasteries, including most of the large ones. By 1539 the majority had actually surrendered, and the Act of 1539 represented a *fait accompli*, passed not so much to dissolve as to recognise the dissolutions already made and make sure that the king's right to the monastic property was unchallengeable by law. The question arises as to why there was so little opposition and why so many houses surrendered voluntarily to Cromwell and his agents, even before the 1539 Act made their dissolution compulsory. There is a combination of reasons:

1 There was a lack of any real religious vocation on the part of many monks, and there were also frequent bickering and petty animosities within communities, which Cromwell's agents were able to exploit.

2 The king's offensive had developed gradually, making it difficult for potential opposition to know when to make a stand. By 1536 all monks had been softened up by having had to swear the oath of succession (see chapter 7), and an oath to obey the king as head of the church.

3 Monks who behaved themselves received pensions and if they wished, they could have 'capacities' (*i.e.* permission to obtain posts as secular clergy in the outside world).

4 Priors and abbots could expect to get particularly large pensions and favourable treatment if they agreed to cooperate with Cromwell (see profile of Prior More on page 63).

5 Monks who opposed government policy were punished ruthlessly. Eighteen Carthusian monks who had refused to swear to the headship were killed. Either they were executed with particular cruelty or they died a lingering death in prison.

6 Those who resisted could expect little support from laymen in their area because in most cases the local gentry stood to gain from the dissolution by being able to buy monastic land.

No wonder that when the dissolution commissioners arrived at a particular house and invited the prior to sign a deed of gift surrendering his monastery and all its property to the king, many did so without a murmur. They knew the alternatives before them: comfortable retirement with a pension – or disembowelment on the scaffold!

Results of the Dissolution

One obvious result was that the Crown took over the total net income of the monasteries, as estimated in the *Valor*. In addition, there was a very large lump sum from the sale of bullion, plate, jewellery and other valuables, including lead from the roofs and bell metal. All this wealth was handled by a new government department created by Cromwell, the Court of Augmentations, which for a time became almost the national treasury. However, it declined in importance as monastic land was sold, and was finally incorporated into the Exchequer in 1554.

If the monarchy had managed to hang on to this new source of income it

Figure 8.2 The ruins of Rievaulx Abbey, North Yorkshire

would have enormously strengthened its position in relation to Parliament, and the history of the next century or so might have turned out differently. But by the end of Henry's reign over half the land had gone to pay for his wars and other expenses, and the rest was mostly disposed of by the end of the century. Humanists such as Thomas Starkey (see chapter 5) had hoped that some of the new wealth would be used for reform of the church and for education. In the event, something was done in these areas, but not much. Six former abbeys – Westminster, Gloucester, Peterborough, Chester, Oxford and Bristol – became the centres for new bishoprics, although Westminster was taken off the list in 1550. At Oxford and Cambridge some new professorships were created and two new colleges set up – Christ Church, Oxford, which was an enlargement of Wolsey's foundation of Cardinal College, and Trinity, Cambridge. Some existing cathedral grammar schools were re-endowed, but very little was spent on founding entirely new schools. Generally, it was an opportunity missed.

The monastic buildings were mostly pulled down, or at least de-roofed, so as to be uninhabitable (see Figure 8.2). In a few cases the new owners purchased the buildings intact and were able to put them to new use: William Stumpe set up a rudimentary factory to spin woollen cloth at Malmesbury Abbey; Thomas Wriothesley converted the cloister and nave of Titchfield Abbey into a private house. One irreparable loss was the melting down of reliquaries, images and other medieval art and jewellery, and the loss of thousands of books from monastic libraries, although a few ended up in private collections, including the king's.

67

Case study

Margaret Basforth was born in Thornaby-on-Tees and became a nun at the Benedictine house of Moxby, near York, at the age of 14. When she was 20 the nunnery was dissolved and 'she having no pension appointed nor other living towards her finding, and so continued unmarried to about a xiii years after and then for lack of living she married with Roger Newstead'.

In 1555, during Mary's reign, the couple were brought before a church court and the marriage declared invalid. The judgement of the court was 'that they shall from henceforth live separately the one from the other; and that they shall not accompany together by day nor by night, specially in one house, but in church and market; and that they shall not common nor talk together except in the presence of three or four persons at least; and that the said Margaret shall provide her nun's apparell and specially for her hood, betwixt this and Whitsuntide next, and the other apparell as shortly after as ye may conveniently'. She was to live 'in any honest place without the said house of Mounsby'. No marriage, no pension, no monastic community, but compulsory uniform, self-provided, and kind permission to live outside the disused buildings of the dissolved nunnery! However, there was a happy ending. In another legal case, in 1586, she appears as a witness and is described as 'Margaret, wife of Roger Newstead, gresman [shepherd ?] of Thornaby'.

A. G. Dickens, *The Marian Reaction in the Diocese of York* (1957).

The treatment of the ex-monks, provided they had not been a nuisance to the government, was relatively generous. Heads of houses were awarded large pensions and some went on to hold high office in the Church. Four Elizabethan bishops, including John Scory, Bishop of Hereford (1559–85), had been monks or friars. Ordinary monks usually received five or six pounds a year, equivalent to the wage of an unskilled worker or a chantry priest. Two categories which were treated more shabbily were friars and nuns. In the case of the friars the government felt under no obligation to grant pensions because their houses yielded up little or no wealth when they were dissolved. As for the nuns, they received either no pension (see case study), or a very small one, and of course they did not have the alternative of becoming secular priests, as did friars and monks.

It is unlikely that many of the employees or servants of the monasteries suffered too badly from the dissolution of the monasteries. Many were paid off with a 'reward' amounting to a year's wages, and the majority, especially the outdoor servants and those who farmed the demesne land, would probably have been needed by the new owners. Of the 84 employees listed at Butley Priory, the 12 agricultural labourers as well as the carters, shepherds, woodkeepers, swineherds, wheelwrights, warreners, slaughterers and coopers would all surely have been re-employed by the Frith family who took over the monastic site.

Who got the monastic lands? This is a difficult question requiring many local studies, but at the present state of research it seems that the new owners tended to be those already well established in the locality, and not 'new men'. In Devon, Professor Youings has shown how the Crown deliberately encouraged the Russells to build up their land holdings so that they might replace the Courtenays, who had been convicted of treason, as the leading government supporters in the area. Apart from the Russells, most Devon monastic land went to a number of minor gentry families rather than to the very rich.

The economic results of the Dissolution have been exaggerated. The monasteries were not replaced by a new type of landlord who ground the faces of the poor by rack-renting or enclosure. Nor was it a major cause of vagrancy and poverty in the countryside. The mid-century inflation, which caused economic dislocation and unemployment, had European causes, especially the silver influx, and insofar as the English government contributed, it did so by successive debasements of the coinage rather than by its treatment of the monks (see chapters 11, 13 and 16). Nevertheless, the decline of clerical and monastic influence, and the corresponding rise in status of gentry families, represented long-term alterations in the nation's social structure which also had important political implications.

Task: class discussion

Divide into groups to discuss whether, by the 1530s, the monasteries had outlived their usefulness or whether they still had a role to play. Imagine that you are living in 1539. Many smaller monasteries have already been dissolved. Then Cromwell announces that the government intends to dissolve the greater monasteries as well. Discuss in groups the arguments, both for and against, this move. Make a list of these and show them to other groups. How much agreement is there between the groups?

Further reading

A. G. Dickens (ed.), *The Register or Chronicle of Butley Priory* (Winchester, 1951) – a good study of the Dissolution at a local level.

D. Knowles, *The Religious Orders in England*, volume III, 'The Tudor Age' (Cambridge University Press, 1971) – the classic account, beautifully written.

J. Youings, *The Dissolution of the Monasteries* (Allen and Unwin, 1971).

9 The Pilgrimage of Grace

Time chart

1536: **2 October** Start of Lincolnshire rising. Bishop of Lincoln's official seized at Louth

4 October Gentry assume leadership. Murder of Dr Raynes, the Bishop's chancellor, at Horncastle. **Robert Aske** crosses Humber to meet leaders

6 October Hussey writes to Shrewsbury to sound him out

8 October Hussey receives Shrewsbury's reply ordering him to join him, which he does. Ten thousand rebels march on Lincoln. List of grievances sent to the king

10 October King's reply repudiating grievances reaches Lincoln. Gentry involved in rebellion disperse

13 October Rising in South Yorkshire. Aske proclaimed 'Grand Captain' and speaks of a Pilgrimage

16 October Rebel force under Aske enters York and is acclaimed by the citizens. Other risings in Northumberland, Durham and North Yorkshire. Barnard Castle surrenders to rebels, but Skipton resists. Contingents from Cumberland assemble at Penrith

21 October Darcy surrenders Pontefract Castle to Aske. Henry orders Shrewsbury to advance towards Doncaster

27 October 30,000-strong Pilgrim army confronts royal army of 8,000 under Duke of Norfolk at Doncaster. Meeting between Norfolk and Pilgrim leaders, including Darcy, on Doncaster Bridge. Agreement that two Pilgrims should carry petition to king at Windsor. Uneasy truce while king's reply awaited

21 November Robert Bowes gives Pilgrim Council account of visit to Windsor. Henry has requested clarification

4 December Pilgrim Council at Pontefract issues detailed Articles

6 December Second meeting at Doncaster between Norfolk and Pilgrim leaders. Norfolk agrees to general pardon and calling of Parliament to address grievances. Aske persuades Pilgrims to accept terms and tears off his Pilgrim badge (see Figure 9.1). Henry delays confirmation of agreement

1537: **16 January** Sir Francis Bigod leads new rising in Yorkshire. His force enters Beverley but fails to take Hull or Scarborough

10 February Bigod is captured. Another rising in Cumberland fails to take Carlisle and is put down. Henry now has excuse he needs to punish original leaders. In following months 178 Pilgrims are executed, including Darcy and Aske

PROFILE: *Robert Aske*

Robert Aske was born at the beginning of the sixteenth century. From an East Riding of Yorkshire gentry family, he was a successful lawyer with a London practice when the rebellion in the north erupted. According to Professor Knowles in volume III of *The Religious Orders in England* he was 'one of the few men of his age whom we recognise at once to have been utterly frank and single-minded. Although he appears on the stage of history for only six months of his 36 years of age, it is clear that he had an intelligence, a capacity for leadership and a sense of justice and generosity quite out of the common.'

Having crossed the Humber to meet the leaders of the Lincolnshire Rising, Aske speedily took over sole command of the Pilgrimage, leading his forces into York, accepting the surrender of Pontefract Castle and negotiating with the Duke of Norfolk (see time chart). He always stressed the religious nature of the Rising and was particularly concerned with the restoration of the suppressed monasteries, emphasising their social and economic role in the North. He later admitted that he alone had been responsible for the demand in the Pontefract Articles that the Pope should be restored as head of the English Church.

After the failure of the Bigod rising in early 1537, Aske was arrested and interrogated. He was executed at Clifford's Tower, York, in July.

This chapter is about historical causation. It concerns the causes of the Pilgrimage of Grace, the rebellion that swept the north of England in the autumn and winter of 1536. The Pilgrimage was the most serious revolt against any Tudor government. Owing to thorough investigations by the authorities after its suppression, it is easily the best documented – though depositions by prisoners whose main aim was to avoid the scaffold must be treated with caution. It was a complex movement, not confined to one area and involving many social elements. Here we discuss three inter-connected issues, all the subject of current historical debate:

1 Was the Pilgrims' motivation mainly secular or religious?

2 How far was the Pilgrimage a spontaneous mass-movement, and how far was it dominated, or even manipulated, by the upper classes?

3 Insofar as the gentry and nobility did assume the leadership, were their motives 'feudal' or 'factional'?

Religious or secular?

From the sheer numbers involved (10,000 in Lincoln; a 30,000-strong army at Doncaster) it is likely that there were many different reasons for joining the Pilgrimage. Some of these are stated in the Articles sent up to the king from Lincoln – which became the basis for Aske's York Articles of 15 October – and in the more detailed Pontefract Articles of early December 1536. Both sets of Articles are a mixture of economic, political and religious grievances, although such distinctions may not always be meaningful. There is disagreement among historians as to whether secular or religious factors dominated the Pilgrimage. According to Rachel Reid, writing in 1921, 'Even if there had been no Reformation, there must have been a rising in the North about this time.' Dr Reid emphasised the high food prices caused by a disastrous harvest in 1535, followed by a disappointing one in 1536. She also examined the discontent of tenants at rises in rent and 'gressoms' (*i.e.* the entry fines payable to a landlord when a new tenant took over a farm). However, this factor, it is now acknowledged, was really significant as a cause for rebellion only in Westmorland and Cumberland, and particularly among the tenants of the grasping Henry Clifford, Earl of Cumberland.

A recent article by M. L. Bush also comes down on the side of secular motivation. Dr Bush shows that both clergy and laity were angered by recent innovations in taxation. The Act of First Fruits and Tenths (1534) meant that Henry took a much larger slice of clerical wealth than ever the Pope had, and this was compounded by the *Valor Ecclesiasticus* (see chapter 8) which provided a more realistic assessment of that wealth. Meanwhile, tax-paying laymen were disquieted by the fact that the 1534 Parliamentary subsidy (which was in process of being collected in Lincolnshire when the revolt broke out) was not justified by the usual pretext of military need, and therefore implied the innovatory precedent of regular peacetime taxation.

However, more significant than issues of tax or entry fines was the cumulative effect on conservative northerners of the many sweeping religious changes that Cromwell's government was imposing. The dissolution of the smaller monasteries, under the Act of 1536, was proceeding and was much resented, but for most the chief threat, real or perceived, was to their local churches and their traditional religion. It was through the parish church that people obtained their sense of belonging to a community; they joined in its rituals and they contributed to its upkeep over the years.

One of the three sets of government commissioners who were visiting

Figure 9.1 *'The Five Wounds of Christ – the badge of the Pilgrims*

Louth when the revolt started (the others being to raise the subsidy and to dissolve the monasteries) was enforcing Cromwell's 1536 Injunctions which empowered them to check the credentials of the local clergy and to get rid of 'superstitious practices'. One example of the sort of government measure that got people's backs up was the abolition of local 'holy-days' in honour of parochial patron saints. On top of all this there were many rumours of worse to come, including that Cromwell planned to pull down certain churches, leaving only one every five miles. Another rumour was that the government intended to seize all church plate, and to introduce a series of indirect taxes: 6/8d [33p] for every plough, 4d per baptism. In a time of uncertainty and change, such stories spread like wildfire. As John Hallom, one of the ring-leaders from Yorkshire, later said, 'The people saw many abbeys pulled down in deed, they believed all the rest to be true'.

In Yorkshire, Robert Aske made religion into the mainspring of the revolt. It was he, early on, who called what they were doing a pilgrimage, and who evoked powerful religious imagery, including the badge of the five wounds of Christ, to sanctify their enterprise (see Figure 9.1). He also composed the Pilgrims' oath, which started:

> '*Ye shall not enter into this our Pilgrimage of Grace for the Commonwealth, but only for the love that ye do bear unto Almighty God his faith, and the Holy Church militant and the maintenance thereof . . .*'

What other justification could there have been for daring to pit themselves against their anointed sovereign? As C. S. L. Davies says:

> '*Religious factors were an essential feature of the Pilgrimage; they figured large among the causes, they served to give the movement cohesion, to bind together different classes with widely different interests, providing slogans and scapegoats, in the last resort legitimating resistance to the king.*'
>
> C. S. L. Davies, 'Popular Religion and the Pilgrimage of Grace' in Anthony Fletcher and John Stevenson (eds), *Order and Disorder in Early Modern England* (1985).

A spontaneous movement?

Was the Pilgrimage a spontaneous mass-movement, or was it the creation of certain interested parties? Professor Elton believed the latter. He pointed to some of the Pontefract Articles as being clearly the work of an educated elite. For example, Article 8 reads:

> Item   *to have the Lord Cromwell, the Lord Chancellor, and Sir Richard Rich knight to have condign punishment, as the subverters of the good laws of this realm and maintainers of the false sect of those heretics and the first inventors and bringers in of the same.*

Elton comments, in *Reform and Reformation; England 1509–58*, 'one wonders whether the peasants had even heard of Cromwell, let alone Rich'. In both Lincolnshire and Yorkshire, he claims, the rebels 'needed to have their enemies pointed out to them'. There are other articles which were clearly inserted on behalf of either gentry or clergy, and were unlikely to interest anyone else. An example of the latter is Article 5, concerning First Fruits and Tenths, and of the former, Article 20, which demanded the repeal of the **Statute of Uses**.

KEY TERM:

Statute of Uses, 1536

The Use was a legal device which enabled nobles and gentry who were tenants-in-chief of the king to avoid paying feudal dues. By setting up a use, or perpetual trust, a landowner could effectively bypass this obligation, but the king resented the way in which he was being cheated of his legitimate rights and income, and more or less forced Parliament to pass the 1536 statute outlawing such uses.

It was now the turn of the landowners to show resentment (*e.g.* in the Pilgrimage of Grace). Henry therefore accepted a compromise embodied in the Statute of Wills, 1540. As long as feudal dues were paid on one-third of his land, a tenant-in-chief could pass on the rest to his heirs free of charge.

As to the spontaneous origins of the revolt, either south or north of the Humber, Elton argued that there was evidence of pre-planning. Witnesses who were interrogated later stated that the rumours about new taxes and the destruction of churches all started to circulate about four to six weeks before the outbreak. There is testimony that commoners received payment for joining rebellious crowds. William Leech of Horncastle is said to have given a shilling each to 40 'poor men' to be at Horncastle the following Tuesday, seize control of the church from the churchwardens and ring the bells to summon the town. Leech, however, was not a **gentleman** but a prosperous **yeoman**, and it may be that the instigators of the Pilgrimage were yeomen and tradesmen rather than the gentry.

In view of the variety of rumours and grievances and the speed with which the revolt spread, it may very well have been a spontaneous rising to start with, but there is no doubt that, both in Lincolnshire and further north, the gentry soon took over the leadership role. For instance, all the members of the king's Council of the North, important dignitaries and landowners in their localities, supported the rising, and several of them served on the Pilgrims' Council, the body that directed the pilgrims' strategy. Our final question is about their motives for so doing.

Feudal or factional?

One explanation of the Pilgrimage is to see it as a feudal reaction against the government in London led by the Percies, the leading family in the north, with extensive estates in Yorkshire, Northumberland and Cumberland. Many Pilgrims were **Percy** tenants or employees, including

PROFILE: *Henry Percy*

Henry Percy, sixth Earl of Northumberland, was regarded by the government with great suspicion as the head of the powerful Percy family and a known conservative. However, he was 'a weakling, physically and mentally', who had incurred heavy debts as warden of the East and Middle Marches. In 1536 he was induced to make the king his only heir in return for a pension and the settlement of his debts. As he was childless, this meant the disinheritance of his brother, Sir Thomas Percy. The earl played no part in the Pilgrimage, but he did surrender Wressle Castle, where he was lying sick, to the rebels without resistance. His death a year later allowed Henry VIII to take over all the Percy lands.

Aske, who was the earl's legal adviser. Although the Earl himself was ill throughout the rebellion, his brothers became prominent leaders – Sir Thomas in Yorkshire, and Sir Ingram leading a Northumberland force down from Alnwick, one of the Percy strongholds. Sir Thomas's motive was clear – anger at the way he had been disinherited through the pressure put on his brother by the government.

However, against this interpretation is the fact that none of the other heads of the great feudal families joined the rising. Lord Dacre and Ralph Neville, Earl of Westmorland, lay low, Lord Derby in Lancashire remained neutral, and Shrewsbury and Norfolk played a crucial part in suppressing it. The tenants of Henry Clifford, Earl of Cumberland, actually rose against their landlord, who remained loyal, holding Carlisle for the government against a rebel siege. So, with the partial exception of the Percies, the feudal explanation does not seem to fit.

An alternative explanation is the 'factional' model developed by Professor Elton, and for Lincolnshire by Mervyn James. James maintains that the conservative Lincolnshire gentry disagreed profoundly with several of Henry's policies, and in particular that they much resented the territorial ambitions in that county of the upstart nobleman, Charles Brandon, Duke of Suffolk, who was the king's friend and brother-in-law. The only way open to them of putting pressure on Henry to change his policies was to organise and lead a revolt of the commons which they could then use as a bargaining point, but duck all responsibility for it if things went wrong. This was a delicate technique which required the revolt to be serious enough to worry the government, but not to develop into all-out civil war, in which case Henry would be forced to retaliate and would lose face if any concessions were made. The model for a successful movement of this kind was the 1525 riots against Wolsey's Amicable Grant, which resulted in a climb-down by the government.

To have any chance of success the gentry needed a spokesman at court who might act as a mediator between them and the king, and this role (according to Mervyn James) was to be taken by Lord Hussey, an elderly peer with estates in the county who was reckoned to be a member of the 'Aragonese' faction (*i.e.* those supporting the claims to the succession of Mary, daughter of Catherine of Aragon). The idea was that once the revolt was under way Hussey could use his powerful contacts to achieve the goal earnestly sought by all conservatives – the downfall of the hated Cromwell.

All started according to plan. The revolt, thinks James, was probably planned by the gentry, who subsequently were able to pretend that they had only joined it because they had been forced to swear the holy Pilgrim

PROFILE: *Darcy*

Thomas, **Lord Darcy** (?1467–1537), from Templehurst, Yorkshire, was the first of his family to be made a peer. He served Henry VII as an experienced military leader, becoming warden of the East March and constable of the key royal fortress of Pontefract. However, in 1527 he openly stated his opposition to Henry VIII's annulment of his marriage with Catherine and consequently for the next five years he was prevented from leaving London for Yorkshire. In 1534 he suggested to Chapuys, Charles V's ambassador in London, that if Charles were to send an army to restore Princess Mary, disinherited by Henry, he would receive his support along with that of many other peers and gentry. On 21 October 1536, Darcy surrendered Pontefract Castle to Aske without resistance, claiming that he had no food or powder for a siege. But thereafter he supported the rebellion and was one of the leaders of the Pilgrims who met with Norfolk on Doncaster Bridge in December. Darcy was granted a free pardon along with the other leaders but, after Bigod's revolt the following January, he was arrested and executed.

oath, and once sworn they could not go back on their word. But soon things began going wrong. Hussey found he could not carry out the role assigned to him, for he received a specific order from Henry's general, Shrewsbury, to join him at Nottingham. Since the only alternative to obedience was open – and treasonable – defiance of the order, Hussey complied. When the local gentry heard about his defection they realised the game was up and speedily dispersed, leaving the commoners to face the music.

Professor Elton broadened this explanation of gentry involvement to take in the main Pilgrimage north of the Humber. He saw **Darcy** and Hussey as the chief organisers of the entire affair. Darcy, too, intended to use the rebellion in order to stage a modest protest against Henry's policies, only to find himself overwhelmed by the size and speed of the movement. One crucial pointer towards Darcy being implicated in the initial planning of the revolt is the curious fact that, when he surrendered Pontefract Castle, he just happened to have – left over from an earlier expedition – a number of badges of the five wounds of Christ, badges which the Pilgrims found suitable to wear!

The James–Elton explanation has not gone unchallenged. S. J. Gunn questions the ability of the Lincolnshire gentry to combine in the fashion suggested, and he sees Hussey as ineffective and hesitant rather than as a calculating planner. Other historians, while admitting the importance of

Hussey and Darcy, have found the 'factional' explanation too narrow in view of the scale and nature of the Pilgrimage. It might be argued that the speed with which the rebellion spread suggests that there was much combustible material ready to set off, in the shape of popular grievances against the authorities.

Task

This chapter, on the causes of the Pilgrimage of Grace, has deliberately included the conflicting views of several historians. This is not intended to confuse you but to show that there are areas of history in which even the experts disagree. To help clarify the issues they disagree about, try this exercise:

Write a paragraph to support each of the following statements. Each paragraph should contain as much factual backing as possible. Explain in each paragraph which historian(s) mentioned in this chapter might support each statement.

- The Pilgrimage of Grace was a popular movement with mainly economic causes.
- The Pilgrims were mainly motivated by religion.
- The Lincolnshire rebellion was planned and organised by discontented gentry.
- The Pilgrimage was planned by courtiers opposed to Henry's rejection of Catherine of Aragon.

Further reading

There is no single modern work on the Pilgrimage of Grace. The best brief introduction is to be found in Anthony Fletcher, *Tudor Rebellions*, Seminar Studies in History (Addison Wesley Longman, 3rd edn, 1983).

M. L. Bush, 'Up the Commonweal: The Significance of Tax Grievances in the English Rebellions of 1536', *English Historical Review*, vol. CVI, 1991.

C. S. L. Davies, 'Popular Religion and the Pilgrimage of Grace', in Anthony Fletcher and John Stevenson (eds), *Order and Disorder in Early Modern England* (Cambridge University Press, 1985).

G. R. Elton, *Reform and Reformation; England 1509–1558* (Edward Arnold, 1977) – puts the Pilgrimage into context.

S. J. Gunn, 'Peers, Commons and Gentry in the Lincolnshire Revolt of 1536', *Past and Present*, vol. 33, 1989.

M. E. James, 'Obedience and Dissent in Henrician England: The Lincolnshire Rebellion 1536', *Past and Present*, No. 48, 1970.

10 Was there a 'revolution in government'?

Time chart

1529: Wolsey falls from office having failed to persuade the Pope to annul Henry VIII's marriage to Catherine of Aragon
Reformation Parliament summoned; it lasted until 1536

1531: **Thomas Cromwell** joins the inner ring of the King's Council

1532: Cromwell becomes Henry's chief minister

1533: Henry secretly marries Anne Boleyn. Act in Restraint of Appeals prohibits appeals from English church courts to Rome in cases concerning marriages and wills. Thomas Cranmer, newly appointed archbishop of Canterbury, pronounces the king's marriage to Anne legal

1534: Act of Supremacy acknowledges the king as head of the English church. Other Acts confirm the breach with Rome. Cromwell becomes Secretary of State

1536: Anne Boleyn accused of adultery and executed
Act for the dissolution of monasteries with an income of less than £200 a year; Act of Union with Wales which creates new shires out of the marcher lordships and provides Wales with representation in parliament; Act abolishing franchises and liberties ends the semi-independent status of certain English lordships, including Durham, and brings the whole country under the direct rule of the King's government. Court of Augmentations is established to control the wealth acquired from the monasteries. Pilgrimage of Grace breaks out against the recent reforms. A Privy Council of about 19 members appears, at least temporarily

1537: Pilgrimage of Grace is crushed and its leaders executed. Cromwell re-asserts his personal authority over the Council. First authorised English translation of the Bible is published, at Cromwell's behest. Cromwell, as Vicar-General (Henry's deputy as head of the church), issues Injunctions requiring all parish priests to keep a register to record births and deaths, and to provide an English Bible for their parish

1539: Proclamations Act states that royal proclamations should be obeyed 'as though they were made by Act of Parliament'
Act for the dissolution of the greater monasteries

1540: Court of First Fruits and Tenths set up to handle revenues received by the Crown from the Church. Cromwell is arrested and executed for treason. His fall results from political intrigue by his enemies and from loss of favour with Henry due to having arranged the king's marriage to Anne of Cleves. Privy Council is reconstituted with a clerk, a minute book and a register

---

PROFILE: *Thomas Cromwell*

Thomas Cromwell was born in Putney about 1485. His father was an ale-house keeper. Cromwell later told Cranmer that he had been 'a bit of a ruffian' when young. He took off for the continent in his late teens, and is said to have fought in the French army at the Battle of Garigliano (1503). Later he turned to trade and travelled widely, learning French, Italian and Latin. He settled in England but continued to make journeys abroad, on one of which he is supposed to have learned the New Testament by heart. He had no formal education, not even in the law, but he managed to build up a successful legal practice. He took service with Wolsey and became an MP.

From 1531 he was in the royal service, becoming the King's Secretary and subsequently Vicar-General, with authority over the church. He drafted the Acts passed by the Reformation Parliament and carried out many other reforms including the dissolution of the monasteries. Among the reasons for his fall from power were that Henry disliked Anne of Cleves whom Cromwell had brought from Germany for him to marry, and that Henry suspected him of being a crypto-Lutheran. Cromwell was beheaded in June 1540 after being charged with treason and heresy.

The 1530s were a time of much activity, and many aspects of life in England and Wales underwent major alterations. This was the decade in which Henry's dissatisfaction with his wife Catherine led to a religious revolution. Other events included faction struggles at Court, the dissolution of the monasteries and a serious rebellion in the countryside, all of which are considered in other chapters. In this chapter we look at an issue of major historical controversy – the so-called revolution in government.

In 1953 Geoffrey Elton published his famous book, *The Tudor Revolution in Government*, in which he first put forward the thesis that the changes introduced by Henry's energetic minister Thomas Cromwell (1532–40) amounted to an administrative revolution. There are three key words

Imperial

This term in the sixteenth century did not mean having an empire in the sense of owning colonies. It referred to a particular view of monarchy – namely that England was a totally independent nation (*i.e.* an 'empire' in its own right, owing allegiance to no outside power). Its **imperial** ruler had authority in spiritual as well as secular matters, just like the Roman emperor Constantine (306–337 AD) who made Christianity the official religion of the Roman empire. The theory is set out clearly in the preamble to the Act of Appeals (1533) which was the first act in English history to define the powers of the monarch. (See also chapter 7.)

which encapsulate the main points of Elton's thesis: *sovereignty; Parliament; bureaucracy*.

1 *Sovereignty* Cromwell held the view that England was (or ought to be) a unified sovereign state, meaning that there should be just one power governing the lives of all those who lived within the realm – that power being the king. This principle of national sovereignty became established during the 1530s in the course of a struggle between the king and the pope, which ended by Henry becoming head of the English Church. From now on, all subjects owed exclusive allegiance to their **imperial** ruler.

2 *Parliament* All through the 1530s the important changes were embodied in statutes (Acts of Parliament), made by the king, Lords and Commons. Henry's supremacy over the Church was God-given – or so he and Cromwell asserted – but Parliament was needed to enforce it. Until Parliament had decreed that certain actions were criminal (such as denying that Henry was head of the church) there was no way that the supremacy could be enforced. So the break with Rome served to strengthen the authority of Parliament instead of creating a royal despotism.

3 *Bureaucracy* Cromwell took over a government dominated by the Household (*i.e.* a government which was run by the personal efforts of the king and the court officials surrounding him). But this system tended to break down when the king was not active and powerful. Cromwell downgraded the Household, and replaced it by a series of bureaucratic institutions which did not depend on the king's personal efforts but functioned efficiently whatever the monarch was like. This marked the transition to modern administration.

To sum up the Elton thesis, Cromwell is said to have bequeathed England:

- a unified, independent sovereign state
- a constitutional monarchy in which all law was made by Parliament
- a modern, bureaucratic administration.

Professor Elton revised and expanded his ideas in many books and articles since the 1950s, but never fundamentally altered them. However, other historians have criticised several aspects of the Elton thesis. In fact, owing to these controversies the 1530s is one of the most widely discussed decades in the whole of British history.

Areas of agreement

Much of the Elton thesis has been generally accepted. For instance, there is no doubt that the monarch's power did increase during the 1530s. Supremacy over the church augmented Henry's authority, and the dissolution of the monasteries his wealth (although it is true that the increase in wealth did not last very long – see chapter 8). One could even argue that Henry's reign marked a high point in the monarchy's power, before decline set in.

Secondly, most historians would accept that the decade saw an increase in the status of Parliament (see chapter 7). One dissenting voice was that of Joel Hurstfield, who claimed that Thomas Cromwell basically held Parliament in contempt, and that the Statute of Proclamations (see time chart) was originally intended as a way of giving Henry powers to make future laws by proclamation, so that he could later dispense with Parliament. However, this view has not been generally accepted. It was crucial for the development of Parliament that Henry and Cromwell used it for their Reformation, and the precedents established in the 1530s affected the relationship between the monarch and the Commons throughout the Tudor period and beyond.

A third area in which the 'revolution in government' seems indisputable involved Cromwell's efforts to extend the royal sovereignty throughout the country so as to provide more efficient government and to ensure that the religious changes were enforced without opposition. Important here was the Act of 1536 against franchises, which abolished the various separate legal jurisdictions which had existed in England for centuries. The main franchise abolished was that of the bishopric of Durham where, since 1066, royal laws had only been implemented when the Bishop of Durham agreed with them. This special status now disappeared. The same year another Act brought Wales fully under English law, with new counties, JPs, and the right to elect members to Westminster. Both these measures were crucial in the work of turning the nation into a unified sovereign state.

Controversies

We now turn to the parts of Elton's thesis which have been significantly challenged by other historians. Elton always maintained that Cromwell had a systematic approach to his reforms, but other historians regard him as a pragmatist who reacted to circumstances and to the political needs of the moment. Again, Elton believed that Cromwell was advised by a group of like-minded and far-sighted reformers; others have seen this so-called 'commonwealth' group as a collection of random individuals who approached Cromwell for patronage at different times. Thirdly, Elton singled out Cromwell as the initiator of the series of statutes which brought in the 1530s Reformation, and gave him the credit for the famous preamble to the 1533 Act of Appeals. Other historians have argued that, while Cromwell may have drafted the preamble, the king dictated the contents. It was a statement of Henry's beliefs, which he probably derived from a collection of texts known as the *Collectanea* which had been presented to him in 1530 by scholars who had been researching into the case for his divorce. Henry genuinely believed that he possessed an *imperium*, a divine right to rule over both spiritual and temporal affairs. Even if Cromwell would have preferred a greater emphasis on Parliament, he was merely the servant who carried through his master's wishes.

There are two particular areas where there has been considerable argument between Elton and his critics. The best way to proceed in each case is: first, to state a few relevant facts which are not in dispute; second, to give Elton's view; finally, to present those of his critics.

1 The privy council

The facts

- Under the Yorkists and Henry VII there was a large Council to advise the monarch, consisting of scores of councillors, including peers, courtiers, judges and others. Many did not actually attend Council meetings; most of the work was done by an inner ring. By the end of Henry VIII's reign there was a Privy Council of about 20 members, mainly office holders, who all met regularly, with a clerk to record the minutes of their meetings.

- Historians can attempt to work out when the change took place by (rare) surviving lists of councillors, and by whether letters or warrants issued by the (Privy) Council were signed collectively by the entire body, or by particular members only.

- From such evidence it appears that a Privy Council emerged for a few months only during 1536/7, and re-emerged in 1540 after the fall of Cromwell.

Elton's view

The new Privy Council was constituted in the autumn of 1536 by Thomas Cromwell. However, he was reforming for the future and he wished to keep the system under his control while he remained in charge (especially as some of the Privy Councillors were his potential opponents).

This is why the Privy Council had to be reconstituted in 1540 after he had gone. But it was basically his achievement.

Critics' views

John Guy argues that Cromwell would never have had the time to undertake such a fundamental reform during 1536, the year in which he overthrew the Boleyn faction in the spring and faced the Pilgrimage of Grace in the autumn. Secondly, even if he had, he would not have staffed the new Privy Council with his enemies (religious conservatives who, in fact, did eventually engineer his fall). Thirdly, between 1537 and 1540 Cromwell reasserted his personal control of government, thus preventing the Privy Council from acting as a corporate body. So the new body was created 'less because he lived than because he died'.

2 Finance and bureaucracy

The facts

■ Up to 1530 government finances were dominated by a system where-by the monarch personally used his Chamber and Privy Chamber (see chapter 4) to receive and to spend revenue. These two departments of the Household were undifferentiated – meaning, firstly, that their funds came from different sources and could be spent on anything the monarch wanted; secondly, that these two departments did not deal only with finance, but also with politics, foreign policy, and so on.

■ By the end of Henry VIII's reign four new financial departments had emerged. These were the Courts of Augmentations; First Fruits and Tenths; Wards and Liveries; and General Surveyors. Now there were six specialised departments to control different kinds of revenue. The two which already existed were the Exchequer and the Duchy of Lancaster. The Chamber and Privy Chamber survived but lost their earlier importance, since they were no longer revenue departments in their own right but depended for funds upon transfers from the other institutions which had supplanted them.

Elton's view

This was a revolution by Cromwell. He deliberately set out to end the domination of the Household over finances because this system was too informal and relied too heavily on the personal characteristics of whoever happened to be monarch. Instead, he set up a bureaucratic system along modern lines, in which properly trained officials operated with clearly-defined job descriptions within specialist departments.

Critics' views

J. D. Alsop denies that the new departments were more bureaucratic than the old: all the institutions, old and new, changed their methods over the course of time (see Coleman and Starkey's *Revolution Reassessed*). And if some element of modernisation did occur – such as, for example, the substitution of arabic numerals for Roman numerals in the accounts – it could happen equally well in a Household or a non-Household department. Moreover, many officials moved in the course of their careers from Exchequer to Household, or vice versa. In Alsop's view the attempt to distinguish between personalised and bureaucratic institutions is false and misleading. Alsop also argues that, although Cromwell may have made an important contribution, the changes that did take place were over a long time-scale, and not really due to any one minister. They came about largely because financial affairs were steadily becoming more complicated and requiring different methods.

David Starkey's view is that the importance of the Privy Chamber throughout Henry VIII's reign shows that the Household continued to dominate government. In particular, he explains that the 'revolution' in financial administration was never completed because, late in the reign, Henry decided to accumulate large sums of money to be reserved for his own personal use (either for war or for palace-building). This private war-chest was kept by Henry 'if not under the bed, at least at the back of the bedchamber in the secret jewel-house, a dramatic reassertion of the vitality of household administration'.

Starkey also claims that Cromwell, far from trying to reduce the importance of the Privy Chamber, actually worked through it (at least, he did so after 1536, when he had gained power over the other factions at Court). Cromwell even managed to get his own nominee, Thomas Heneage, made Groom of the Stool. This was important to Cromwell because of Henry's laziness. There were always numerous documents which had to have the king's signature and the best way to get them signed was for someone who was close to the king to catch him in a good mood.

Conclusion

Our two topics of the Council and finance overlap because after 1540 the new Privy Council was in place, overseeing the new revenue departments. A non-Household system had taken over from the personal methods of Henry VII. The revolution in government had occurred. But had it? This surely depends on the meaning of the word 'revolution', and this in turn partly depends on the time-scale. A revolution has to be rapid. If the crucial developments we have been concerned with all took place during the 1530s, then this might be 'revolutionary'; if they took the whole reign, then perhaps not.

Some historians want to extend the time-scale still further. G. L. Harriss has argued that the national sovereign state which Cromwell is supposed to have set up was, in fact, a return to the more formalised government of the late Middle Ages, which had been disrupted by the Wars of the Roses. Harriss sees the Household administration of Edward IV and Henry VII as a temporary response to the weakness of the monarchy in the mid fifteenth century. He writes: 'although Dr Elton is right to see the 1530s as a turning-point, by equating early Tudor with medieval government he has mistaken a part for the whole, and interpreted as a revolution what was in fact a return'.

David Starkey, on the other hand, has advised us to judge Cromwell's work in the context of the whole of the following century. He argues that under the early Stuarts, James I and Charles I, 'the revived power of the royal bedchamber made itself felt and led to a return to the strategies characteristic of the power politics of the reigns of Henry VIII and Edward VI'. He concludes: 'Stop the clock with Elizabeth's death, as Tudor historians are all too inclined to do, and it is possible (just) to argue that government by the monarch was developing into government under the monarch by the Council. But let the clock move forward, as of course it did, into the reign of James, and the argument for long-term change collapses.' In other words, according to Starkey, there was no permanent revolution at all, and to see one under Cromwell is just a failure of perspective.

The fact that no consensus has emerged about the significance of the 1530s is due to various factors, including variations in the period of time over which the changes are judged, differences in the interpretation of the evidence, and concentration on different aspects of government. It would be foolish to end a chapter like this by trying to give a definitive judgement on all the issues at stake, but from what has been said it does seem dangerous to argue that there was a revolution in administration in this decade, or that government shifted decisively from Household to bureaucratic methods at this time. Nevertheless, it is clear that Thomas Cromwell was an administrator of genius who made important changes in the relatively short time available to him. But he may not have been either 'the most remarkable revolutionary in English history', or 'a man who knew precisely where he was going and who nearly always achieved the end he had in view' (two of Elton's past claims for him). Perhaps one might leave the last word with Christopher Coleman: 'Thirty years after the publication of [Elton's] *The Tudor Revolution in Government*, historians are as far as ever from agreeing with either Professor Elton or with each other on the extent to which its central ideas are, or are not, valid.'

Task: essay-writing

You will know by now that the essay has an important part to play in historical studies as a way for you to show your ability to think logically and to write clearly. Writing a good essay is not easy. It takes a lot of effort and practice; many students find it the hardest part of a history course. Here are some suggestions which might help.

1 Think about the question very carefully. If possible, divide it into two or more aspects. Remember, too, you don't have to agree with the wording of a question, especially if it involves a quotation which you are asked to discuss or 'debate'.

2 Read any class notes, handouts or chapters in the books you use, looking for points that are relevant to the various aspects of the question, and noting them down.

3 Make an essay plan. This will let you see if you have enough points to answer the question. Making a plan means getting your points into a logical order. It will also help when you actually write the essay. A good plan prevents repetition and waffle and helps you decide about what to write next in the essay.

4 The plan should break down your argument into paragraphs. Each paragraph should deal with a different topic connected with the question.

5 Your various points should be supported by facts and examples. Note them down in the right places in the plan. But make sure you don't put in facts just for the sake of it. Facts should only be used to illustrate or support particular points or opinions.

6 The first paragraph should be the introduction. This should not be too factual but should discuss/define the question and set out your general argument: that is, it should tell the reader what the rest of the essay is going to be about.

7 It is important to have a good concluding paragraph. The conclusion should not bring in any new facts. It should go back to the question and explain how your essay has tried to answer it.

Essay question
'Henry VIII was a conservative but the results of his policies were revolutionary.' Discuss this statement in relation to English government policies in the 1530s.

Essay plan
Here is a suggested essay plan to help you tackle the essay question above. Remember, though, that you don't have to agree with the

line taken here. Essays at this level are about *debate*; debate implies different viewpoints. Don't be afraid to defend your own view – but always from a careful consideration of the evidence.

---

1   Introduction. 'Conservative' = maintaining status quo? 'Revolutionary changes' = intended, long-term changes? Look at 'conservative' first, then 'revolutionary', arguing that some changes may have been long term, though unintended by Henry.

2   H = conservative? Conventional upbringing. Hobbies of tournaments, hunting giving way by 1530s to taste for theology. Conservative aims: an heir; rivalry with Francis I & Charles V; hence, money; honour & status. True, new kingship ('imperial') – but based on historical precedent (chronicles, Old Testament).

3   Conservative also in religion. *Fidei defensor*, 1521. Never a Protestant. Publishes Bible merely to enhance kingship. Claims headship of church & dissolves monasteries mainly for power/money. Reverts to ultra-conservative, 1536 – end of reign.

4   Revolutionary results? Elton says rev. in government (extension of royal power over England; Council more bureaucratic) but (a) much of Elton thesis disputed now & (b) if true, it was Cromwell, not H.

5   True, headship of church & dissolution are long-term changes. Other long-term changes quite unintended by H. *e.g.* weakening of monarchy due to over-spending, sale of Crown lands, debasements.

6   Conclusion. 1st part of statement right; 2nd part, only partly so. 'Revolutionary' change implies someone planned it. If so, H. certainly didn't, though Cromwell might be called revolutionary.

Further reading

C. Coleman and D. Starkey (eds), *Revolution Reassessed: Revisions in the History of Tudor Government and Administration* (Clarendon Press, 1986).

G. R. Elton, *The Tudor Constitution* (Cambridge University Press, 2nd edn, 1982) – summarises the Elton version.

John Guy, 'Thomas Wolsey, Thomas Cromwell and the Reform of Henrician Government' in Diarmaid MacCulloch (ed.), *The Reign of Henry VIII: Politics, Policy and Piety* (Macmillan, 1995).

G. R. Elton, *Thomas Cromwell* (Headstart History Papers, 1991).

D. Starkey, *The English Court from the Wars of the Roses to the Civil War* (Addison Wesley Longman, 1987).

G. L. Harriss, 'Medieval Government and Statecraft', *Past and Present*, 25, 1963.

11 Somerset v. Northumberland

Time chart

1547: January Death of Henry VIII. Hertford (Edward Seymour) secures his position as Lord Protector and makes himself Duke of Somerset
September English invade Scotland and win Battle of Pinkie
November Somerset starts to construct garrison forts in Scotland. Act of Six Articles and Henrician treason laws repealed
December Dissolution of chantries authorised by Parliament

1548: February Demolition of all images in churches decreed
June French army lands at Leith and proceeds to attack English garrisons. Mary Stuart taken to France.
Commissioners appointed to examine recent enclosures

1549: January Thomas Seymour, Somerset's brother, is arrested and executed for plotting against state.
New prayer book, in English but conservative in tone, is approved
April Enclosure commissioners given powers to 'reform' forbidden enclosures
May–August Revolts break out in several parts of the country
August Henry II of France declares war over Boulogne. Western rebels finally crushed by Lord Russell at Sampford Courtenay. Kett's rebellion defeated by Earl of Warwick (John Dudley) at Dussindale
October Warwick arrests Somerset and takes possession of Edward's person

1550: February Warwick, in alliance with Cranmer, defeats Wriothesley and conservative faction. Somerset is released from prison and reappointed to Council
March Treaty of Boulogne; French obtain town in exchange for subsidy

1551: February New guard of 900 horsemen, 'gendarmes', is created
July Treaty of Angers. Edward is bethrothed to Elizabeth, daughter of Henry II of France (but marriage never takes place)
October Warwick promotes himself Duke of Northumberland. Somerset is re-arrested, tried for felony and executed

1552: October 'Gendarmes' abolished for reasons of economy
November Under Second Act of Uniformity new prayer book

comes into use in all churches: Protestant in tone, reflecting influence of continental radicals such as Martin Bucer

1553: **Spring** Edward ill with tuberculosis. Northumberland persuades him to copy out 'Device for the succession' which disinherits both Mary and Elizabeth. Subsequent draft names Lady Jane Grey, who marries Northumberland's eldest son in May

July Death of Edward. Northumberland proclaims Jane Grey Queen. Mary flees to Norfolk where her support grows. Northumberland gives himself up and is imprisoned

August Execution of Northumberland

Edward VI was 9 when he came to the throne on his father's death; he was nearly 16 when he died of tuberculosis in 1553. During these six years the country was governed successively by two noblemen: Edward Seymour, Duke of Somerset, and John Dudley, Duke of Northumberland (see Figures 11.1 and 11.2). These two self-created dukes had much in common: both came from families recently arrived on the political scene; both had originally been promoted by Henry VIII for their military skills; both controlled and manipulated the young king for their own purposes.

Until quite recently, however, historians have treated them very differently. Somerset was 'the good duke' – a ruler of liberal, if not socialist, views – who was eventually brought down because his co-rulers resented

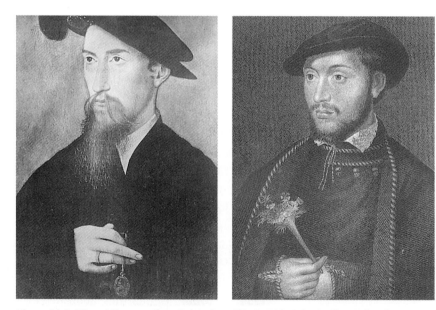

Figure 11.1 *Edward Seymour, later Duke of Somerset (c. 1506–52)*

Figure 11.2 *John Dudley, Duke of Northumberland (c. 1502–53)*

the way he took the side of the poor in their struggle against greedy landowners. Northumberland, 'the bad duke', was – as Lady Jane Grey is supposed to have said just before she was executed – 'wicked and full of dissimulation ... he hath brought me and our stock into most miserable calamity and misery by his exceeding ambition'. This chapter investigates these verdicts in the light of recent historical research. We can compare the two leaders under four headings: the nature of their rule; their foreign, fiscal and religious policies.

Nature of rule

Edward Seymour possessed the great advantage of being the young Prince Edward's maternal uncle, but investigations into the events surrounding Henry's death suggest that he more or less bribed himself into his dominant position as Lord Protector. Extra clauses were inserted into Henry's will as he lay dying, one of which allowed the Council to grant any awards which the king might have intended but never legally conveyed. This clause gave Seymour the excuse not only to make himself duke but also to shower titles on the members of his own faction so as to ensure their continued support.

Once in power, Somerset acted more like a king than a regent. Just before his arrest in October 1549 he ordered officials to destroy the records of his Protectorate. Some papers survived, including a copy of the Privy Council's proceedings, and this shows clearly how he tried to govern without using the Council, taking advice instead from members of his own household. Just as Wolsey's palace at York Place had once seemed to be the centre of government, so now it was Somerset House, a little further down the Strand. This neglect of the Council was not illegal, but it had the effect of isolating Somerset politically, so that when he needed the support of councillors in the 1549 crisis, he did not get it.

Somerset lacked charm and made enemies easily. His arrogance and pride created resentment and he took his exalted position too much for granted, as when letters to him spoke of 'your navy', 'your foreign affairs'. Also, he was a weak administrator with a misplaced faith in his own judgement, who refused to listen to acknowledged experts. Even when he performed a necessary action – as when he was forced to have his own foolhardy and disreputable brother executed for treason – he managed to do it in such a way as to arouse maximum resentment. The crisis for Somerset came in the autumn of 1549 when he failed to deal decisively with the rebellions in the West and in Norfolk which had been partly caused by his own policies. As Dale Hoak points out (see 'Further reading' at the end of chapter), his colleagues decided to get rid of him at this point, not because he supported the poor but because he was incompetent.

After his military success in putting down Kett's rebellion, John Dudley (Earl of Warwick, and soon to become Duke of Northumberland) succeeded Somerset as ruler of the country. But Warwick's path to power was not easy. Between October 1549 and February 1550 there was a period of bitter factional in-fighting which has been described as the fiercest struggle for power in England since the previous century. Having had Somerset arrested, Warwick found himself the victim of a second coup, this time organised by Thomas Wriothesley, Earl of Southampton, the leader of a group of conservative peers. Warwick showed his political skills in outmanoeuvring them, but to do so he had to release Somerset from the Tower of London and re-install him as a councillor because Wriothesley was trying to associate him with Somerset's alleged treason. Somerset survived for another two years, though never again approaching the centre of power.

Warwick did not make himself Protector, partly because the title had been discredited by Somerset and partly because, not being a relative of Edward's, he had no possible claim. Instead, he ruled by simultaneously holding two key offices: Lord President of the Council and Great Steward of the King's Household. Through the first he dominated the Privy Council, which was now revived, bringing to an end Somerset's short bout of personal-style rule. Warwick was helped in this revival by the man he appointed to be one of the secretaries to the Council, William Cecil, who was later to fill the same office under Elizabeth.

As Great Steward, Warwick also controlled Edward's household, which he staffed with his supporters. Edward was now at an age to have his own opinions, both about which courtiers he preferred and trusted and on questions of religion, so it was necessary for Northumberland – as he became in 1551 – to tread carefully and make sure he always enlisted the young king's support. He did this through his own personal charm – which was considerably greater than Somerset's – and by controlling all access to the royal person. As regards religion, he was lucky that Cranmer, who was Archbishop of Canterbury and Northumberland's ally, was one of the people Edward trusted most.

Northumberland obtained such an influence over Edward that the king was ready to make it appear as if decisions which had actually originated with the duke came from him. When Edward was dying, he and Northumberland together – nobody can be sure whose idea it was first – concocted a document called the Device which barred both Elizabeth and Mary, Edward's two sisters, from the throne in favour of Jane Grey, the granddaughter of Henry VIII's sister, who just happened to marry the duke's son.

Nevertheless, although he controlled both Council and Household, Northumberland never felt himself secure. He knew that basically he was only a faction leader who had been lucky, and that another coup like the one against Somerset could erupt at any time. Another constant fear was of a new rebellion in the countryside – the government had been deeply shaken by the rebels of 1549. Northumberland's remedy against either possibility was to create the nearest thing England had ever seen to a standing army in peacetime. Several of the new councillors picked by him, such as the earls of Huntingdon and Westmorland, were experienced military leaders whom he allowed to retain bands of horsemen at royal expense. This force, nicknamed the 'gendarmes', was there to deal with any possible rebellion or counter-coup. However, it was disbanded for reasons of economy in 1552 and so was unavailable when Northumberland needed it most, on Edward's death.

War and peace

Somerset's obsessive desire was to do what noblemen thought they did best – go to war. He shared this trait with Henry VIII, except that for Henry the main enemy was France; for Somerset it was Scotland. He had major plans for that country which involved bringing about a union of the crowns through a marriage between Edward and Mary, the daughter of James V of Scotland, who was aged five in 1547. Unfortunately the Scots were not interested, so Somerset personally led an army across the border and won the Battle of Pinkie. He then commenced building and garrisoning a chain of forts intended to keep Scotland in permanent submission. However, this policy turned out to be an expensive failure. Firstly, the forts were not always well positioned, especially Haddington, the largest, which was too close to Edinburgh, a Scottish stronghold that Somerset had omitted to subdue. Secondly, he failed to blockade the Firth of Forth, with the result that the French, allies of the Scots, were able to land an army, together with siege artillery, and capture some of the English forts (see time chart).

Somerset mounted two other invasions of Scotland, but the main result was that the French spirited Mary away to France, where she was betrothed to a French prince. Altogether, Somerset spent half a million pounds on Scotland, half as much again as Henry VIII had in the campaigns of the 1540s, yet in half the time. Another result of Somerset's aggressive policy was that the new and energetic young king of France, Henry II, decided to retaliate by attacking Boulogne, a town only acquired by England in 1544. So Somerset found he had a second expensive campaign on his hands, and one there was little chance of winning.

On taking over power, Northumberland saw that the only way to balance the books and achieve financial and political stability was to end Somerset's wars as quickly as possible. By the Treaty of Boulogne, the town was returned to the French in exchange for a subsidy, thus leaving only Calais in English hands, to be lost in the following reign. The involvement with Scotland was also ended and the troops withdrawn from the remaining forts. In a second treaty with the French, Edward was betrothed to a French princess instead of to the unavailable Mary, although this arrangement never came to anything.

The 'commonwealth'

Somerset's expensive foreign policy meant that he had to exploit every possible source of revenue. The dissolution of the chantries (see chapter 3) and the continued sale of crown and ex-monastic lands were both lucrative, but Somerset also continued the policy of systematically reducing the silver content of the coinage, copying the precedents set by Wolsey in 1526 and Henry in 1544–6. Unfortunately his wars, and especially his debasements, contributed to the price inflation which was rampant in the mid sixteenth century. Somerset may have genuinely wished to tackle the price rises, but he was not prepared to give up his military aims in order to do so. He refused to listen to Sir Thomas Smith (see chapter 16), author of an outstandingly perceptive treatise on the economy, who advised a restoration of the coinage, as this would have reduced government income drastically. Instead, he chose the soft option, advocated by **John Hales**, of going for enclosures and greedy landowners as scapegoats on whom to blame the inflation.

Another point which tends to contradict the image of Somerset as a ruler bound on helping the poor is that he himself was a highly acquisitive landowner. During his Protectorship he built up huge estates in Somerset and Wiltshire, partly at the expense of the Bishop of Bath and Wells whom he forced to enter into unfavourable exchanges of property.

Northumberland inherited a dangerous situation caused not only by Somerset's actions but also by a bad harvest in 1549 and a disastrous slump in the cloth trade due to a glut of unsold cloth piling up at Antwerp. He knew he could not survive politically without sound finance, so, as with France and Scotland, he speedily reversed the policies of his predecessor. A halt was brought to the **debasement** of the coinage, though not before he had debased one more time. In April 1551

KEY TERM:

Debasement

In an age when coins were supposed to contain precious metal worth their face value, England's coinage traditionally had the reputation of being sound as to weight and fineness (*i.e.* the proportion of silver or gold to alloy). Wolsey first reduced the fineness of silver coins in 1526, and this was followed between 1544 and 1551 by five successive issues of coins of ever-decreasing weight and silver content. The teston (silver shilling) of 1546 was so small it was mistaken for a groat (four-penny piece) and, on handling, soon showed a coppery tinge. Over the same period the number of coins issued was increased, and several new mints opened.

Henry VIII and Somerset made their profit from debasement by the difference between what they paid for minting the coins (including the cost of the metal) and their face value. The total profit between 1544 and 1551 was £1,300,000 – mostly spent on war.

Debasement may have helped trade by reducing the price of English goods for foreigners, and by increasing the number of coins in circulation, but these advantages were considerably outweighed by its bad effects: inflation, and the destruction of confidence in the English coinage. It was Northumberland who finally called a halt to the process, but a total recoinage had to wait until Elizabeth's reign.

PROFILE: *John Hales*

John Hales was a Chancery civil servant and member for Coventry in
the Parliament of 1547–52. He was a leader of the small group of
intellectual radicals known as the Commonwealth School, who tried to
find solutions to the economic and social problems of the day. His
belief was that the main cause of the price inflation of the late 1540s
was enclosure for sheep, which led to a shortage of food. Somerset
accepted this opinion and allowed him virtually to run the
government's economic policy. Regional commissions were set up to
investigate the effects of enclosure, and Hales served on the most
active commission, for the Midlands. He died in 1571.

It was probably at Hales's suggestion that Somerset persuaded
parliament to authorise a tax of a penny per sheep to make enclosure
less profitable. Such policies were unpopular with landowners and did
little to reduce inflation. Moreover, Hales's incendiary language as an
enclosure commissioner – talking about a conspiracy of landowners to
obstruct legislation – probably contributed to the revolts of 1549 during
which people took the law into their own hands, tearing down hedges
and filling in ditches. Hales was well-meaning, but historians have
judged him harshly as 'a notable example of the confident economic
expert who gets it all wrong' (Elton).

---

a sound money policy was introduced whereby the nominal value of the
(debased) silver shilling was reduced, first to nine, and later to six, pence
– something like its real value. This deflationary move had the effect of
actually bringing down some food prices, a major achievement. It was
followed up by a partial recoinage, with an increased silver content,
though a full recoinage had to wait until Elizabeth's reign.

Northumberland turned out to be adept at financial administration. He
succeeded in making economies in government spending and forced a
stricter accounting of income. He did not live long enough to see the
major reform of the financial system he was working towards –
the replacement of Cromwell's separate revenue departments by a single
financial agency, an up-graded exchequer – but this finally took place
under Mary.

Religion

Under Somerset there was a steady move towards Protestantism. The government tolerated a rash of Protestant publishing; the Act of Six Articles and Cromwell's treason laws were repealed; the chantries were dissolved; and a new English Prayer Book was enforced. These moves probably reflected Somerset's own views, but they were also a response to the pressures of a vocal minority of Protestants who were especially influential in London and the South-East and who, on the death of Henry, had already started to take the law into their own hands, destroying images in churches and preaching against 'superstition'. Nevertheless, the government did not want to go too far in a Protestant direction, as was shown by the ambiguities of the 1549 Prayer Book and its retention of the Catholic version of the mass in the new service:

> And when he delivereth the Sacrament of the body of Christ, he shall say to every one these words.
>
> *The body of our Lord Jesus Christ which was given for thee, preserve thy body and soul unto everlasting life.*

KEY TERM:

Radicalism

Radicalism is a term which often causes confusion. Literally, it means a belief associated with getting to the root of something. It follows that radicals can hold very different views. What they have in common is a desire to institute significant change, quite possibly on the basis of belief in a particular political or religious philosophy.

The main factor making for restraint was the desire not to alarm the Catholic emperor, Charles V, whom Somerset needed to appease owing to the war against Scotland and France. For this reason **radicalism** was kept in bounds; Somerset also tolerated Mary's Catholicism and kept denial of the royal supremacy as a capital offence. The policy was successful insofar as Charles did remain neutral, closing his ports to French shipping during hostilities. However, it led to an uncertain, transitional situation which satisfied few, either conservatives or radicals. In fact, Somerset's religious policy was a cause of the revolts of 1549, as one of his more perceptive colleagues in government, Sir William Paget, pointed out to him in a critical letter:

> *'Society in a realm doth consist and is maintained by means of religion and law. And these two or one wanting, farewell all just society, farewell king, government, justice and all other virtue ... Look well whether you have either law or religion at home and I fear you shall find neither. The use of the old religion is forbidden by a law, and the use of the new is not yet printed in the stomachs of the eleven of twelve parts in the realm, what countenance so ever men make outwardly to please them in whom they see this power resteth.'*

Northumberland's religious changes were much more thoroughgoing than Somerset's. At first sight this is puzzling, as Northumberland himself seems to have been a less committed Protestant. Nevertheless, it was during the period 1550–53 that the Church of England acquired its essential nature, a church which could accommodate the majority of Protestants but which retained a number of Catholic features. In these years continental reformers dominated the universities, tables replaced altars in parish churches, and Cranmer's Prayer Book of 1552 did away with all mention of the real presence in the communion service.

However, even now there were limits to England's advance towards Calvin's Geneva or Zwingli's Zurich. A crucial confrontation between the radical John Hooper and other bishops led by **Thomas Cranmer** ended when Hooper, an ally of the Zurich reformers, was forced to wear the traditional vestments on his consecration as Bishop of Gloucester. Northumberland took Cranmer's side, and his stand marked a vital decision for the future of the church, confirming that it would remain distinguished from the continental churches in structure and appearance.

PROFILE: *Thomas Cranmer*

Thomas Cranmer (1489–1556) spent the first half of his career as an obscure academic at Cambridge until he came to Henry VIII's notice over his views about the divorce. He was unexpectedly made Archbishop of Canterbury and worked with Cromwell to achieve the Henrician Reformation. In 1532 on a mission to Germany he met and married the niece of a Lutheran minister, but as archbishop he had to keep her so much under wraps that there was a story he took her round in a trunk.

Cranmer's views gradually moved towards the **Zwinglian position**, which made things difficult for him in the final years of the reign. But after Henry's death he was able to realise his ideas for reform. The 1549 Prayer Book was his work, although modified in a conservative direction by Parliament. He was trusted by Edward, and his alliance with Northumberland in 1549 helped to defeat the conservative faction led by Wriothesley. His crowning achievement was the 1552 Prayer Book which marked the official arrival of Protestantism in England and became the basis for the Elizabethan Prayer Book of 1559.

Cranmer was arrested for heresy early in Mary's reign. At his trial he typically had some doubts about whether he was justified in resisting the Queen's authority, but he recovered his determination and was burnt in 1556, a martyr for the Protestant faith.

KEY TERM:

Zwinglian position

Ulrich Zwingli was a Swiss reformer who took the city of Zurich into the Protestant camp in the 1520s. The Zwinglian 'position' means principally Zwingli's attitude to the Eucharist or Mass, which he saw simply as a memorial of the Last Supper, denying any real presence in the Sacrament. Zwingli died in battle in 1531. For more detail on Zwingli see the companion title in this series *The Development of Early Modern Europe 1480–1648*.

Northumberland himself was a *politique*, someone who saw religion primarily in political terms, as a binding and unifying factor in society. Why then did he preside over these sweeping changes? In the first place he needed the support of the radicals in the struggle against his conservative enemies led by Wriothesley. For this purpose he formed an alliance with Cranmer; once allied, he followed where Cranmer led. In this rather haphazard way Protestantism was officially introduced into England as a by-product of the factional struggles of 1549–50.

Northumberland may also have been influenced towards sweeping changes by the fact that there was money to be made. Many parish churches owned valuable collections of silver plate, including chalices and patens (vessels used in the Mass), and these could now be confiscated by the authorities in the name of reform. Bishops, too, could be coerced into giving up some of their estates and endowments. Yet another factor was that there was now less need to go carefully in order to conciliate Charles V, who was much too busy fighting German princes and Turks to worry about what was going on in England.

The two dukes

It should be clear by now that the old verdict on Somerset, 'the good duke', is quite misplaced. He failed in most of what he tried to do; nor was he especially sympathetic to the lower classes, as was once thought. His colleagues got rid of him because he was irresolute and incompetent, not least when it came to putting down rebellions.

As for Northumberland, there is perhaps now a risk that his rehabilitation can be taken too far. Like Somerset, he seems to have been motivated by a desire for wealth and power, for himself and his family. Both were insecure faction leaders who weakened the financial status of the monarchy by giving away crown lands in order to retain their supporters. It is difficult, too, to admire, even if one can understand, Northumberland's convenient changes of personal religion. He conformed to the conservative Act of Six Articles after 1539, introduced radical Protestantism after 1550, and then, when Mary succeeded, tried to avoid execution by proclaiming himself a Catholic.

Nevertheless, of the two, it was Northumberland who left the more permanent legacy. His foreign policy of peace with Scotland and France foreshadows Elizabeth's, and his reform of government finances laid the foundations for future accountability. Above all, his return to rule by the Privy Council, ably seconded by Cecil, showed the path that the English government was to take in the second half of the century. One might end by quoting Hoak's verdict that 'the Duke of Northumberland appears to have been one of the most remarkably able governors of any European state during the sixteenth century'.

Task: finding out more

Remember how to go about this work by looking at the advice given at the end of chapter 5.

1 Investigate the two rebellions of 1549 – Kett's rebellion and the Western Rising. What were the causes of each? Examine in particular how far Somerset's policies may have helped cause these rebellions, and his role in putting them down.

2 Investigate Northumberland's attempt in 1553 to place his son and Lady Jane Grey on the throne. How, and why, did Mary Tudor succeed in defeating this attempt?

Further reading

G. R. Elton, *Reform and Reformation; England 1509–1558* (Edward Arnold, 1977).

Dale Hoak, 'Rehabilitating the Duke of Northumberland', in *The Mid-Tudor Polity c. 1540–1560,* edited by Jennifer Loach and Robert Tittler (Macmillan, 1980).

David Loades, *Essays on the Reign of Edward VI* (Headstart History, 1994).

David Loades, *Two Tudor Conspiracies* (Cambridge University Press, 1965).

David Loades, *John Dudley: Duke of Northumberland 1504–1553* (Clarendon Press, 1996) – a recent and authoritative account.

M. L. Bush, *The Government Policy of Protector Somerset* (Edward Arnold, 1975) – a pioneering account which broke with the conventional view of Somerset as 'the good duke'.

12 Was Mary I a failure?

Time chart

1516: February Birth of Mary Tudor

1553: July Death of Edward VI. Failure of Northumberland's plot and accession of Mary
October–December Mary's first Parliament. Her first Act of repeal revokes Edwardian religious laws
December Marriage treaty approved by Parliament

1554: January–February Wyatt's rebellion
February Lady Jane Grey beheaded
March Royal Injunctions order bishops to suppress heresy and remove married clergy
April–May Second Parliament. Quarrel in Lords between Paget and Gardiner
July Marriage of Mary and Philip II
November Cardinal Pole lands in England
November 1554–January 1555 Third Parliament. Mary's second act of repeal revokes Henrician Reformation but incorporates Pole's dispensation to owners of ex-monastic lands

1555: February Campaign of persecution starts with burning of John Rogers, followed by Hooper, Ridley, Latimer, Cranmer and others
November Death of Stephen Gardiner
December First meeting of Pole's legatine synod which issues decrees for church reform and initiates survey of all English parishes

1557: April Pole is deprived of legatine powers by Pope Paul IV
June England declares war on France

1558: January–May Mary's last Parliament. Acts passed for reorganisation of militia
May New Book of Rates for customs is issued
June Loss of Calais
17 November Death of Mary, and of Pole a few hours later

Mary's political talents

Historians are often more interested in developments with long-term significance than in those that turn out to have none. It is partly for this reason that Mary Tudor has had such a bad press. Her reign has usually been seen as an unfortunate disruption of the natural progress of six-teenth-century England – progress in the Reformation, in the growth of nationalism, in modernisation. According to the imperial ambassador Simon Renard, Mary was 'good, easily influenced, inexpert in worldly matters, and a novice all round'. Historians have been even more unkind. Elton called Mary 'arrogant, assertive, bigoted, stubborn, suspicious and (not to put too fine a point upon it) rather stupid . . .'.

Leaving aside the question of whether someone can be both easily influenced and stubborn at the same time, might there not have been more to Mary than these verdicts indicate? On at least two important occasions she seems to have shown political skills of a high order. The first was when negotiating with Pope Julius III at the beginning of her reign over the terms of England's return to obedience to Rome. The Pope clearly assumed that, before he agreed to absolve the English from the 'schism' of Edward's reign, the wealth of the church confiscated over the previous 20 years, and in particular the ex-monastic lands, would be returned. But Mary knew that politically this was quite impossible. Hence her task was to bargain with the Pope until he gave his legate, **Cardinal Pole**, the power to dispense the present owners of these lands from having to give them back. During the bargaining – which went on for over a year – Mary showed that she was quite prepared to stand up to papal pressure, and in this she had the support of her future father-in-law, the emperor Charles V. Together, the two of them 'bullied the papacy until Pole was given a brief on church lands which was acceptable to the English'. The deal was concluded in November 1554 and Pole was allowed to cross to England from Charles's territory of the Netherlands, where he had been impatiently kicking his heels. The papal dispensation concerning the lands, which he brought with him, was then incorporated into an Act of Parliament (see time chart).

The second occasion when Mary revealed political acumen was over her marriage negotiations. Before becoming queen it had not been possible for her to make a suitable marriage because her father had declared her illegitimate. Now she was nearly 37 and had to hurry if she were to have a reasonable chance of conceiving a child. She needed an heir if she did not want her policies to cease with her death, as her younger half-sister, Elizabeth, was reputed to harbour Protestant sympathies.

But whom to marry? Just as Elizabeth herself was to discover a few years later, this was a major problem. Everyone expected her to marry, but equally there was bound to be widespread protest against whichever candidate she picked. There were two English possibilities, Pole and Courtenay, but neither were realistic choices. Henry Courtenay had spent most of his life in the Tower, ever since his family had been charged with

---

PROFILE: *Cardinal Pole*

B orn in 1500 of royal blood – his mother, Countess of Salisbury, was of the House of York – **Reginald Pole** was educated for the priesthood, but his career was blighted when he opposed the royal divorce, and he was forced to go into exile. From 1532 he lived in Italy, from where he orchestrated opposition to Henry's rule, especially after the execution of his mother for treason in 1541. He became a cardinal, a leading church reformer, and twice narrowly missed being elected pope.

On Mary's accession he was appointed papal legate to England, and Mary made him Archbishop of Canterbury, but his arrival was delayed owing to the argument over returning church lands. When he finally reached England he did his best to restore Catholicism but was hindered by lack of time and money. He always tended to underestimate the strength of Protestantism, and his policy of persecution was a failure.

In 1557 his legateship was taken away by Pope Paul IV and he was summoned to Rome to answer charges of Lutheranism, but Mary refused to let him go and he continued as archbishop until his death a few hours after the Queen's in November 1558.

---

treason in 1538; Pole was too closely identified with Rome, and had spent much of the two previous reigns trying to persuade foreigners to invade England. Mary's choice fell on Philip, son of Charles V and heir to Spain and the Netherlands. From England's point of view this was a sensible match, as Spain at this date was still regarded as England's natural ally against France. In a way, the match was a continuation of Henry VIII's policy of planning a marriage between Mary and Charles in 1525.

There was nevertheless some anti-Spanish feeling among a minority of Mary's subjects, as Wyatt's rebellion in 1554 demonstrated, and this is where Mary's political skills were called on. By stressing the weakness of her own position in the face of a nationalistic Council and House of Commons, Mary was able to obtain astonishingly generous terms for the marriage from Charles. Any son by the marriage was to inherit the Netherlands and Naples (and Spain too if Philip's existing son, Don Carlos, died first). Philip was to be king of England during Mary's lifetime but to have no rights in the country after her death. Without her permission he could carry no jewels, ships or guns out of the kingdom, nor involve England in his wars. Mary's position was safeguarded in every possible way, and the terms were so favourable that the government took the unusual step of publishing the articles for public consumption.

Figure 12.2 *The Great Seal of Philip and Mary*

Mary was also capable of determined and effective action when under pressure. As her half-brother Edward lay dying, she fled in disguise under cover of darkness from her home in Hertfordshire, first to the houses of friends in Cambridgeshire and Suffolk and then to her own house at Kenninghall. There she summoned her supporters to join her and wrote to towns across England for help. The revolt against the Duke of Northumberland, which swept her to power, was due in large part to her own vigorous action.

A year later there was another striking instance of her courage when in danger. The marriage plans had given some of her Protestant opponents the chance to pose as patriots and mobilise support under the guise of outraged nationalism. Sir Thomas Wyatt's rebellion in Kent lasted only two weeks and recruited less than a tenth as many supporters as had the Pilgrimage of Grace, but it still caused some sticky moments for the government, especially when a force of 500 Londoners sent against the rebels defected to Wyatt at Rochester, crying (allegedly): 'We are all Englishmen'. It was at this crisis point that Mary went to the Guildhall in the City of London and made her famous speech which turned the tide against Wyatt. It was reported back to Charles V in glowing terms by that same Simon Renard who had such a low opinion of her political talents:

'She spoke to the people, and said that the objects she had ever had in view since coming to the throne were to administer justice, keep order and protect the people's peace and tranquillity. The rebel, Wyatt, had taken up arms under the pretext that she had married his Highness [Philip], but his reply showed clearly that he aimed at the Crown, and meant to tyrannise and molest the people; and she read out Wyatt's answer in full. Her action as to her marriage, she went on, had been advised by her Council as conducive to the welfare of the realm, and in no wise adopted in accordance with her own personal desires; if the reasons in favour of it had not been sufficiently understood, they might be repeated in Parliament. Now, however, that Wyatt was nearing London, she wished to hear from her people whether they meant to behave like good subjects and defend her against this rebel, for if they did, she was minded to live and die with them and strain every nerve in their cause; for this time their fortunes, goods, honour, personal safety, wives and children were in the balance. If they bore themselves like good subjects she would be bound to stand by them, for they would deserve the care of their sovereign lady. And thus, with befitting persuasions, she urged them to take up arms.

'So elegant and eloquent was her speech, that all the people cried out loudly that they would live and die in her service, and that Wyatt was a traitor; and they all threw up their caps to show their goodwill.'

Religious policies

Mary's policy regarding the Church was also Cardinal Pole's policy, as the two worked closely together after his belated arrival in England. Both of them underrated the strength of Protestant opposition to their efforts to restore the Catholic Church. Pole thought that the English people were like children (or sheep) who had been led astray by a small group of evil heretics. Once these wicked leaders had been dealt with, the sheep would return voluntarily to their fold. He did not believe in strident evangelism or emotional preaching, feeling that people had experienced enough of these under Edward, and that what was now required was a period of peace. This is why he declined Ignatius Loyola's offer to send Jesuits to help in the reconversion of England.

Unfortunately, Pole did believe that the wicked leaders who had spread heresy must be treated ruthlessly, and this was the rationale behind the destruction by burning of about 280 people during the reign. The authorities never actually intended such a holocaust; they preferred converts to martyrs and they were taken aback by the determination of so many Protestants – of both sexes, and all ages and classes – to die as a witness to their truth. But the statistics and the stories make horrifying reading, and Mary's opponents were quick to exploit them. By far the best known of the many books and pamphlets which poured from Protestant presses was John Foxe's *Book of Martyrs*, although this was not published until 1563 (see Figure 12.3). It became one of the century's bestsellers, which was to influence generations of Englishmen against the Catholic Church.

The persecution policy was certainly not a success, but neither was it as disastrous as historians have made out. There was a widespread fear and hatred of heresy after the excesses of Edward's reign, and the heresy Bill of December 1554 which empowered the courts to condemn Protestant heretics to death passed both Houses without opposition. One has to remember, too, that most of the people burnt and their supporters believed in the burning of heretics just as much as Mary's bishops did; they would merely have chosen other victims.

At the legatine synod which he called on his arrival, Pole initiated a promising programme of church reform, including the proposal to set up seminaries (special training colleges) to train priests, and the publication of a Catholic prayer book in English. But there were enormous administrative problems to be dealt with first. For one thing, were bishops and parish priests from Henry's and Edward's reigns to be allowed to keep their jobs? Because it was not possible to find hundreds of new priests at a moment's notice, Pole ruled that they could – provided that those who

Figure 12.3 *The burning of Latimer and Ridley at Oxford in 1555: a woodcut from Foxe's* Book of Martyrs *(1570 edition)*

had married now renounced their wives. Most agreed to do so, although no doubt this led to much heart-searching. An odd result of the new rule of celibacy was that an ex-husband might get into trouble for not abandoning his wife completely! At the Norwich visitation of 1556 two clergy were denounced for behaving as caring husbands in visiting their ex-wives and supporting them with food and money.

Pole lacked two essentials – time and money. He wanted to improve the incomes and the education of the clergy, end pluralism and restore 'beauty of holiness' to the Church by replacing the vestments, ornaments and church fabric which had been confiscated by the Protestants and the images which had been destroyed. However, the Church had lost much of its wealth in the previous reigns. Mary was prepared to give back First Fruits and Tenths, the clerical taxes taken over by Henry VIII, but this was not enough. At the synod of December 1555 Pole called for a survey of the state of the parishes, so as to have sound information on which to base his reforms, but this took so long to collect that by the time it arrived he had lost his legatine powers and hence his status.

Mary's and Pole's ecclesiastical policies have been called negative and lacking in a sense of direction. This is partly true, but the obstacles facing them were immense. Given more time, perhaps those obstacles could have been overcome. Christopher Haigh in *English Reformations* goes further than most experts on the period would, in claiming: 'The Marian reconstruction of Catholicism was a success . . . Pole was leading a promising reform programme which tackled the structural problems of the English Church . . . If there were failures in Mary's reign, they were political and economic, not ecclesiastical.'

Faction and the Council

Our final topic in this chapter is the Marian Council. It has been argued that Mary's regime was weak because her Council was too large and was riven by factions which she failed to control. It is true that Mary did nominate a Council of 43 when she became Queen, but there was a good reason for so many. She needed councillors she could trust and who were of her faith, so she chose from among the Catholic gentry who had first rallied to her standard in Suffolk. However, these 'Kenninghall loyalists' lacked experience of government, so she had to bring into the Council 'Edwardians' such as **William Paget** and Winchester who had such experience, even though they had supported Northumberland. Others, like **Stephen Gardiner**, were 'Henricians', having gained their experience under Henry but fallen out of favour under Edward.

In fact, what happened was that the Kenninghall councillors rapidly ceased to attend Council meetings, although they retained posts at court and played some part on committees appointed for specific purposes. The more experienced councillors soon came to dominate the Council, and average attendance figures went down to 10 or 12, creating an effective inner ring. Among these regulars, the two leaders were Gardiner and Paget.

Although their basic philosophies were not dissimilar and although they were both loyal to Mary, Paget and Gardiner hated each other, and their quarrels must have made Council meetings extremely lively. On one occasion the dispute was so fierce that it spread to the House of Lords. This was in the spring of 1554, when Gardiner was trying to get a new law against heretics through Parliament but Paget used his influence to defeat it because he thought that the question of the ex-monastic lands should be settled first. Mary was so angry with Paget's disruptive tactics that she banned him from Council meetings, but he was allowed back when Philip arrived in July and requested his rehabilitation. Historians have blamed Mary for not clamping down harder on this quarrelsome

---

PROFILE: *William Paget*

William Paget (1506–63) became principal secretary of state in 1543, and from then until the death of Mary made himself indispensable to successive regimes. He was a first-class administrator and 'a true bureaucrat to whom the work always came first'. He gave Somerset much good advice, was made a peer in 1550, and in Mary's reign worked closely with the imperial ambassador, Simon Renard. Paget opposed his rival, Gardiner, whom he greatly disliked, on a range of issues. He supported the Spanish marriage, was unenthusiastic about Pole's persecution of Protestants, and advised Mary against executing Princess Elizabeth after Wyatt's rebellion. In 1558 his political career came to an end when he was not invited to join Elizabeth's Council.

PROFILE: *Stephen Gardiner*

Cambridge-educated like Paget, **Gardiner** rose rapidly in the Church, becoming Bishop of Winchester in 1531. He pleased Henry by publishing a book, *De Vera Obedientia*, which ably supported the royal headship of the Church. A conservative in religion, he was imprisoned during Edward's reign, but appointed Lord Chancellor by Mary. On the Council he frequently clashed with Paget; he wanted Mary to marry Courtenay, supported the burning of Protestants, and tried to have Elizabeth executed. His death in 1555, aged about 73, allowed Paget to dominate the Council for the rest of the reign.

---

pair, and it does seem that she kept her councillors on a looser rein than Elizabeth did when she became queen.

However, the arguments between Paget and Gardiner were not factional. Factions are groups with a constant allegiance, either to a leader or to a political programme. No such permanent groups existed on Mary's Council. For example, over the marriage issue, in the autumn of 1554, most of the Council first supported Gardiner, who wanted Mary to marry Courtenay, but as soon as they understood that Mary was determined on Philip, they swung round. On the other hand, over the question of whether or not to execute Elizabeth, which arose after Wyatt's rebellion, most of the Council supported Paget, who wanted her spared.

Those historians who have discerned faction have been unduly influenced by the despatches of Simon Renard, who tended towards a conflict view of the political scene, painting a picture of confusion and impotence, perhaps to emphasise his own importance as an adviser to Mary. It seems, then, that the Marian Council was stronger and more coherent than used to be thought, although Mary did not always control it properly, or take its advice (*e.g.* over whom to marry). Nevertheless, much in the way of positive administrative measures was achieved during the reign: a new Book of Rates for the customs, and a reform of the militia, to take two examples (for the militia, see chapter 14).

Conclusion: the final years

In this chapter some points have been made which tend towards the verdict that Mary was not such a dismal failure as she is sometimes portrayed. If one stopped the clock at the end of 1555 her achievements would appear obvious: the link with Rome restored and a programme of church reform under way; England in firm alliance with the most powerful force in Europe, the House of Habsburg, yet with a marriage treaty that protected vital English interests; Mary pregnant, so that it looked as if her policies would be carried on even after her death.

However, a series of disasters, mostly due to bad luck rather than mismanagement, changed everything. Mary was not pregnant after all – she turned into a sick, unloved, pathetic figure, pining for a husband who was never there. A series of bad harvests and accompanying epidemics decimated the population (see the next chapter). Pole was accused of heresy and stripped of his legatine powers, causing a dispute between Mary, who refused to let him go to Rome, and the Pope. The nation was dragged into a war during which Calais, the last English possession in France, was shamefully lost. And the final blow was over the succession. Mary had reluctantly to recognise Elizabeth as her successor because there was no one else (the only other candidate, Mary, Queen of Scots, was disqualified because of her link with France, with whom England was at war). So Mary died in the certain knowledge that all her work would be undone, and in this sense she must be classed as a failure.

Task

Disagreement and controversy are the lifeblood of history. Historians may disagree either because new evidence comes to light, or (as is more likely with widely studied figures like Mary Tudor) because different interpretations are placed on the existing evidence. In the case of Mary it can hardly be denied that she sometimes gave the impression – especially when talking to the imperial ambassador, Simon Renard – of being weak and indecisive. Many historians have accepted this at face value. Here, for instance, is Geoffrey Elton's judgement:

> '*She was ill prepared to be England's first woman sovereign. She had ever been her mother's daughter rather than her father's; devoid of political skill, unable to compromise, set only on the wholesale reversal of a generation's history, she was a manifest portent of strife ... Thirty-seven years old, she seized a power rightfully hers for the exercise of which she was utterly unsuited.*'
>
> G. R. Elton, *Reform and Reformation; England 1509–1558* (1977).

On the other hand, Elizabeth Russell argues that Mary deliberately fostered this negative image of herself:

> '*Mary herself created her own reputation for weakness and lack of skill, in order to serve her own political ends ... She exploited the unhelpful activities of the French, the heretics and the schismatics, while parliament and the Council made plausible scapegoats. They, and not she, were held responsible for delays, and they, and not she, insisted on better terms for a marriage treaty and reconciliation on England's own terms. The pope, Pole, Philip and even the Emperor Charles V, all bowed to the inevitable. In so doing, they delivered into Mary's hands political conditions and treaties which were essential for her success on the English throne, and for the complete implementation of her policies.*'
>
> Elizabeth Russell, 'Mary Tudor and Mr Jorkins', in the *Bulletin of the Institute of Historical Research*, vol. 63 (1990).

You should make up your own mind on this issue, after considering the evidence in this chapter and any other information you have.

Further reading

Christopher Haigh, *English Reformations* (Clarendon Press, Oxford, 1993).

Elizabeth Russell, 'Mary Tudor and Mr Jorkins', in *Historical Research*, vol. 63, 1990 – puts the case *for* Mary.

Jennifer Loach and Robert Tittler (eds), *The Mid-Tudor Polity c.1540–1560* (Macmillan, 1980).

G. R. Elton, *Reform and Reformation; England 1509–1558* (Edward Arnold, 1977).

R. H. Pogson, 'Revival and Reform in Mary Tudor's Church: a Question of Money', *Journal of Ecclesiastical History*, No. 25 (1974) and 'Reginald Pole and the Priorities of Government in Mary Tudor's Reign', *Historical Journal*, No. 18 (1975) – these two important articles show the positive side of Mary's reign.

13 Was there a 'mid-century crisis'?

This is a topic that cuts across the dividing line between political and economic history, exploiting some of the points made in the last two chapters. We ask whether the term 'crisis' is appropriate to describe the various difficulties facing the English state and people in the mid six-teenth century.

The traditional view is that the reigns of Edward VI and Mary – a sickly boy followed by a bigoted female – were a period of stagnation and failure sandwiched between the more stable and successful reigns of Henry VIII and Elizabeth. In 1973 Whitney Jones published *The Mid-Tudor Crisis 1539–1563*, which extended this interim period from just before the fall of Thomas Cromwell in 1540 until the year after the young Queen Elizabeth nearly died of smallpox (1562). His pessimistic message was that this entire quarter-century was a time of crisis. In successive chapters he analysed the ineptitude and factional nature of the govern-ments, the increasing religious polarisation and the mounting social and economic problems. He saw the focal point in all this as the weakness of the monarchy; a strong monarch would never have allowed the other problems to proliferate as they did. The situation of mid-Tudor England, according to this view, was much the same as the situation in France in 1559, after the death of Henry II, when a series of weak monarchs permitted nearly half a century of civil war and anarchy.

Whitney Jones's problem, of course, was to explain why this did not happen in England, and how, if the situation was as serious as he claimed, the Tudor dynasty escaped catastrophe. As David Loades subse-quently pointed out, 'the true significance of the reigns of Edward VI and Mary lies less in what happened than in what did not happen'. A royal minority could have led to an aristocratic reaction which undid the work of Henry VIII; Mary's uncompromising Catholicism could have produced civil war; her marriage to Philip could have converted England into a Habsburg province. None of this happened. Incidentally, Loades's recent book is also entitled *The Mid-Tudor Crisis* (this time subtitled, *1545 to 1565*) yet, in spite of the title, he writes in the introduction that these years 'should be seen in a very positive light, not as years of crisis but as years of achievement'.

Continuity

New work on the central administration during the mid-century period has undermined the notion of crisis and substituted that of continuity instead. In spite of their differences, especially in religion, the governments of Edward and Mary were preoccupied with much the same problems – for example, the lack of finance and the need to control inflation – and they tended to adopt the same solutions. There is, too, considerable continuity among the senior ministers during the two reigns. Skilled administrators such as **Sir William Paulet** and Sir William Petre, or the financier, Sir Thomas Gresham, served under both monarchs, a fact which contributed to the efficiency and vitality of the government under Northumberland and Mary.

Unexpectedly, there was even continuity of a sort in the religious policy of the two reigns. Both governments had the same problem in trying to enforce their brand of religion – the lack of well-qualified clergy. Mary and Pole were forced to use 'schismatical' clergy (*i.e.* clergy who had been ordained, or who had served, under the previous Protestant regime). The fact that so many of them were prepared to transfer their loyalties to the new regime seems to show that the average clergyman was more open to compromise than used to be thought. The same, only more so, goes for the average English layman, who compliantly accepted and obeyed both Cranmer's Protestant revolution and the Marian restoration.

PROFILE: *Sir William Paulet*

Paulet entered the king's Household in the 1520s and rose rapidly, due to his outstanding abilities, becoming successively Lord St John, Earl of Wiltshire and Marquis of Winchester. From 1550 until his death in 1572, aged about 87, he was in charge of the Exchequer as Lord Treasurer. During this period he carried out important reforms, including a reorganisation of the revenue courts, the customs and the navy. His aims were the same as Burghley, who succeeded him as Treasurer: to balance the budget and keep the Crown solvent by all possible means.

Although Elton describes him as 'probably the outstanding example of the Tudor civil servant in high places who avoided the complications of politics' (*England under the Tudors*), this verdict does not seem entirely valid, because Paulet helped Northumberland against the Wriothesley faction in 1549, supported Gardiner against Paget in Mary's reign, and voted against Elizabeth's 1559 Uniformity Bill in the Lords.

Elton argued that, despite faction and despite major differences in their personal religion, the post-Cromwellian generation of leaders showed 'a coherence in attitudes, purposes and ethos which overrode political and religious disagreements'. They all agreed on the new order, especially on the royal supremacy, the predominance of the laity in the affairs of the Church and the need to try to solve the problems of the 'commonwealth'. This consensus helps account for the stability of a potentially unstable situation.

Centralisation

Another reason why the dynasty survived the mid-century years without major upheaval is centralisation. Since 1485 the importance of the regions as centres of political power had diminished and territorial magnates had grown weaker in comparison with the powers of the central government. The royal court had become the political and social centre for the elite, and the new nobles who had come into prominence by the 1540s, especially the Seymours and Dudleys, were primarily courtiers and privy councillors, without a strong power-base in the country.

The result of all this was that in the factional struggles of Edward's reign, it was difficult – if not impossible – for those involved to take the struggle out of court and call up armies of supporters to fight for them, as might have happened in earlier times. Somerset did try to broaden the struggle in this way when he had his back to the wall in 1549, but without success. He issued a proclamation in the king's name which charged 'all his loving subjects with all haste to repair to his highness at his majesty's manor of Hampton Court, in most defensible array, with harness and weapons, to defend his most royal person and his most entirely beloved uncle the Lord Protector, against whom certain hath attempted a most dangerous conspiracy'. But adequate support was not forthcoming, and the Council supported Warwick's bloodless *coup d'état*, while strongly condemning Somerset's tactics:

> *'Your grace's proclamation and billets put abroad for the raising of the Commons we mislike very much. The wicked and evil disposed persons shall stir as well as the faithful subjects.'*

Continuity and centralisation help explain why the mid-century Tudor state, although facing serious difficulties, was never in 'crisis'. It could be argued that the one time there was a serious threat of a breakdown of law and order – surely the real test of crisis for the state – came in 1549, when two rebellions, in the West and in Norfolk, erupted simultaneously. Again, however, recent research has somewhat altered our perceptions of these events. The 1549 rebellions certainly reveal Somerset's deficiencies as a decision-maker, and they led directly to his fall from power. Nevertheless, considering the demands of the moment, which included maintaining an army in Scotland and damping down widespread social unrest in England, the Council performed with resource and energy, and both sets of rebels were decisively defeated.

Inflation

One might at this point make a distinction between the Tudor state and the people it governed; there is much evidence that the mid-century was a time of real crisis, or crises, for the majority of ordinary people, if not for the state. Prices had been rising since the 1490s, but in the 1540s they started to soar. Food prices doubled during that decade, most of the increase being after 1544; whereas wages barely rose at all, which meant that real wages (*i.e.* their purchasing power) went down by 50 per cent. From now on those who lived off any kind of fixed income, whether wages, salaries or rents, were in trouble (see chapter 16).

It is true that there were mitigating factors. Few people depended exclusively on money wages; many labourers, for instance, were fed by their employers, and many grew their own food or lived principally by barter. One has to remember that retail shops were almost non-existent at this time, except in towns. Nevertheless, the hike in prices must have been a severe shock, especially to the poor, and above all to the urban poor, who were probably more involved in the money economy than were peasants. It was at this time (1550–51), too, that the cloth trade which employed so many, directly or indirectly, was suddenly hit by the collapse of the Antwerp market (see chapter 30).

The underlying cause of the inflation was population expansion plus the effect of European price movements, which were in turn affected by the silver influx from the New World. The particularly rapid inflation of the 1540s was the fault of the English government and was caused firstly by the very expensive series of wars against France and Scotland fought between 1544 and 1551, which put far too much extra money into circulation, and secondly by the main way the government tried to finance the wars – debasement of the coinage (see key term, page 94).

Demographic crisis

The greatest crisis of all came towards the end of Mary's reign and was not caused by governments at all, but by a combination of bad weather and disease. For most of the population the upward trend of prices was not nearly so significant as the violent short-term fluctuations caused by a failure of the harvest.

As can be seen in Figure 13.2, harvests between 1530 and 1548 were generally good (with the exceptions of 1535 and 1545), but in 1549–51 there were three bad years in a row, and further disastrous ones in 1555 and 1556. The latter year was the worst of the century, due to 'the greatest rain and floods that ever was seen in England', according to one witness, who added, 'in divers places both men and cattle drowned'. The result was that the price of wheat rocketed to twice its normal level and – as William Cecil recalled many years later – 'there was such a scarcity of corn within the realm of England that the common people, in most parts of the land, were glad to make their bread of acorns'.

Moreover, as if that were not enough, the country was now swept, between 1556 and 1558, by a major epidemic. Described by contemporaries as 'the new ague', this produced burning fevers, and resulted in a high mortality rate. Unlike plague, which always struck in high summer, it was not seasonal. It seemed – again unlike plague – to affect country folk just as much as town dwellers.

Figure 13.2 *The quality of English harvests, 1480–1620*

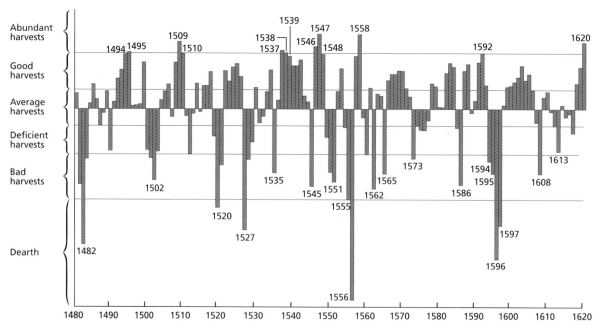

Historians' estimates of the numbers who died during these disastrous years vary from 11 to 20 per cent of the population. It is difficult to know whether most deaths were caused by the disease itself or by starvation consequent on harvest failure, but clearly the two were closely interconnected because:

■ those weakened by months of malnutrition were more likely to contract a fatal dose of the ague;

■ increased geographical mobility due to starving people quitting their villages in search of food led to a more rapid spread of infection.

The close of the 1530s saw the worst demographic disaster in English history since the Black Death of 1349. There may not have been a 'mid-century crisis' for the state but there definitely was for many English men and women. It consisted not of doubts over the government's religious policy or distrust of its new coinage, but in disease, starvation and the fear of death.

Task: class discussion

Divide into groups to discuss the 'mid-century crisis'. In particular consider:

1 What does the word 'crisis' actually mean? Compare it to 'revolution'. Do you think that either, or both, terms involve a certain limited time-scale?

2 Of the following years, which would you argue was the time of greatest crisis, and why: 1549; 1553; 1556–7?

3 After considering the evidence, would you conclude that there was indeed a 'mid-century crisis'?

Further reading

G. R. Elton, *Reform and Reformation; England 1509–1558* (Edward Arnold, 1977).

Whitney R. D. Jones, *The Mid-Tudor Crisis 1539–1563* (Macmillan, 1973) – this is the work which sparked off the controversy over whether or not there was a mid-Tudor crisis.

Jennifer Loach, *A Mid-Tudor Crisis?* New Appreciations in History No. 25 (Historical Association, 1992) – a balanced survey.

David Loades, *The Mid-Tudor Crisis, 1545–1565* (Macmillan, 1992).

D. M. Palliser, *The Age of Elizabeth* (Addison Wesley Longman, 2nd edn, 1992) – has a useful chapter on the topic.

Diarmaid MacCulloch, 'The Reign of Edward VI: a Mid-Tudor Crisis?', *History Review* No. 16 (1993) – a most useful survey of the current debate.

14 War and foreign policy 1: the early Tudors

Time chart

1477: Death of Charles the Bold, leading to break-up of Duchy of Burgundy

1479: Union of Aragon and Castile under Ferdinand and Isabella

1485: Accession of Henry VII

1488–9: English force sent to Brittany fails to prevent its assimilation by France

1489: Henry and Ferdinand sign Treaty of Medina del Campo creating a Spanish alliance and promoting marriage of Prince Arthur and Catherine of Aragon

1491: Perkin Warbeck impersonates Richard, Duke of York, and is supported by French king

1492: Henry leads English army to France. By Treaty of Etaples he withdraws in return for pension and promise that French would not support pretenders

1496: *Magnus Intercursus* means restoration of trade between England and Netherlands after three-year boycott due to Margaret of Burgundy's support for Warbeck

1497: After seeking support in Scotland and then in Ireland, Warbeck attempts to raise the West country and is taken prisoner

1501: Catherine of Aragon marries Arthur (who dies in following year)

1506: Philip of Burgundy is persuaded to sign trade treaty highly favourable to England (he dies the same year)

1509: Accession of Henry VIII

1513: Henry leads army to France and wins Battle of Spurs, gaining Tournai
James IV of Scotland is defeated and killed by English at Flodden

1514: Treaty with France whereby Henry's sister, Mary, marries Louis XII

1515: Death of Louis and accession of Francis I

1516: Death of Ferdinand who is succeeded by Charles of Burgundy

1518: Treaty of London, Henry's and Wolsey's attempt to secure universal peace. Tournai is returned to French

1519: Death of Maximilian. Charles elected emperor (in addition to his existing Habsburg, Burgundian and Spanish inheritances)

1520: Field of Cloth of Gold (meeting between Henry and Francis), and two meetings between Henry and Charles V

1522–3: Henry declares war against France and despatches two successive military expeditions

1525: Charles defeats France and captures Francis at Pavia
Amicable Grant, imposed by Wolsey to pay for projected invasion of France, is abandoned due to opposition

1527: Henry subordinates other foreign-policy considerations to decision to annul marriage with Catherine
Sack of Rome by imperial troops

1529: Dismissal of Wolsey. Thomas Cromwell subsequently emerges as Henry's leading minister

1539: Pope publishes Bull deposing Henry. Fear of joint invasion of England by Francis and Charles

1540: Henry marries and then rejects Anne of Cleves. Fall of Cromwell

1542: English victory over Scots at Solway Moss, followed by death of James V

1543: Treaty of Greenwich with Scotland. War is declared on France

1544: English armies invade Scotland and France. Capture of Boulogne

1547: Death of Henry VIII. Somerset invades Scotland and wins Battle of Pinkie. English garrisons established in Scotland

1550: Warwick gives up Boulogne in treaty with French

1553: Accession of Mary

1554: Marriage of Mary and Philip II of Spain

1557: England joins Habsburg side in war against France

1558: French capture Calais. Death of Mary and accession of Elizabeth

1559: Treaty of Cateau Cambresis signed by Philip II, Henry II of France and Elizabeth

The making of policy

It was the monarch who was solely responsible for relations with other countries. Diplomacy, along with war, was seen as too important for

KEY TERM:

Prerogative

The Crown's **prerogative** meant those powers possessed by monarchs which allowed them to perform their role effectively. According to Geoffrey Elton in *The Tudor Constitution*, 'prerogative was the great Tudor word, stressed in particular by Henry VII and Elizabeth. The former needed it to restore the ascendancy and finances of the Crown; the latter opposed it to the interference of her subjects in delicate matters of policy.' Henry VIII believed in it just as much as his father and daughter but used the term more rarely, being more likely to talk about his dignity and honour.

One area in which the royal prerogative was never questioned was foreign policy. Sir Thomas Smith wrote in 1565 that: 'The monarch of England, king or queen, hath absolutely in his power the authority of war and peace, to defy what prince it shall please him and to bid him war, and again to reconcile himself and enter into league or truce with him, at his pleasure or the advice only of his Privy Council.'

anyone except rulers. Once, when Henry VIII was feeling critical of Thomas Cromwell's efforts to build up a Protestant alliance abroad, he informed the French ambassador that Cromwell was 'a good household manager, but not fit to intermeddle in the affairs of kings'. A monarch could always ask his council for advice, and usually did, but he was under no obligation to take it. Foreign affairs belonged to his **prerogative**.

Parliament officially had no role to play in the making of foreign policy; however, it did hold the purse strings. Usually, the taxes requested by the monarch were granted, but often only after heated debate – and occasionally such debate might even involve criticism of royal policy, as on the following occasion:

> From a letter to Charles V by his ambassador, Eustace Chapuys, 2 May 1532:
>
> *'The King has again applied to Parliament for a subsidy in money to fortify the frontiers of Scotland. During the debate two worthy members of that assembly were bold enough to declare openly and in plain terms that there was no need at all of such military preparations.'*

Another constraint on the monarch's freedom to make policy might be the unwillingness of the country to pay taxes, whether or not they had been sanctioned by Parliament. The Cornish rebels of 1497, who protested against having to pay for Henry VII's projected war against Scotland, were one of the factors causing him to make peace with the Scots. Again, resistance to Wolsey's unparliamentary 'Amicable Grant' of 1525 effectively sabotaged the plan for another invasion of France. These cases were exceptional, but they do show that royal power in this area had its limits.

Decisions regarding foreign policy often had to be made on the basis of incomplete or biased information. International diplomacy, in the early sixteenth century, was in its infancy, and it was only owing to the Italian wars that the leading powers had even started to maintain resident ambassadors in each others' capitals. England was represented only in Rome at the beginning of Henry VII's reign, although by Wolsey's time there were also English ambassadors in Spain, the Netherlands, France and Venice. But they had no special training; those chosen were often unsuitable, lacked the necessary skills and found themselves isolated in a hostile and suspicious environment.

Figure 14.1 *'The Ambassadors' by Hans Holbein*

Qualifications needed for an ambassador

1 Have private means – because they were badly paid and their salary was often in arrears, yet they were expected to live elegantly and entertain lavishly.

2 Be well-born – so that they could become the intimate friends of influential nobles and even princes in their host country.

3 Have a foreign language. No one in this century except an Englishman was expected to speak English. Latin was still an international medium. Italian was useful, and so was French, especially as it happened to be Charles V's mother tongue.

4 Be healthy – sick or delicate constitutions could never cope with the strains of travel and of foreign climates and food.

These early ambassadors (described by one wit as men sent to lie abroad for their country's good) were very much left to their own initiative. The more enterprising set up private networks of agents to gather information, as did Eustace Chapuys, quoted on page 118. Chapuys' successor,

Simon Renard, was even more successful, in that he gained Mary Tudor's confidence and helped to arrange her marriage to Philip II (see chapter 12). But others were quite inadequate, and their despatches must have thoroughly confused their own governments. John Stile, who represented England in Spain after 1505, was 'neither learned nor intelligent. In all the years of his embassy he never acquired much Spanish. Ferdinand thought him an ass, and deceived him again and again outrageously'.

The objectives of policy

It is important not to judge sixteenth-century foreign policy exclusively by modern criteria. Today we tend to ask, of a military campaign or a treaty, how it benefitted the strategic or the economic needs of the nation concerned. However, this attitude, while not unknown, was not the pre-vailing one. The concept of nationality itself was still imprecise in the first half of the century. For most people in Europe their 'nation', which attracted their primary loyalty, was their province – Normandy, Anjou – or even their city – Lübeck, Valencia. It is true that England started to achieve nationalism – a sense of the wider community – sooner than most countries, probably due to the early strength of the monarchy, and, of course, geography. However, even in England this spirit was slow to develop.

A case often cited as evidence of national feeling was the attack by a mob of Londoners on the Steelyard, the headquarters of the German Hanseatic League, in 1494. But on this occasion the attackers had eco-nomic motives – they believed that the privileged German merchants were reducing their prospects of employment. The most that can be said is that the episode showed a degree of xenophobia, a negative form of nationalism. It was not until half a century later that a more stridently nationalistic spirit appears, as evidenced by Sir Thomas Wyatt's rebellion against Mary's Spanish marriage, and the Londoners sent against him who changed sides crying, 'We are all Englishmen' (see chapter 12).

After Elizabeth's accession this concept of Englishness deepened, no doubt because of English hostility to the Catholic Church, and subse-quently to Spain. However, in the first half of the century most people, when they thought about their nation rather than their region, thought exclusively in personal terms. Their loyalty was to an individual – their prince – rather than to an abstract concept. In other words, **dynastic** loyalty had not yet given way to nationalism.

Of course it would be wrong to say that there were no economic motives behind English foreign policy. Successful commerce brought more wealth for everyone, including the monarch, and Henry VII in particular was very conscious of the needs of trade, as his various commercial treaties and navigation acts, and his patronage of the Cabots, bear out. Merchants were a powerful pressure group not to be ignored, especially the well-organised Merchant Adventurers who controlled the cloth trade with the Netherlands. But even here the three-year trade boycott organised by Henry between 1493 and 1496 is a striking illustration of how dynastic considerations – the need to stop Margaret of Burgundy shielding Perkin Warbeck – came before commercial ones.

Henry VIII was less open to commercial pressures, or interested in developing new trade routes, than his father. He would certainly have agreed with the verdict of the Italian writer, Castiglione:

> *'You know in great matters and adventures in wars the true provocation is glory; and who so for lucre's sake [i.e. for money] or for any other consideration taketh it in hand deserveth not the name of a gentleman, but is a most vile merchant.'*
>
> Castiglione, *The Book of the Courtier* (1528).

War and honour

'Glorious war', as Shakespeare's Othello defined it, was the sport of kings, and war was a regular occurrence under the early Tudors. In 1492, 1513, 1522–3, in the 1540s and in the late 1550s, troops were raised to fight in France or Scotland, usually both. Some of these armies were large; in 1513, 35,000 soldiers crossed the Channel, a force of similar size to the Habsburg and Valois armies then fighting in Italy.

These wars mostly seem to us a tremendous waste of time and resources. Why, for instance, did Henry VIII spend £600,000 in the capture of Boulogne, a third-rate port, which subsequently cost another £400,000 to retain, until it finally had to be given back six years after it was taken? The main results of all Henry's aggression seem to have been debasement of the coinage, inflation and, in particular, the massive sale of crown lands, which had the long-term effect of weakening the power of the monarchy.

However, this verdict is anachronistic. Henry viewed his wars mainly as a supremely king-like and honourable activity, and only incidentally in terms of economic advantage or even of territorial gain. It is difficult for

Figure 14.2 *'The royal forces'*
(Henry VIII's army).

us to grasp the significance of this concept of honour, which has virtually disappeared from the modern world along with the feudal aristocracy that maintained it. In pursuing his French adventures Henry consciously imitated chivalric models such as Arthur and Charlemagne, and in particular his renowned ancestor, the warrior-king, Henry V. Henry VIII commissioned a group of scholars to write the first-ever biography of Henry V, on whose chivalric and warlike doings he tended to model himself. We are told that when Henry VIII led his army into France in 1513, after the first day's march it was essential to his role that, refusing to go to bed, he rode about the camp until three in the morning encouraging his troops, because this was what Henry V had done the night before Agincourt.

The vast majority of Henry's contemporaries would have approved of these attitudes. The nobility especially were thoroughly imbued with the concept of honour, had been educated for war, and tended to fret if peace went on for too long. For them and for many gentlemen military action meant a chance for glory and promotion. True, there was a small group of Erasmian intellectuals who criticised the folly and waste of war. Among

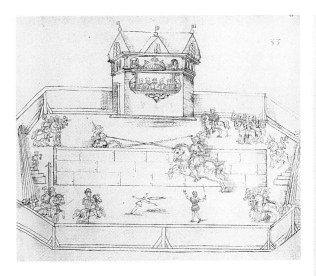

Figure 14.3 Drawings of tournaments in England during the reign of Henry VIII

them was the Archbishop of Canterbury, William Warham, who pointed out in 1525 'what infinite sums of money the King's Grace hath spent already invading France', and that in spite of all this expenditure Henry 'at this hour hath not one foot of land more in France than his most noble father had'. This, however, was very much a minority opinion.

For Henry, war was a form of competition against another monarch – rather like a tournament (see Figure 14.3), only more honourable and satisfying. The two princes most worthy of his rivalry were Francis and Charles V, but unfortunately he was weaker than either of them. A kingdom of three million could hardly compete with sixteen million French or eight million Spanish, to say nothing of all the Germans and Dutch who owed Charles allegiance. England could usually cope with the Scots, but was at a definite disadvantage on the continent.

Military weakness

KEY TERM:

Arquebus

Also known as an 'harquebus' (or hook-gun), the **arquebus** was a portable gun supported on a tripod by a hook or a forked rest.

English armies at this time tended to be less well trained and equipped than their French, German and Spanish counterparts, and lacking in experience. There was too much reliance on archery, regarded as especially English, probably owing to the memory of famous victories like Crecy and Agincourt, said to have been won by the bow. 'Archery,' said Hugh Latimer, was 'a gift of God that He hath given us to excel all other nations withal'. On the continent, however, the bow was giving way to firearms such as the **arquebus**.

123

A further problem was the inefficiency of the recruitment system. There were three ways of assembling an army in this period, and each had its disadvantages.

1 Throughout the Middle Ages and into the sixteenth century English armies consisted mainly of the retinues of various nobles and gentlemen whose military help for a specific campaign the king had requested. But there had always been social and political dangers in permitting powerful subjects to maintain their own armed followers, and since Edward IV monarchs had been trying to restrict the system of retaining (see chapter 2). In addition, the idea that a tenant owed military service to his landlord, who could summon him when necessary, was now beginning to be questioned. There were cases in Henry VIII's reign when the call to arms was refused.

2 Since Norman times the germs of an alternative system of recruitment had existed in the shape of the home militia, which could be called on to meet a threat of foreign invasion. The Statute of Westminster (1285) required all those of a certain wealth to keep a horse and a suit of armour in readiness. In the sixteenth century this was still the law, and commissioners were appointed to hold musters in every shire at regular intervals, to view the able-bodied men and to charge the inhabitants to 'find harness according to their substance'. However, the militia lacked training and was badly armed. Also it tended to be seen as secondary to the retinue system, so that many claimed exemption on the grounds that they belonged to some lord or gentleman's contingent. The Militia Act of 1558 started to remedy this, bringing the landed classes into the national system, and future English armies would be based on an improved militia.

3 Henry VIII, Somerset and Northumberland all hired mercenaries from abroad to stiffen their essentially part-time armies with a core of professionals, but this was extremely expensive. The foreigners expected to be paid about three times as much as English soldiers, and they were often a nuisance and resented by the natives. In the late 1540s Spanish, Italian and German mercenaries were permanently stationed on the **Borders**, but they quarrelled with the householders on whom they were billeted, refused to eat English food and would not pay for their lodgings.

More promising was the development of the navy. Henry VII encouraged shipbuilding generally, although there were only five ships belonging to the state at his death. Under Henry VIII an ambitious building programme produced a navy of 53 ships by 1547. Dockyards were set up, and a navy board established to oversee the new service. In Mary's

KEY TERM:

Borders

This was a wild and mostly mountainous region where the actual boundary was often in dispute, and where feuding, plundering and cattle-rustling were a way of life. Wars between Scotland and England were not usually caused by events in the **Borders**, but border conditions often made such wars longer and were used as the excuse for further military action. The Borders were divided into three regions, the East, West and Central marches, and in both Scotland and England wardens were appointed for each march. The wardens' functions were to try to keep a semblance of law and order when the two nations were at peace, and to fight the enemy when they were at war. They were usually selected from leading Border families, such as, on the English side, the Dacres and the Percies (see chapter 9), because only they had the prestige to build up and maintain the required forces. The turbulence of the Borders was partly caused by economic conditions. This was an impoverished region, with a population too large for the available farming land.

reign there was continued improvement, encouraged by Philip who had an interest in stopping French privateers in the Channel. However, before Elizabeth the navy was always a small-scale affair, designed to protect English coastlines but not to take on enemies in distant waters, as it did under Drake and Hawkins (see chapters 22 and 24).

With hindsight, and viewing the sixteenth century as a whole, we can see how England gradually changed from a continental to a maritime power. Elizabeth gave up its claims to French territory, sent fewer armies abroad, and concentrated on the navy instead. But this development is less clear when one looks only at the first half of the century, and it was certainly not evident to contemporaries. Foreign policy between Henry VII and Mary is full of discontinuities and changes of tack, as the objectives and priorities altered, and as ambassadors and rulers tried to keep up with the day-to-day pressure of events. Perhaps foreign policies are always like that.

Further reading

Susan Doran, *England and Europe 1485–1603*, Seminar Studies in History (Addison Wesley Longman, 2nd edn, 1996) – an up-to-date account with a comprehensive bibliography.

J. J. Scarisbrick, *Henry VIII* (Penguin, 1972).

Jeremy Goring, 'Social Change and Military Decline in Mid-Tudor England', *History*, vol. 60, 1975.

L. B. Smith, *Henry VIII: The Mask of Royalty* (Cape, 1971) – good on the ideology of honour.

Garrett Mattingly, *Renaissance Diplomacy* (Penguin, 1973) – describes the development of the ambassadorial system.

R. B. Wernham, *Before the Armada: The Growth of English Foreign Policy 1485–1588* (Cape, 1966) – the standard account.

15 Scotland and the French connection

Time chart

1496: James IV, in support of Perkin Warbeck, makes an unsuccessful raid on northern England

1502: 'Treaty of Perpetual Peace' between England and Scotland

1503: Marriage of James IV and Margaret Tudor

1509: Accession of Henry VIII; worsening relations between England and Scotland

1512: Attempts by James IV to unite Christendom in crusade against Turks. Renewal of 'auld alliance' with Louis XII

1513: Battle of Flodden. Death of James IV and many leading Scotsmen. Accession of infant James V

1515–17: First period of regency of John, Duke of Albany

1517–21: Albany's absence in France

1521–4: Second period of Albany's regency. Unsuccessful attempts by French to persuade Scots to fight English

1528: James V's escape from control by Archibald Douglas, Earl of Angus; end of minority

1536–7: James's visit to France and marriage to Madeleine, daughter of Francis I; death of Madeleine

1538: Marriage of James V to Mary of Guise

1541: Failure of James to turn up to meeting with Henry VIII at York

1542: Scots heavily defeated by English at Solway Moss. Death of James V and accession of his week-old daughter, Mary

1543–54: Regency of James Hamilton, Earl of Arran

1543: Treaty of Greenwich; Mary bethrothed to prince Edward. Arran deserts English cause, and Scots Parliament repudiates treaty

1544: Beginning of 'Rough Wooing'; English punitive raid into Scotland

1545: Scots victory at Ancrum; second English raid

1546: Murder of Cardinal Beaton by group of Scots lairds who occupy St Andrews Castle

1547:	Death of Henry VIII. Fall of St Andrews to French force; John Knox made prisoner. English invade Scotland and win Battle of Pinkie
1548:	Scots treaty with France; Mary sent to France to marry the Dauphin
1550:	Mary of Guise arrives in Scotland
1554:	Arran ousted from regency by Mary of Guise
1557:	First 'Band' of Lords of the Congregation
1558:	Marriage of Mary and the Dauphin, Francis. Death of Mary Tudor and accession of Elizabeth
1559:	Return to Scotland of John Knox; call to arms by Protestants
1560:	**January** English fleet blockades Leith, in Scotland **March** Tumult of Amboise starts French wars of religion **June** Death of Mary of Guise **July** Treaty of Edinburgh and withdrawal of English and French troops **December** Death of Mary's husband, Francis II
1561:	Mary's return to Scotland

For centuries the Scots had maintained the 'auld alliance' with France in order to cope with their 'auld enemy', England, but at the beginning of the sixteenth century this looked like changing. In 1503 there took place the marriage of James IV of Scotland with Henry VII's elder daughter, Margaret, the so-called marriage of the Thistle and the Rose. The previous year James had signed a treaty of perpetual peace with Henry, which confirmed the truce made after the ending of James's support for the pretender, Perkin Warbeck. In 1503, then, it seemed that the age-old enmity between the two nations might have at last worked itself out. Also, the old link between France and Scotland was now being questioned. France had become the strongest power in Europe and was engaged, after 1494, in an expansionist programme in Italy. From the Scottish point of view there was a danger that their country would be used merely as a pawn by the French in order to keep the English at bay.

However, the 1503 treaty turned out to be far from 'perpetual', the alliance with France and the enmity with England continued, and the next half-century was one of the stormiest periods in the entire history of Anglo-Scottish relations. It was not until 1560 that, by a fortunate combination of circumstances, a really lasting peace was achieved between the two nations. In this chapter we ask, firstly, why there was such hostility between England and Scotland during this period, and, secondly, why 1560 saw a turning-point in their relationship.

Figure 15.1 Margaret Tudor

Scotland

Scotland at this time was a separate nation under the rule of its own king, but it was a much poorer nation than England, with a population perhaps one-fifth the size. It contained a lower proportion of fertile, arable land than England, and there was no equivalent to the profitable English cloth trade. Scotland's foreign trade, such as it was, consisted of primary products, including raw wool, hides, fish and animals on the hoof; practically all manufactured and luxury goods had to be imported – for the few who could afford them. Furthermore, in the late Middle Ages the economy stagnated, leading to a fall in the value of the Scottish pound, which, from being once equal to the English pound, had fallen by 1560 to the equivalent of four English shillings [20p].

The House of Stewart, kings of Scotland since the fourteenth century, had its share of talented rulers, but had been particularly unlucky in that most of its members came to the throne as children; between 1460 and 1625 there were 60 years of royal minority, when the country was ruled by regents. This had the effect of lowering the crown's prestige and its already low income, because regents, lacking natural authority by birth, had to conciliate potential opposition by buying support (as did Somerset and Northumberland during Edward VI's reign).

Surrounding the monarch, and as often as not related to him, were the Scottish nobility, a quarrelsome and touchy lot, who jealously maintained their feudal prerogatives as well as their fortified castles and their bands of retainers. It was these bands on whom the king had to rely when he wanted an army, because there was no way he could afford to hire mercenaries, as did Henry VIII and other monarchs. Central government in Scotland was weak and informal compared to England; there was a one-chamber parliament and a king's council, but they lacked the means to dominate the countryside. Consequently much power stayed in the hands of local magnates and lairds. All through Scotland the bonds of kinship were strong, not only among the Highland clans but also among powerful Lowland families such as the Douglases and the Hamiltons.

The Church was corrupt and disproportionately wealthy in a poor country, owning far more land than the king. Ordinary parish clergy were wretchedly paid, but the top positions were occupied by powerful nobles, and the king had a considerable say in appointments to bishoprics. In 1504 James IV created a minor scandal by making his 11-year-old illegitimate son, Alexander, archbishop of St Andrews. The fact that the lay elite dominated and exploited the Church meant that they had little incentive to seek its reform.

An uneasy relationship, 1503–42

Figure 15.2 From James II to James VI

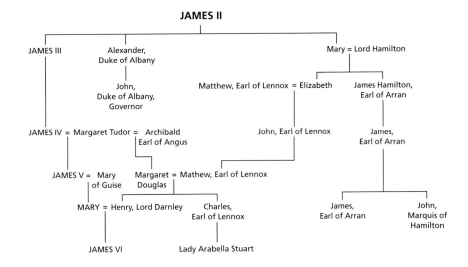

After Henry VIII's accession, relations between Scotland and England deteriorated. James IV was obsessed with the idea of heading the nations of Europe on a crusade against the Turks, and when only Louis XII of France seemed interested, he was flattered into renewing the Franco-Scottish alliance. This meant that he found himself leading an army into England in the interests of France, and suffering a massive defeat at Flodden. Ten thousand Scots died, including James himself and many nobles. It was a major psychological shock to the Scottish ruling class, and over the next few decades they were cautious about again being drawn into war with England.

After Flodden, it seemed as though Henry VIII had every chance of bending Scotland to his will through the regency of his sister, Margaret, but this was not to be. Margaret took as her second husband John Douglas, Earl of Angus, who was young, handsome and one of the richest noblemen in Scotland. But the couple soon became highly unpopular. Other noble families resented the enhanced status of the Douglases, the marriage turned sour, and Margaret became a lonely, unhappy and vacillating figure, more concerned with her own comfort than with the politics of Scotland.

In 1515 the Scottish Parliament invited the **Duke of Albany** to replace Margaret as regent for the young James V. During his regency (1515–24), Scotland once more moved closer to France.

Henry VIII, in impotent fury, attempted crude and ineffective tactics against Albany's rule. He instructed Lord Dacre, warden of the West

PROFILE: *Duke of Albany*

John Stewart, Duke of Albany, was the son of James III's brother, but he was brought up in France and was, to all intents and purposes, a Frenchman. Before arriving in Scotland, in 1515, to succeed the unpopular Margaret Tudor as regent, he had earned a reputation as a successful French general in the Italian wars. He was welcomed by the Scots, and was named next in line to the throne if James were to have no children.

In 1517 Albany returned to France for what was planned as a brief visit, to see his wife and family, but Francis forced him to stay, as he wanted to maintain friendship with Henry. In 1521, when war broke out between France and England, Albany was finally allowed back to Scotland for his second period of regency. In 1522 and 1523 he twice tried to invade England, but the Scots refused to fight for him, and both expeditions ended in humiliation. The following year he quit Scotland for good. He resumed his career as a French commander and died in 1536, full of honours from the French king.

Albany's regency achieved little militarily, yet he successfully helped Scotland retain her independence from England, and kept up the 'auld alliance'.

March, to make regular raids into Scotland. He also resorted to propaganda, letting it be suggested that Albany planned to do away with the young king and himself succeed to the throne (see John Skelton's poem opposite).

After Albany had left Scotland for good, Angus again dominated the government for a few years. His power rested on the fact that he had gained possession of James, now a teenager, whom he kept a virtual prisoner in Falkland Castle. However, one night in 1528, James, disguised as a groom, managed to escape and make his way to Stirling, where he proclaimed the start of his personal rule. This was the end of Angus's influence. James somewhat naturally hated him and the whole Douglas clan, whose lands he confiscated and whose members he forbade ever to approach within 7 miles of himself. The same year Margaret persuaded the Pope to annul her marriage to Angus, and proceeded to marry another Scottish nobleman.

During his 14 years as king in his own right, James was not unsuccessful. He managed to raise royal revenues considerably, in particular by preying on the wealth of the Church, and he kept the nobility fairly well in their place. His main preoccupation was to avoid falling under the domination of his uncle, Henry; consequently he looked to France for support, linking himself by marriage, first with the daughter of the French king, and then, after her death, with the capable and dynamic **Mary of Guise.** In 1541 James roused Henry's particular ire by failing to meet him, as arranged, at York because the Scots royal council had advised him not to go for fear of kidnap. The direct result of this episode was that Henry provoked James into war, and the Scots suffered an ignoble defeat at Solway Moss, when many of their leaders were captured. The news of this humiliation is said to have precipitated James's death a few days later from nervous exhaustion, at the age of 30.

The 'rough wooing', 1543–50

At this point we might take a look at the problem of Scotland as seen from Henry VIII's point of view. Was the conquest of the country his ultimate aim? After all, he had been crowned king of Ireland, and had integrated Wales into his kingdom; perhaps he had a vision of a united British Isles under one realm? However, Henry was a traditionalist, not a visionary. True, he attacked and defeated James V, but there were personal reasons here. James, although Henry's nephew, had continually rejected his advice, particularly over the question of the Scottish Church, which Henry suggested he should take over, as he himself had done in England. James had chosen to befriend the French, and had dared to marry Mary of Guise, whom Henry had also considered as a wife. Above all, James had insulted Henry by keeping him waiting for several days at York. It was, for Henry, a question of honour that James should be punished for these crimes on the battlefield; once James was dead, however, honour was satisfied. As Henry said to Lord Lisle, there was no longer any honour in continuing to fight against 'a dead body, or upon a widow or on a young suckling'.

So Solway Moss was not followed up by a plan of conquest. Henry merely wished to ensure that Scotland would remain in the English camp, and the best way of doing this was through the betrothal of Henry's son Edward to the baby Mary, an arrangement which would ultimately lead to the union of the two crowns, as had occurred in Spain almost a century earlier. These terms were agreed at the Treaty of Greenwich, and to make doubly sure of the outcome Henry set about creating a pro-English party in Scotland. He had the new regent, the Earl of Arran, on his side, and before their release he bribed a number of important Scottish prisoners captured at Solway Moss to support his policy.

Unfortunately for Henry his project rapidly fell apart. The Assured Scots,

How ye pretend
For to defend
The young Scottish
*   king,*
But ye mean a thing,
An [i.e. if] ye could
*   bring*
The matter about,
To put his eyes out
And put him down,
And set his crown
On your own head
When he were dead.
Such treachery
And traitory
Is all your cast;
Thus ye have
*   compassed*
With the French king
A false reckoning
To invade England . . .

From John Skelton's poem,
'The Duke of Albany' (1524).

PROFILE: *Mary of Guise*

One of the ten surviving children of Claude, Duke of Guise, **Mary** was a member of the most powerful noble family in France. When James V met her in 1537 she was a young widow of 22 with a little boy, who had to be left behind when he married her and she left her home for Scotland. Mary was tall and healthy – just the type to appeal to a prince in search of heirs. She bore James two sons, both of whom died, and six days after James himself died, in 1542, she gave birth to a daughter, Mary.

Mary of Guise was a prudent and skilful administrator, as she demonstrated over the next 18 years. 'How this wonderful woman, alone in a strange and violently disturbed country, managed to outwit Henry and his agents makes a remarkable story', writes the historian William Ferguson. She built up a pro-French party which came to dominate Scotland, and in 1554, after taking over the regency from the Earl of Arran, she brought in French administrators and tried to reform both the government and the Church.

She died during the siege of Leith, in June 1560, of dropsy, a painful disease involving swelling of the stomach and limbs. She was a gifted and attractive figure, although her reputation was systematically blackened by her leading opponent, John Knox.

as those bribed by England were called, proved to be shifty and untrustworthy. Worse, Henry's manoeuvres were circumvented by Mary of Guise, whose pro-French faction, headed by Cardinal Beaton, rapidly gained support, including that of the regent, Arran. The final blow to Henry was when the Scots Parliament formally repudiated the Treaty of Greenwich, in December 1543.

Henry's anger at the behaviour of the Scots can be imagined. He decided to teach them a lesson, the 'rough wooing', and sent an army under the Earl of Hertford to ravage the Lowlands. Henry's instructions were to 'put all to fire and sword, burn Edinburgh town, so rased and defaced when you have sacked and gotten what you can of it, as there may remain forever a perpetual memory of the vengeance of God lightened upon them for their falsehood and disloyalty'.

However, Hertford's punitive expedition merely strengthened Scottish resistance. Even Angus now changed sides, angry at damage to his own property, and the next year he defeated an English force in a skirmish at Ancrum. A second devastating raid by Hertford, in 1545, meant that only 'the godly party' (*i.e.* the small Protestant group in Scotland) now supported Henry. It was some of these who assassinated Cardinal Beaton at St Andrews the following year. But Henry died with his Scottish policy in ruins and the Scottish nation united against the English.

Somerset's Scottish policy was discussed in chapter 11. He won another resounding victory at Pinkie, and then tried to control the country through a network of garrison-forts, but the only result of his efforts was the sending of the young Mary to France, where she was betrothed to the Dauphin, Francis. Somerset's successor, Northumberland, was forced to withdraw the English troops and agree to give up Edward's claim to marry Mary.

Reformation and lasting peace, 1550–60

By 1550 Scotland appeared to be firmly in the French camp. Under Mary of Guise French influence increased and, under the protection of French troops, French administrators started to bring some order to the chaotic Scottish government. Yet in 1560 the Treaty of Edinburgh provided for the withdrawal of the French, and in the same year a Scots Parliament ushered in the Protestant religion and abolished the Mass and the Pope's jurisdiction. The following factors contributed to this turn-around:

1 The corruption and conservatism of the Scottish Church stimulated the growth of anti-clericalism and Protestantism, especially after the charismatic **John Knox** returned to Scotland to lead the reformers.

2 Some leading Scottish nobles, while not necessarily supporting Knox's Calvinism, decided that they stood to lose financially by Mary of Guise's attempts to reform the Church. These 'Lords of the Cong-regation' therefore threw in their lot with the reformers and started a revolt against Mary's rule.

3 Elizabeth's accession to the English throne encouraged the Prot-estant party in Scotland. Elizabeth and her leading minister, Cecil, hoped that by sending a modest amount of military and naval assistance to the rebels they could permanently eliminate French influence in Scotland. Cecil realised that without English help the Lords of the Congregation, who were not particularly concerned with religious principle, might make a deal with the French. The result would be a Catholic Scotland whose queen, with her claim to the English throne, represented a permanent threat to Elizabeth.

PROFILE: *John Knox*

Born in 1505, **John Knox** became a priest, but was converted to Protestantism and rescued from 'the puddle of papistry' (as he later wrote) in the 1540s. In 1547 he was chaplain to the garrison at St Andrews when the French captured the castle and sent him to serve on the galleys. In 1549 Somerset's government interceded for him, he was released from captivity, came to England and became an influential preacher. On Mary's accession he fled, first to Frankfurt and later to Calvin's Geneva. In 1559 he returned permanently to Scotland where his international reputation and powerful preaching won many important converts to Calvinism.

Knox was a domineering egoist, savage in his hatred of opponents, especially Mary of Guise and her daughter. He held that rebellion against 'ungodly' rulers was a duty, and he openly preached violence. He also believed that women were unsuitable to be rulers, a doctrine which got him into trouble with Elizabeth. Until his death in 1572 he dominated the Scottish Church, making life very difficult for the young queen, Mary Stuart. His epitaph reads, 'Here lies one who never feared the face of man'.

4 The Scottish rebels, even with English help, could never have taken the powerful fortress of Leith, where Mary of Guise and a French force were undergoing a siege, had it not been for the start of the religious wars in France. This meant that the French government could not afford to divert the necessary resources to supply and reinforce Leith.

5 The death of Mary of Guise in June 1560 allowed negotiations between the two sides to be speeded up, leading to the Treaty of Edinburgh, under which all English and French forces were to leave Scotland.

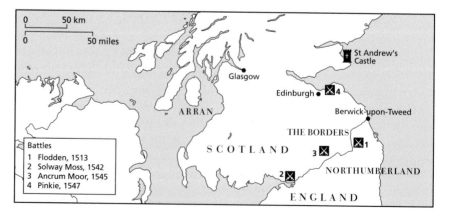

Figure 15.5 Southern Scotland and the Borders

Task: essay-writing

'Account for the failure of Henry VIII's and Somerset's Scottish policies.'

For suggestions about essay-writing look at the end of chapter 10.

Hints on how to approach this question:

Even when one knows the facts it is not a simple matter to plan an answer to this typical A-Level question. To start with, it is crucial – as with most such questions – to avoid a narrative answer. Just saying what happened between 1509 and 1550 in regard to Scottish–English relations explains nothing. 'Account for' means 'give reasons for', and a simple narrative never does this. It is also important to avoid giving irrelevant detail. If you find yourself recounting that Mary of Guise died of dropsy, or that John Knox was an egoist – merely because it says so in this chapter – you are doing just that, and it doesn't help answer this particular question.

When planning an essay, take a close look at the wording of the question. In this instance, there seem to be three components:
(a) Henry VIII's and Somerset's Scottish policies – what were they?
(b) the failure of – is that right? (One doesn't always have to agree with the assumptions behind the wording of a question.) So how far were they a failure?
(c) Account for (*i.e.* think of some reasons why they did fail [in so far as they did]).

This analysis gives us a possible way of planning the essay. Here is a suggestion for a plan (but you still need to construct your own more detailed plan!):

para 1	introduction – explain how your essay is going to be shaped, and perhaps also something about the nature of relations between England and Scotland generally at this period.
2	component (a) i – Henry VIII's policy – here, as well as this chapter one could look at chapter 14.
3	(a) ii – Somerset's policy – see this chapter and chapter 11
4	(b) – did they fail?
5 6 7	(c) – some reasons why.
perhaps 8	conclusion – summarising the key point(s) made in the essay.

Further reading

William Ferguson, *Scotland's Relations with England: a Survey to 1707* (John Donald Publishers Ltd, Edinburgh, 1977).

Jenny Wormald, *Court, Kirk, and Community, Scotland 1470–1625* (Edward Arnold, 1981) – the best introduction to Scottish history.

Richard Glen Eaves, *Henry VIII and James V's Regency 1524–1528* (University Press of America, 1987) – a detailed study of a short period.

16 A price revolution?

Apart from the period since the First World War, the Tudor age saw the most sustained inflation of any time since the Norman Conquest. It has been called a price revolution, although modest by twentieth-century standards. It posed major problems for a society which did not understand what was happening and had inadequate machinery for coping. In this chapter we look at the nature and extent of the inflation, and its possible causes.

Wages and prices

Not surprisingly, the sources available for measuring sixteenth-century inflation are very inadequate. What is needed is, firstly, a price series – that is, a list of the average prices paid for certain goods on a year-by-year basis. But the few institutions whose accounts have survived – some Oxford and Cambridge colleges, certain leading schools – were hardly typical of the majority of people. There also has to be a wage series, a list of average annual wages for particular workers – again, hard to come by. Finally, wages and prices need to be put together to establish 'real' wages (*i.e.* what people could actually buy for their money).

It is worth considering a specific example to see the difficulties of producing a prices and wages index. The most recently published attempt is that of S. Rappaport (see 'Further reading' at the end of chapter). His price series is based on over 4,000 prices from the records of London livery companies such as the Carpenters and the Grocers. These wealthy organisations held regular 'feasts' throughout the year and they kept meticulous accounts of how much they spent. Rappaport examined the prices paid for eight commodities: flour, meat (mutton and rabbit), poultry, fish, milk, drink (ale or beer), suet, and wood for fuel. For each year all prices paid for a particular item were averaged out, and then that average price compared to the average price paid during the base period 1457–71. This period was chosen because it was before any inflation started, when prices were more stable. The going price during 1457–71 for a particular food was labelled 100, and later years computed relative to this. For instance, if milk sold at an average price of 4d a gallon in 1457–71, and a gallon cost 5d in 1535, then the price index for that year was 125 (5d divided by 4d, multiplied by 100). This technique makes it easy to detect price increases and to compare the different items. If the price index for a bushel of flour is 150 in 1535, then we know that flour has gone up by 50 per cent since 1457–71 (*i.e.* by twice as much as milk).

From the individual price series for flour, meat, and so on, a composite price series was constructed by averaging out the various items in proportion to what a typical family might have been expected to spend: flour and drink were each given weightings of 20 per cent; the other items, 10 per cent each. This produced a price index based on a 'basketful of consumables', as in the table and graph in Figure 16.1.

There are, of course, some drawbacks to using this price index as a firm indication of inflation (as the author himself points out):

1 Can we be sure that the particular prices on which this index is based are typical? Might not livery companies, who bought in bulk, have paid less than ordinary people?

2 The index makes assumptions about what people actually did spend their money on. For instance, would they really have spent twice as much on flour as, say, on fish?

Figure 16.1 *Composite price indices, 1490–1609*

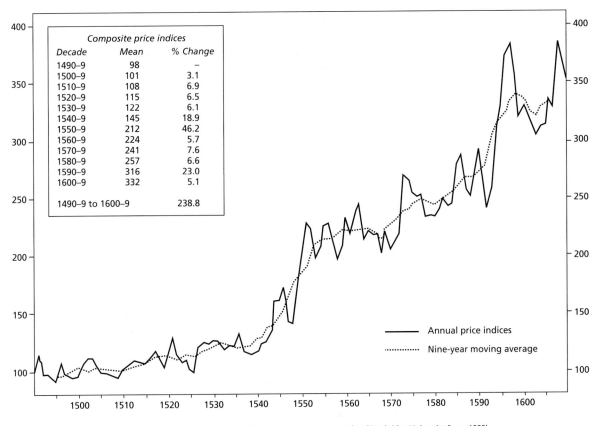

Composite price indices		
Decade	*Mean*	*% Change*
1490–9	98	–
1500–9	101	3.1
1510–9	108	6.9
1520–9	115	6.5
1530–9	122	6.1
1540–9	145	18.9
1550–9	212	46.2
1560–9	224	5.7
1570–9	241	7.6
1580–9	257	6.6
1590–9	316	23.0
1600–9	332	5.1
1490–9 to 1600–9		238.8

——— Annual price indices

············· Nine-year moving average

Adapted from S. Rappaport, Worlds within Worlds; Structures of Life in Sixteenth-century London *(Cambridge University Press, 1989).*

3 It blurs the distinction between classes. What was typical for a wealthy grocer might have been the height of luxury for a labourer. For instance, poorer people very likely never bought any meat at all.

4 Why should we assume that families went on buying the same items over the years? When prices started to go up, might not consumption have shifted from more to less expensive types of food – for example, from mutton to rabbit?

Rappaport used the same livery-company accounts to construct a wage index, based on the daily wages of skilled and semi-skilled workers, such as carpenters and bricklayers, employed by the companies from time to time. Again, the index is correlated to a base of 100, which represents the average wages of such workers in the period 1457–71. At this time, in fact, most skilled craftsworkers were paid 8d per day, and most semi- or unskilled labourers, 5d.

The graph in Figure 16.2 does not mean, of course, that in the 1570s

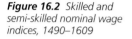

Figure 16.2 *Skilled and semi-skilled nominal wage indices, 1490–1609*

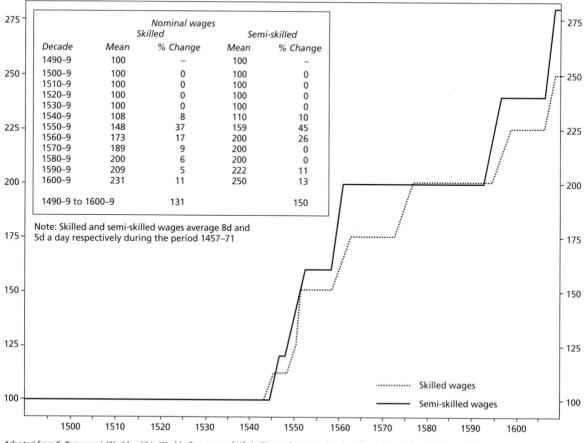

| | Nominal wages | | | |
| | Skilled | | Semi-skilled | |
Decade	Mean	% Change	Mean	% Change
1490–9	100	–	100	–
1500–9	100	0	100	0
1510–9	100	0	100	0
1520–9	100	0	100	0
1530–9	100	0	100	0
1540–9	108	8	110	10
1550–9	148	37	159	45
1560–9	173	17	200	26
1570–9	189	9	200	0
1580–9	200	6	200	0
1590–9	209	5	222	11
1600–9	231	11	250	13
1490–9 to 1600–9		131		150

Note: Skilled and semi-skilled wages average 8d and 5d a day respectively during the period 1457–71

··········· Skilled wages

———— Semi-skilled wages

Adapted from S. Rappaport, Worlds within Worlds; Structures of Life in Sixteenth-century London *(Cambridge University Press, 1989).*

semi-skilled workers were being paid the same as skilled ones. It just shows that at that time both kinds of workers were getting twice as much as they respectively earned in 1457–71. As with the prices index, there are problems to be faced here before one can assume that it gives a good indication even of the nominal income of sixteenth-century workers.

1 It is not always clear from the sources used whether a given worker was skilled or semi-skilled, so some assumptions have to be made.

2 This index represents only the fairly specialised workers employed to repair or extend the various buildings owned by livery companies. Other workers, even other building workers, may not have received the same rates.

3 Another objection, which also applies to the price index, is that these figures are for London. Can we assume that rates were similar in the rest of the country?

We now come to what the wages could actually buy. A 'real' wage index was calculated for each year by dividing the nominal wages index by the composite price index. But first the skilled and semi-skilled wages had to be averaged out. This average was weighted in the proportion 3:5 for semi-skilled and 2:5 for skilled, because this was believed to be the proportion of skilled to semi-skilled workers living within the City of London. A real wage index of 100 means that in that year both prices and wages had risen by the same proportion since the base period of 1457–71. A lower figure means that prices had risen relatively higher than wages, and hence workers could buy less with their money (see Figure 16.3).

Again, as with the other two graphs, there are problems in assuming that this really shows how much purchasing power the average building worker had at any given time during the century. It may be that they were not quite so badly off as the table in Figure 16.3 seems to suggest:

1 Average daily rates take no account of possible overtime payments. Overtime working in the evening or at weekends may well have increased during the century to compensate for higher prices. For instance, in July 1561, 12 men employed on repairing St Paul's Cathedral received six shillings 'reward' each for working on a Sunday.

2 The table is based on day-wages, but perhaps the number of days worked per year went up. We do know that the Reformation substantially reduced the number of religious holidays.

3 Many workers (but we do not know how many) received food and drink from their employers as well as wages.

These three factors might all have helped cushion the effect of rising

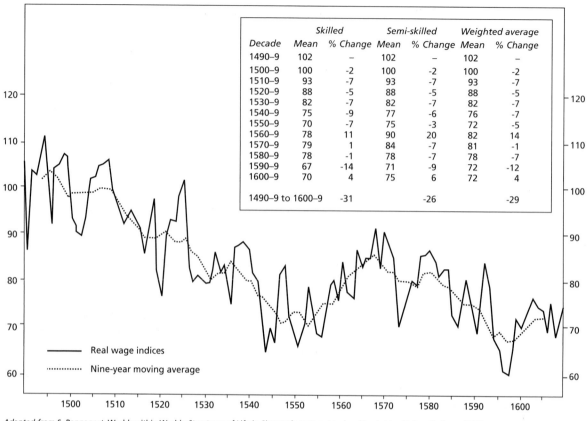

Decade	Skilled		Semi-skilled		Weighted average	
	Mean	% Change	Mean	% Change	Mean	% Change
1490–9	102	–	102	–	102	–
1500–9	100	-2	100	-2	100	-2
1510–9	93	-7	93	-7	93	-7
1520–9	88	-5	88	-5	88	-5
1530–9	82	-7	82	-7	82	-7
1540–9	75	-9	77	-6	76	-7
1550–9	70	-7	75	-3	72	-5
1560–9	78	11	90	20	82	14
1570–9	79	1	84	-7	81	-1
1580–9	78	-1	78	-7	78	-7
1590–9	67	-14	71	-9	72	-12
1600–9	70	4	75	6	72	4
1490–9 to 1600–9		-31		-26		-29

Real wage indices

Nine-year moving average

Adapted from S. Rappaport, Worlds within Worlds; Structures of Life in Sixteenth-century London *(Cambridge University Press, 1989).*

Figure 16.3 *Weighted average of skilled and semi-skilled real wage indices, 1490–1609*

prices, which in general may not have been quite as drastic as some historians have argued. What can, in fact, be deduced about inflation from these three graphs (Figures 16.1–16.3)? The trend in prices can be divided into four distinct phases: a gradual rise of only 22 per cent from the end of the fifteenth century through to the 1540s; then ten years (1542–51) of severe inflation when prices rose by more than 75 per cent; followed by another moderate rise of 23 per cent from the 1550s to the early 1590s; and finally a short period (1593–7) when prices jumped by nearly 50 per cent. By Elizabeth's death in 1603 prices had more than tripled since her father's accession in 1509.

As far as real wages are concerned, these fell gradually through to the early 1540s, and then declined more sharply over the next decade. However, by the 1560s they had staged a recovery, returning to the level of the 1530s. During the first three decades of Elizabeth's reign they fell by only 5 per cent from an average index of 82 in the 1560s. But in the late 1580s and the 1590s they plunged down to 68 (and to 61 in 1596–8, the lowest level throughout the 120-year Tudor period), although they had started to climb again by the end of the century.

Contemporary views

We now turn to the possible causes of the price increase, bearing in mind that neither contemporaries nor historians have ever reached a consensus – this perhaps would be expecting too much, considering that modern economists fail to agree about how to handle our present inflation!

In the mid sixteenth century people were well aware that prices were rising unprecedently, but the reasons were far from clear. Everyone understood that after a bad harvest the price of bread went up, due to the scarcity of grain. However, they had a problem recognising the opposite experience whereby prices rose, not because commodities were scarce, but because money was too plentiful. Contemporaries used the word, 'dearth' – which really means scarcity – to cover both these kinds of inflationary situations, leading to some confusion:

> 'I marvel much, Master Doctor, what should be the cause of this dearth; seeing all things are (thanks be to God) so plentiful. There was never more plenty of cattle than there is now, and yet it is scarcity of things which commonly marketh dearth. This is a marvellous dearth, that in such plenty cometh, contrary to his kind.'
>
> Sir Thomas Smith, *A Discourse of the Commonweal of this Realm of England* (written in 1549, published in 1581).

Faced with inexplicable inflation there was a tendency to look for scapegoats. Popular candidates were the greedy landowner who enclosed or rack-rented, and the unscrupulous merchant who **forestalled** or **regrated.**

Behind such views lurked the medieval theory of the 'just price' (*i.e.* that everything had its normal, appropriate price, and if it had gone up, then some greedy, evil-minded person must be responsible). This was the moral view of society, born of centuries in which prices hardly rose at all from decade to decade. What contemporaries lacked was a quantity theory of money, which would have provided alternative ('monetary') explanations for inflation. Such theories gradually came in during the course of the century. Latimer, for instance, as early as 1549, preached against the government's debasement of the coinage, alleging that 'the naughtiness of the silver was the occasion of dearth of all things in the realm'. The anonymously published *Discourse of the Commonweal*, now known to have been written by **Sir Thomas Smith**, discusses both the debasement and the influx of silver from America as principal causes.

KEY TERMS:

Forestallers and regraters

Forestallers cornered supplies of scarce goods before they reached the market and then forced up prices by exploiting a temporary local monopoly. **Regraters** bought and sold the same goods, thus taking a profit for services of no use to anyone. How far they really were a menace and how far they merely shared with enclosing landowners the role of universal scapegoat is unclear, but there was an exaggerated suspicion of all middlemen in trade, and repeated attacks were made in pamphlets and sermons:
'I have heard how that even this last year there was certain acres of corn growing on the ground bought for viii pounds: he that bought it for viii sold it for x. He that gave x pounds, sold it to another above xii pounds: and at last, he that carried it of the ground paid xiiii pounds . . . I say these merchants of mischief, coming betwixte the bark and the tree, do make all things dear to the buyers . . . Take away regraters and all such as by buying and selling make things more dear, and when they be gone, all things will be more plenty and better cheap.'
(Thomas Lever, in a sermon at St Paul's Cross, December 1550)

141

Figure 16.4 *Regulations concerned with bread-making, published by the Company of Bakers in York*

PROFILE: *Sir Thomas Smith and The Discourse*

A *Discourse of the Commonweal of this Realm of England* has been described as 'the most advanced statement of economic thought in Tudor England'. Its author was almost certainly **Sir Thomas Smith** (1513–77), a leading administrator and principal Secretary of State in 1548–9, and again during the 1570s. The *Discourse* was only published in 1581, but Smith probably wrote it in 1549, and revised it in the 1570s. In the first draft he ascribes inflation to the current debasement of the coinage, but in his revised version he – unlike most of his contemporaries who were still looking for scapegoats – blames 'the great store and plenty of treasure which is walking in these parts of the world, far more in these our days than ever our forefathers have seen in times past. Who doth not understand of the infinite sums of gold and silver which are gathered from the Indies and other countries, and so yearly transported unto these coasts?'

Monetary causes

Explanations for the Tudor inflation from modern historians fall into two categories: those relying on the quantity theory of money and those emphasising non-monetary factors. The principal monetarist explanations are the debasements and the influx of bullion.

Debasement

For more detail on the state's debasement of the coinage see chapter 13. The debasements took place between 1542 and 1551, and this period coincides exactly with the rapid mid-century rise in prices. It is argued that debasement brought about inflation in two related ways. Firstly, the government approximately doubled the amount of money in circulation during these years, because the silver which was saved by issuing inferior coins was used to mint more coins. Therefore, more money was now chasing the same amount of goods, and the result was inflationary. Secondly, it was a question of public confidence. People knew that the new coins were inferior – sometimes they could even see the differences in thickness or colour. Hence, shopkeepers and others offering goods and services would have been likely to demand more money than previously. The debasements thus contributed to inflation not only by increasing the money supply but also by creating a mood of currency instability and lack of public confidence.

There are, however, difficulties in making debasement the only, or even the primary, cause of inflation:

■ Inflation was well under way long before 1541 – admittedly, at a much slower rate than during the mid-century period.

■ If the doubling of the money supply through debasement caused the inflation, then the reduction in the money supply after 1551, by Northumberland, and later by Elizabeth, ought to have brought about a fall in prices. But inflation continued, although at a much reduced rate.

■ Inflation was a European phenomenon. Hence, other reasons apart from the actions of the English government are required to explain it.

Bullion

The theory here is that vast amounts of bullion – principally silver – imported into Spain from America found their way to other European countries and were partly used by governments to increase the amount of coins in circulation, thus having an inflationary effect. The two problems with this explanation are:

■ The main silver influx into Spain came after the opening of the huge mines at Potosi (in modern Bolivia) in 1545, and therefore arrived in Europe too late to account for the inflation of the 1540s, or earlier.

■ How exactly did this Spanish silver get to England in large enough quantities to affect prices, given that for the last two decades of the century England was at war with Spain?

These objections can be overcome to some extent in that:

■ The output of silver mines in central Europe increased some five times between 1460 and 1530, so a combination of European and American silver can be used as evidence to back up the bullion theory.

■ Much Spanish bullion *did* enter England throughout Elizabeth's reign because trade between Spain and England continued in spite of the war, and because English privateers captured large quantities (*e.g.* Drake brought back £1.5 million from attacks on Spanish possessions during his round-the-world voyage, 1577–80).

The main problem with the monetary explanations is that we do not know enough about the role of money in the sixteenth-century English economy to prove or disprove them. We do not even know how much money was circulating at any given time. True, the output of the various mints is recorded, but how many foreign coins were also in circulation, how much was hoarded and how many counterfeit coins were there? Yet another factor which is unknown is the velocity of circulation of the coinage; if it increased, for instance, due to increasing urbanisation, this too would have had an inflationary effect.

'Real' causes

These are factors which push up demand for goods and services without a corresponding increase in supply, thus leading to an increase in prices. The most obvious are population increases and war costs.

Population

The population of early sixteenth-century England (before Thomas Cromwell ordered the keeping of parish registers in 1538) is extremely difficult to estimate. There may have been a very gradual increase – something of the order of 0.03 per cent per annum – from about 1510 onwards, after two centuries of stagnation or decline. But in the 1540s the evidence of the registers shows a steady surplus of baptisms over burials, and the increase from this date on may have been about 1 per cent per annum, with the exception of the disastrous years 1556–8 (see chapter 13). The population of England and Wales probably went up from about 2,700,000 in 1541 to 3,000,000 in the 1560s and 4,000,000 by the 1590s. Thus the date when the population started to go up faster matches the date when inflation started to increase, and a causal link is highly likely. Two known facts about the inflation tend to back this theory:

1 Agricultural prices went up faster than industrial prices, which is what one would expect if there was growing population pressure on food supplies.

2 Grain prices went up faster than meat, dairy or wool prices, which is also to be expected if more people needed to be fed.

War

Heavy government expenditure would also tend to increase demand, and therefore be inflationary. It was war that drastically increased the expenses of the state, compelling it to borrow large sums of money in order to feed and clothe armies, build fortifications, and so on. It is significant that Tudor inflation starts just when Henry VII's peaceful policies give way to the more aggressive policies of Henry VIII. The inflationary 1540s were also years of heavy military expenditure, as were the 1590s. Nevertheless, too much should not be made of this factor. Tudor government spending, even in wartime, was very slight by modern standards, and its inflationary effect could only have been marginal.

Conclusion

It would be a mistake to make too sharp a distinction between monetary and real causes of inflation. Clearly, they are often linked: for example, Henry VIII's and Somerset's wars led to their debasement of the coinage; again, a rising European population would have created a growing demand for money, making the mining of silver more profitable and therefore more likely. It seems evident that there was no single cause for inflation, and all we can do in the fragmentary state of our knowledge is to try and apportion weight to the various factors on offer.

Task: roleplay

The failure to agree on the causes of sixteenth-century inflation allows an opportunity for roleplaying. Your class could divide into three groups, each representing people with a different view about inflation. Each group has to use evidence from this book, or elsewhere, to support its point of view. Groups can then each make a report, or you could set up a mock-debate.

Group 1 should defend the view held by most people at the time that certain categories of scapegoat were responsible for price rises. Support for this might be found in this chapter or in chapter 29, on enclosure. *Group 2* believes in monetary explanations, including debasement and the influx of silver. You can find evidence either in this chapter or in chapter 13 on the mid-century crisis. *Group 3* supports 'real' explanations, such as the rise in population and the effects of war. Again, this chapter and chapter 13 should be useful. Remember you are **not** allowed to make things up, or even to say how things 'must have been' without having the evidence to support your view.

Further reading

R. B. Outhwaite, *Inflation in Tudor and Early Stuart England* (Macmillan, 1970) – a lucid analysis of the causes of inflation.

Joyce Youings, *Sixteenth-Century England* (Penguin, 1984).

D. M. Palliser, *The Age of Elizabeth, 1547–1603* (Addison Wesley Longman, 1992).

S. Rappaport, *Worlds within Worlds: structures of life in sixteenth-century London* (Cambridge University Press, 1989) – provides a new basis for calculating wage and price rises.

Part Two   1559–1603

17 The Elizabethan religious settlement

When Elizabeth I succeeded to the throne, on 17 November 1558, the realm was in urgent need of strong, purposeful government. Armigail Waad, a former clerk to the Council, summarised the situation:

> 'The Queen poor, the realm exhausted, the nobility poor and decayed. Want of good captains and soldiers. The people out of order. Justice not executed. All things dear. Excess in meat, drink and apparel. Divisions amongst ourselves. Wars with France and Scotland. The French king bestriding the realm, having one foot in Calais and the other in Scotland. Steadfast enmity but no steadfast friendship abroad.'

One of the many problems confronting the new queen was to settle the country's religion. Everyone knew that Elizabeth did not share her half-sister's Catholicism, but precisely what kind of settlement she would make was uncertain. To balance the various factors involved was going to require immense delicacy and caution.

Factors behind the settlement

1 Elizabeth's personal views

It is difficult to be definite about the queen's personal religion, which she knew how to keep private, but could also exploit on occasion for political reasons. It is likely that throughout her life she was a committed and conventionally pious Protestant. She had been taught by humanist tutors, and had spent the last years of Henry VIII's reign in the household of the evangelical Catherine Parr. At the start of her own reign she made clear her disbelief in the Catholic doctrine of transubstantiation by walking out of a communion service when the officiating priest refused to obey her order not to elevate the consecrated host. There is no doubt that she always intended to go further than her father, and establish a Protestant settlement. However, she also liked some of the old ceremonial and traditions. She kept the crucifix and candles on the altar of her chapel royal, much to the disgust of reformers, and she continued to employ Catholic musicians such as Thomas Tallis and William Byrd because she liked their music. She also disapproved of clerical marriage, although she never banned it.

2 Opinion in the country

Again, no one can be sure about how many committed Protestants there were in England in 1558, or how many committed supporters of the Pope. In general, the further from London, the fewer Protestants. Probably, most people were prepared to obey whatever settlement their monarch imposed on them, and this included the clergy, a large majority of whom agreed to swear the oath of supremacy. Clearly, the bishops left over from Mary's reign were going to cause difficulty, but luckily for the government several of them had recently died – including Cardinal Pole, the then Archbishop of Canterbury – and there were 11 vacant sees by 1559.

Elizabeth's new Council, under the leadership of William Cecil, was decidedly Protestant. Several of the Councillors, along with other influential figures, had been at Cambridge together in the 1540s, and they formed an unofficial network of humanist reformers who called themselves 'Athenians', and were committed to securing a mildly Protestant settlement. Cecil himself was an Athenian, and so, in a way, was Elizabeth, who had been tutored by Cambridge Humanists. One crucial factor pushing members of the ruling class, including the House of Commons, towards a Protestant settlement was the fear that a restoration of papal authority might threaten their right to keep the lands that many had acquired from the dissolution of the monasteries and chantries.

3 The foreign situation

Elizabeth was surrounded by Catholic powers who saw her as the bastard daughter of a king who had led his realm into schism (division). England was militarily weak and vulnerable to attack from France and Scotland, with both of whom she was still at war. The loss of Calais at the end of Mary's reign meant that France controlled yet another port from which an invasion could be mounted. In Scotland, the young Mary Stuart, wife of the French Dauphin, claimed to be the rightful successor to the English throne, and Henry II's death in June 1559 was to make her husband, Francis, king of France. It was, therefore, crucial not to antagonise England's only ally, Philip II of Spain. It is true that a general peace would be signed at Easter, 1559 – the Treaty of Cateau-Cambresis – but in fact this made the situation potentially even more dangerous because by freeing France from the threat of Spain, it allowed her to concentrate on England. To sum up, it was important for Elizabeth to proceed cautiously towards any Protestant settlement, and keep the world guessing about her intentions for as long as possible.

4 The Marian exiles

Early in Mary's reign several hundred people had left England for Switzerland or Germany. Some went for political reasons, having been involved in Northumberland's plot of 1553; others wanted to avoid the religious persecution. On the continent they saw for themselves churches that had broken away from Rome and had thoroughly reformed their theology and discipline along Calvinist or Zwinglian lines. It has been argued that these exiles, who mostly returned to England after Mary's death, played a major part, especially through their influence in the Commons, in pushing Elizabeth towards a more extreme Protestant settlement than she personally wanted.

However, the importance of these Marian exiles has been inflated. There were not as many of them in the 1559 Parliament as used to be thought, and they did not form a united faction. Apart from a minority of extreme Calvinists most of them were content to accept Elizabeth's leadership, and in fact some, such as Edmund Grindal and Richard Cox, became bishops in the Elizabethan church.

Constructing the settlement

Recent research has produced a revised version of how the settlement came about. According to Sir John Neale, Elizabeth originally wanted a church like the semi-Catholic compromise created by Henry VIII, but was pushed into a more Protestant programme by activists in the Commons, led by the Marian exiles. Subsequent investigators, however, have down-played the role of the activists, and stressed instead Catholic opposition in the Lords.

The new version goes like this: on 9 February 1559, the Council intro-duced into the House of Commons a bill 'to restore the supremacy of the church in England . . . to the crown of the realm', along with two other bills to bring back the church services of Edward's reign. By 21 February these had been amalgamated into a single bill, but although it eventually passed through the Commons, it was wrecked in the Lords. The Elizabethan Settlement had been blocked at its very outset.

During the Easter recess the government discredited the Catholic bishops by staging a rigged public debate on religion in Westminster Abbey, in order to make them appear obscurantist (difficult to understand) and awkward. After this debate, two leading bishops were imprisoned in the Tower, and two others excluded from the Lords. In the next session of Parliament two new bills were introduced, one for the supremacy and one for Protestant services. These were less offensive to the conservatives, as they made substantial concessions, but even so, they only just passed the Lords. Some of the speeches made in opposition have survived, such as the one made by Bishop Scot of Chester, from which this extract is taken:

> *'Our religion, as it was here of late discreetly, godly and learnedly declared, does consist partly in inward things, in faith, hope and charity, and partly in outward things, as in common prayer and the holy sacraments universally administered. Now, as concerning these outward things, this bill does clearly in very deed extinguish them, setting in their places I know not what. And the inward it does also shake, that it leaves them very bare and feeble. And as for the certainty of our faith, whereof the story of the church does speak, a thing of all others most necessary, if it shall hang upon an Act of Parliament we have but a weak staff to lean unto. And that I shall desire you to take me here not as to speak in derogation of the authority of Parliament, which I acknowledge to be of great strength in matters whereto it extends. But for matters of religion, I do not think it ought to meddle withal.'*

Eventually, both bills passed the Lords, the Uniformity Bill by only three votes. Without the government's strong-arm tactics it would have failed. However, Elizabeth had got the settlement she wanted.

The nature of the settlement

1 The royal supremacy

Instead of being 'Head' of the Church of England, like her father, Elizabeth is described in the Act of Supremacy as 'Supreme Governor'. In an age of male chauvinism this change was calculated to appeal not only to Catholics – who wanted no head but the Pope – but also to many Protestants, uneasy at the prospect of a woman taking on this role. The new title actually made no difference in practice; subsequent events, such as the suspension of her Archbishop of Canterbury, Edmund Grindal, in 1576, showed that the queen was just as determined as Henry had been to exercise control over the Church.

The Act contained an oath, which all office holders had to take, with the threat of losing their offices if they refused:

'I, A., B., do utterly testify and declare in my conscience that the Queen's Highness is the only supreme governor of this realm and of all other her Highness' dominions and countries, as well in all spiritual or ecclesiastical things or causes as temporal, and that no foreign prince, person, prelate, state or potentate hath or ought to have any jurisdiction, power, superiority, pre-eminence or authority ecclesiastical or spiritual within this realm.'

2 Uniformity

The Act of Uniformity imposed compulsory church attendance on Sundays, and enforced a new prayer book as the prescribed worship for the whole country. This was similar to the 1552 Prayer Book, but with some crucial alterations so as to make it more acceptable to those conservatives who had opposed the original bills in Parliament:

■ In the communion service, at the point where the minister offered the bread and wine to the communicants, the words spoken by him were a combination of the formula from the 1549 Prayer Book and that of the 1552 Prayer Book:

> And when he delivereth the Bread, he shall say:
>
> *The Body of our Lord Jesu Christ, which was given for thee, preserve thy body and soul unto everlasting life and take and eat this in remembrance that Christ died for thee, [and] feed on him in thine heart by faith with thanksgiving.*

This wording conciliated both those who believed that Christ's body and blood were really present in the bread and wine (*i.e.* Catholics and Lutherans), and those who asserted the memorial aspect of the service (*i.e.* Zwinglians and Calvinists). It has been described as 'among the most brilliant theological compromises of the Reformation'.

■ The following **'Ornaments'** rubric was inserted before Morning and Evening Prayer in the new prayer book:

> *And here is to be noted, that such Ornaments of the Church, and of the Ministers thereof at all times of their Ministration, shall be retained, and be in use, as were in this Church of England by the Authority of Parliament, in the Second Year of the Reign of King Edward the Sixth.'*

KEY TERM:

'Ornaments'

'Ornaments', for ministers, implied the vestments they were expected to wear during services. Here, this meant the alb and cope (Catholic vestments traditionally worn at Mass) at communion, and a surplice (a loose white linen over-garment) at other services. 'Ornaments' for churches included the crosses, candlesticks and other furnishings they had at the start of Edward's reign. According to Elizabeth and her bishops, both clerical vestments and church furnishings were 'things indifferent', meaning that they were not matters which people need argue about, being merely imposed to make the English Church appear disciplined and unified. However, the reformers did not see it that way, and took such 'ornaments' as relics of popery which had to be swept away.

This rubric, which was confirmed by a clause in the Act of Uniformity, had the effect of holding up the process of Protestant change, and hence it did not please the reformers. Many hoped and expected that the queen would not enforce the order, but they were wrong, as was proved in the vestments controversy which erupted a few years later (see chapter 26).

3 The royal *Injunctions*

The *Injunctions* (*i.e.* instructions) of July 1559 filled in the details of the religious settlement. Many were similar to Cromwell's *Injunctions* of 1538; for instance, the order to ministers that they were to keep registers to record parish baptisms, marriages and funerals, and have a bible in English available in their church for all to read. Several items were aimed at improving the quality of the clergy, or specified their duties:

> XLIII. Item, *Forasmuch as in these latter days many have been made priests being children and otherwise utterly unlearned ... the ordinaries [i.e. the bishops] shall not admit any such to any cure or spiritual function.*
>
> XLIV. Item, *every parson, vicar and curate shall upon every holy-day, and every second Sunday in the year, hear and instruct all the youth of the parish ... in the Ten Commandments, the Articles of the Belief, and in the Lord's Prayer, and diligently examine them, and teach the Catechism set forth in the book of public prayer.*

Some of the *Injunctions* were a disappointment to reformers, as they did not go as far as they might have done. Number *XXX*, for instance, instructed the clergy to continue to wear 'seemly habits, garments, and such square caps' as they had under Edward. By insisting that they retain such distinctive clothing for their everyday wear, this tended to emphasise the clergy's separateness from the laity, something the reformers were keen to reduce. Other articles encouraged the use of church music in the Sunday service, which Calvinists frowned on, and insisted that the bread used for communion be specially shaped, so that it still looked like the old communion wafers of the Catholics. Nor was there a specific instruction that 'images' – meaning the pictures of the Virgin Mary and the saints on church walls or in stained glass windows – be destroyed. Instead there was merely an order that the clergy should not 'set forth or extol the dignity of any images, relics or miracles'.

Nevertheless, the royal visitation of the whole country which took place in the summer of 1559 was more to the reformers' liking. Teams of royal commissioners, committed to the destruction of every vestige of 'popery', were sent to tour the parishes and enforce the *Injunctions*. The arrival of these visitors was followed by the removal of altars and images. Bonfires were made of rood screens, statues, pictures, banners and even clerical vestments – although no doubt many churchwardens hid such items in case there should ever be another turn-around in royal policy. The visitors also had the task of administering the oath of supremacy and dealing with those who refused it; it seems, however, that only about two hundred clergy out of several thousand did refuse.

4 The *Thirty-nine Articles*

Possibly to avoid further antagonising Catholics at home and abroad, Elizabeth had not added a definition of doctrine to the 1559 Settlement. However, in 1563 the bishops at last produced one, the *Thirty-nine Articles*, which became the Church of England's statement of faith, and to which, after 1571, all clergy had to subscribe. The Articles were based on Cranmer's *Forty-two Articles* from Edward's reign; they emphasised, wherever possible, common ground between the various shades of Protestantism, trying to satisfy both the Lutherans and the Swiss reformers. For instance, they asserted the doctrine of predestination – the idea that God had chosen certain souls to be saved – which all Protestants agreed on, but they left ambiguous the question of what was to happen to those sinners who were not saved. Here, Calvinists, in opposition to Lutherans, held that certain souls had been irrevocably condemned to damnation.

XVII. Of Predestination and Election

Predestination to life is the everlasting purpose of God, whereby (before the foundations of the world were laid) he hath constantly decreed by his counsel secret to us, to deliver from curse and damnation those whom he hath chosen in Christ out of mankind, and to bring them by Christ to everlasting salvation ... So, for curious and carnal persons, lacking the spirit of Christ, to have continually before their eyes the sentence of God's Predestination, is a most dangerous downfall, whereby the Devil doth thrust them either into desperation, or into wretchlessness [i.e. wretchedness] of most unclean living, no less perilous than desperation.

On the issue of the communion service, too, the *Articles*, while clearly condemning the Catholic doctrine of the mass, tried to leave the door open to the Lutherans, who believed in the 'spiritual presence' of Christ's body and blood after the consecration of the bread and wine:

XXVIII. Of the Lord's Supper

Transubstantiation (or the change of the substance of Bread and Wine) in the Supper of the Lord, cannot be proved by holy Writ; but is repugnant to the plain words of Scripture, overthroweth the nature of a Sacrament, and hath given occasion to many superstitions.

The Body of Christ is given, taken, and eaten, in the Supper, only after an heavenly and spiritual manner. And the mean whereby the Body of Christ is received and eaten in the Supper is Faith.

Conclusion

The Elizabethan Church was something of a hybrid, a compromise containing elements from the Calvinists, the Lutherans and the Catholics. In its doctrines and services it was broadly Protestant, but in its structure, with its bishops, archdeacons, cathedrals and canon law, it still looked very like a branch of the universal Catholic church. It was, of course, a

Figure 17.1 A post-Reformation church service. Compare this with Figure 3.1 on page 20.

1 minister
2 scarf of black silk
3 plain glass in wndow
4 'eagle' lectern
5 Book of Common Prayer at north end of table
6 white linen cloth
7 flagon for wine
8 table
9 ordinary bread
10 wall tablets
11 pulpit for preaching
12 royal coat-of-arms
13 surplice

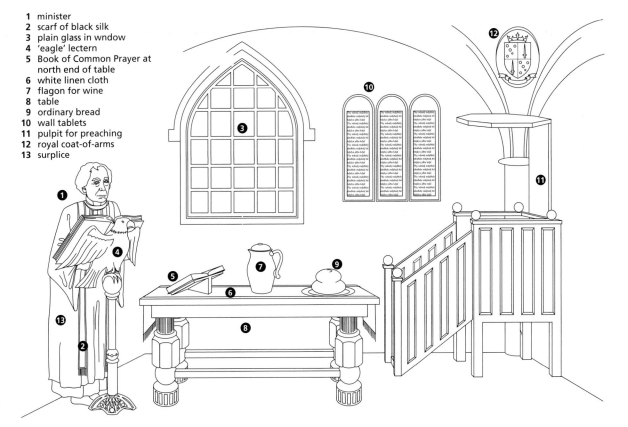

remarkably successful hybrid, which has survived with little alteration until now. For instance, the Elizabethan *Thirty-nine Articles* as well as the *Ornaments* rubric can be found almost unchanged in a prayer book printed today. This chapter has tried to show how the nature of the new church was influenced by the various political factors operating at the time, not least the personality of the queen, as well as the history of England in the previous three reigns.

Task: source evaluation

Before you begin to answer the questions below, read the following hints which are designed to help you get a proper focus.

Q1: This is testing your ability to understand what Bishop Scot is saying and to put his works into the context of events in 1559.

Q2: To answer this you must first understand what the Article is saying. Thus the question relies first on 'comprehension'. However, from this you must move on to relate that comprehension to your understanding of the church doctrine which is involved here.

Q3: This question has a much wider scope than questions 1 and 2. It asks you to use your understanding of three of the documents in this chapter to explain the government's motives. It carries almost as many marks as the other three parts combined and it clearly requires you to write more as a result. You should be thinking of a mini-essay here.

1 Study the extract from the speech by Bishop Scot of Chester (page 151).
  a Why does Bishop Scot allege that the bill he was opposing would 'extinguish' the sacraments?   *3 marks*
  b What view does the Bishop hold about the powers of parliament?   *4 marks*

2 Study Article *XXVIII* of the *Thirty-nine Articles* of 1563 (page 155). Describe in your own words the Church of England's position on the doctrine of transubstantiation and explain the reasons why it took this position.   *6 marks*

3 Study the following three documents: extracts from the Oath of Supremacy; the wording of the Communion Service; the 'Ornaments' rubric (page 152). Use these three documents to explain what the aims of the government were in making the religious settlement of 1559.   *12 marks*

Total: 25 marks

Further reading

Susan Doran, *Elizabeth I and Religion 1558–1603*, Lancaster Pamphlets (Routledge, 1994).

Christopher Haigh, *English Reformations; Religion, Politics, and Society under the Tudors* (Clarendon Press, 1993).

Diarmaid MacCulloch, *The Later Reformation in England 1547–1603* (Macmillan, 1990).

Susan Doran and Christopher Durston, *Princes, Pastors and People; the church and religion in England 1529–1689* (Routledge, 1991).

N. M. Sutherland, 'The Marian Exiles and the Establishment of the Elizabethan regime', *Archiv fur Reformationsgeschichte*, No. 78, 1987 – stresses the diversity of the exiles and their limited influence on the 1559 settlement.

Norman Jones, *The Birth of the Elizabethan Age: England in the 1560s* (Blackwell, 1993) – includes a valuable summary of Jones's revisionist view of how the settlement came about.

David Loades, *Revolution in Religion: the English Reformation 1530–1570* (Wales University Press, 1992).

18 The royal finances

Was the Elizabethan state bankrupt? On the face of it the answer seems to be no, for the financial situation at the end of Elizabeth's reign was similar to what it had been at the beginning. Elizabeth inherited a debt of some £300,000 from Mary and passed on a debt of £360,000 to her successor, James I. When due allowance is made for inflation, this means that she had kept herself solvent despite the costs of the war against Spain which dominated the closing decades of her reign. But appearances can be deceptive, particularly in money matters. We need to look more closely at how much the Crown received and how much it spent.

Ordinary income

Income was traditionally divided into Ordinary and Extraordinary. The essential difference between these two is that extraordinary income had to be granted, usually by Parliament. Ordinary income was derived from the Crown's own resources. The two principal sources of Ordinary income were:

- the crown lands
- **customs**.

The crown lands

Rents and other revenues from lands owned by the Crown had been the basis of the royal finances in the Middle Ages, but during the turbulent reign of Henry VI a great deal of property had passed out of the Crown's possession. The Yorkists and the first Tudor, Henry VII, set about the task of recovering alienated lands (see chapter 2), but there was no significant re-endowment of the Crown until Henry VIII suppressed the monasteries and seized their possessions. This turned out to be a short-term benefit, however, for the heavy cost of his wars against France meant that he had to sell off some two-thirds of what he had confiscated. This process continued under his successors.

At the beginning of Elizabeth's reign the crown lands were bringing in more than £66,000 a year; at the end, just under £89,000. **Wardship** brought in an average of £20,000 a year, giving a total land revenue, by the time Elizabeth died, of close on £110,000. This seems to be a marked improvement on the situation in 1509 when Henry VII died, for his total

---

KEY TERMS:

Customs

These were taxes on imports, the most important of which were called Tonnage and Poundage. Since the reign of Edward IV it had been the practice for the first Parliament of every reign to make a lifetime grant of customs duties to the new sovereign.

Wardship

Wardship was one of the surviving relics of the Norman feudal system which had been imposed on England by William the Conqueror and his successors. The principal landowners were technically 'tenants-in-chief' of the Crown and held their land in return for doing military service. Under-age heirs could not fulfil this obligation and the king therefore had the right to take over their land and make them into royal wards. This was profitable, since he could either exploit the ward's estates himself or sell the wardship to the highest bidder. Henry VII appointed a Master of Wards to handle this source of income, and in 1540, shortly before his fall from power, Thomas Cromwell introduced a bill into Parliament establishing a formal Court of Wards. This remained a major revenue department until its abolition in 1646.

land revenue was only £42,000. But the sixteenth century saw inflation gather pace, at the same time as the range of government expanded, and by 1603 the administrative costs which the Crown had to meet were four to five times higher than they had been in 1509. In other words, for Elizabeth's land revenue to keep pace with the increase in costs she would have needed at least four times what Henry VII had received, namely £168,000, which was well above the £110,000 she was actually getting. In real terms, then – taking due account of inflation on the Crown's expenditure – Elizabeth's income was declining.

Customs

These duties on trade were levied at a rate fixed by the Crown. Mary's Lord Treasurer had increased the income from this source by issuing a new Book of Rates, and the yield subsequently went up to over £80,000 a year. As trade flourished under Elizabeth the customs revenue expanded still further, reaching a peak of £120,000, but by the end of her reign it had fallen back to around £100,000. Here again the comparison with Henry VII is revealing. By the time he died the customs revenue was running at £40,000 a year. When allowance is made for inflation, this was the equivalent of some £160,000 in 1603 – well above the £100,000 or so Elizabeth was receiving.

One final set of figures confirms the impression given so far. Henry VII's total ordinary income from all sources was about £113,000 a year. In real terms this was equivalent to £450,000 by the end of the sixteenth century, but it is unlikely that Elizabeth was receiving more than £300,000. In other words the ordinary revenue had not kept pace with inflation, and the royal administration, despite the fact that it was far more complex and extensive than it had been under the first Tudor, was operating with only two-thirds of the income that he had enjoyed.

Extraordinary income

'We your most obedient and loving subjects the Lords spiritual and temporal and the Commons in this present Parliament assembled, to show our willing hearts and good minds ... have condescended and agreed with one voice and most entire affections to make your Highness at this time [1559] a present ... [of] two whole fifteenths and tenths ... And furthermore, for the great and weighty considerations aforesaid, we ... give and grant to your Highness one entire subsidy.'

It was taken for granted in the Tudor period that the Crown had the right to call upon Parliament for financial assistance to meet exceptional demands upon its resources. Under Elizabeth parliamentary supply was requested in every session except that of 1572 and was duly voted. The medieval fifteenth and tenth continued to be included in parliamentary grants, as you can see from the extract above, and brought in about £30,000. Far more important, however, was the subsidy, which Wolsey had made the standard parliamentary tax.

The advantage of the subsidy was that, unlike the fifteenth and tenth, it was freshly assessed for every grant and therefore reflected the actual distribution of wealth. Despite the fact that the assessors were local gentlemen, they seem to have done their task fairly and thoroughly at first; but by the time Elizabeth ascended the throne there was a growing suspicion that they were undervaluing their own wealth, thereby setting a bad example to those they were assessing. As early as 1558 the Queen reminded them that they should assess themselves 'according to the just value of your lands or goods, without the which ye cannot have authority to call earnestly upon others to do the same'.

Matters did not improve, however, as is shown in a Privy Council letter of 1598:

> 'Subsidies, of later times, have come to far less sums than those of former ages; which cannot grow but by the remiss and neglectful dealing of such as are the Commissioners for the assessment of the same ... You cannot perform the trust reposed in you, nor your duties towards her Majesty and your country, if you proceed not in this service with great care, and endeavour to advance the sums and assessments as much as may be, in assessing all men indifferently that are of ability, without regard of any favour.'

As a result of underassessment, the value of a subsidy declined from £140,000 at the beginning of Elizabeth's reign to £80,000 at the end. During the war years after 1588 Parliament responded by increasing the number of subsidies voted – two in 1589, three in 1593, and four in 1601. This eased the pressure on the Queen's government but did not by any means solve all its financial problems. From 1586 until 1603 parliamentary taxes brought in more than £1,100,000, but the cost of the war against Spain during these years amounted to £4 million. The Queen had to look elsewhere to fill the gap.

Financial expedients

To meet her most pressing needs, Elizabeth resorted to borrowing. During the course of her reign the corporation of London lent her close on £200,000, and she also levied forced loans from her richer subjects which brought her in £330,000.

> ### Privy Seal for a loan 1589
>
> *To our trusty and well-beloved Thomas Lawley of the Coppies, gent.: Whereas for the better withstanding of the intended invasion of this realm, upon the great preparations made by the King of Spain both by sea and land the last year … we were enforced … to be at infinite charges … We have therefore thought it expedient, having always found our good and loving subjects most ready upon such like occasion to furnish us by way of loan of some convenient portions of money agreeable with their estates (which we have a mind always to repay), to have recourse unto them … Wherefore we require you to pay to our use the sum of £25 …*

KEY TERMS:

Purveyance and Monopolies

Purveyance was the right to purchase food and other commodities for the royal court at less than the market price. This affected mainly the southern counties where royal 'progresses' took place during the summer months. The activities of purveyors had long been a cause for complaint, particularly since, as the sovereign's agents, they could not be called to account before the common law courts. Any disputes had to be referred to the Board of Green Cloth, but this was the body which ran the royal household and therefore had a vested interest in supporting the purveyors.

Monopolies had originally been devised to protect new inventions by giving the inventor the sole right to manufacture or trade in them. But under Elizabeth they became little more than a way of raising money. Monopoly rights were sold by the Crown or given away to courtiers who would otherwise have demanded royal pensions or lands. Monopolists could set their own prices, and as more and more goods were covered by monopolies so prices went up – much to the anger of consumers, whose complaints were voiced in Parliament.

Loans provided short-term relief, but since most were eventually repaid they could not be a long-term solution. Elizabeth had therefore to resort to her father's expedient of selling off crown lands, including former monastic property. Land sales raised close on a million pounds during her reign, but by selling off her capital assets the Queen was diminishing her future income. She had no choice, of course, since the threat from Spain was too great to ignore, but she left the English monarchy weaker, in financial terms, than she had found it.

Among other sources of revenue that the Elizabethan government felt compelled to exploit were **Purveyance** and **Monopolies**. Purveyance was the cause of so much ill-will that Elizabeth would have been well advised to abandon it. But had she done so she would have had to pay market prices for supplies to her court, and this would have cost her some £40,000 a year – not a great amount, but more than the hard-pressed Queen could afford. Instead, she instructed her Privy Councillors to improve the existing system, and in the 1590s they extended the practice of 'composition', whereby every county made a contract with the purveyors, agreeing to provide specified amounts of provisions for a fixed sum. The difference between the market price and that which the purveyors were prepared to pay was made up by a local tax. By removing uncertainty from the system, composition made it more acceptable, but purveyance still remained deeply unpopular.

The Queen took the steam out of a bitter debate in the 1597 Parliament by promising to reform abuses in monopolies. But there was no improvement by the time her last Parliament assembled in 1601, and members were in a distinctly bad temper, as is shown by the speech of Francis Moore:

> *'I cannot utter with my tongue, or conceive with my heart, the great grievances that the town and country for which I serve suffer by some of these monopolies. It bringeth the general profit into a private hand, and the end of all is beggary and bondage to the subject ... And to what purpose is it to do anything by Act of Parliament when the Queen will undo the same by her prerogative? ... There is no act of hers that hath been or is more derogatory to her own majesty, or more odious to the subject, or more dangerous to the commonwealth, than the granting of these monopolies.'*

Once again the Queen intervened, assuring members that anyone with a complaint against a monopolist could seek redress in a common law court. She also ordered the cancellation of those monopolies which had been singled out for criticism. In this way she defused a dangerous situation, but the problem of monopolies – which was part and parcel of the problem of the royal finances – remained to plague her Stuart successors.

Corruption

One of the ways in which English rulers – like all other rulers – retained the loyalty of their more important subjects was by giving them titles, pensions and offices. But as the royal finances came under ever greater strain there was less and less money available for outright grants, nor could the Queen afford to increase the salaries of office-holders in line with inflation. They were therefore left to make what they could out of those who needed their services. In other words the customer was made to pay, and as the reign went on payments for services asked or rendered became the rule rather than the exception, and standards of honesty in public life declined.

Another problem for Elizabeth was that the number of people hoping, and expecting, to benefit from royal patronage exceeded what the Crown had to offer. This meant that ministers and courtiers, who were well placed to influence the Queen, acted as intermediaries between her and the suitors who were competing for a share of royal patronage. William Cecil, who was her principal minister, received as many as a hundred letters a day from would-be beneficiaries, as did the royal favourite, the Earl of Leicester. Cecil, Leicester and the handful of other great interme-diaries expected a reward for their mediation, of course, and in many cases it was money rather than merit which determined their attitude.

It was in the 1590s, when the war with Spain was eating up the Crown's resources, that the situation really deteriorated. In 1600 the Queen apologised to one of her courtiers for the fact that the cost of the war compelled her to 'restrain her bountiful hand from rewarding her servants', but although her excuse was genuine it was not the whole truth. Elizabeth had always been reluctant to make grants, and as she grew older she became positively mean. She was unwilling even to bestow titles, which cost her nothing, and at her death there were fewer peers than there had been at her accession. The genuine shortfall in royal patronage was made worse by Elizabeth's refusal to part with what little was available.

Another problem arose from the power struggle between the Cecil family – William Cecil, who died in 1598, and Robert, his son and political heir (see Figure 18.1) – and the Earl of Essex, the Queen's young favourite, which dominated the last decade of the reign. The rival parties were engaged in a battle to gain 'clients' (*i.e.* supporters), and were none too scrupulous about the methods they employed. Since all decisions on the distribution of patronage depended, ultimately, upon the Queen, she came under enormous pressure. In March 1594 Essex wrote from court

Figure 18.1 *William and Robert Cecil, father and son*

163

to Francis Bacon, for whom he was trying to obtain the post of Solicitor General, describing how he had attempted to persuade Elizabeth:

'I find the Queen very reserved, staying herself from giving any kind of hope, yet not passionate against you till I grew passionate for you ... I told her ... I thought that my credit, joined with the approbation and mediation of her greatest Councillors, might prevail in greater matter than this ... [but] ... she said she neither was persuaded, nor would hear of it till Easter ... and therefore in passion bade me go to bed if I would talk of nothing else. Wherefore in passion I went away, saying while I was with her I could not but solicit for the cause and the man I so much affected, and therefore I would retire myself till I might be more graciously heard. And so we parted. Tomorrow ... I will write an expostulating letter to her. That night ... I will be here again and follow on the same course.'

Figure 18.2 *William Cecil, Lord Burghley, presiding over the Court of Wards*

The struggle between the Essex and Cecil factions limited Elizabeth's options, for ultimately she had to choose between one or the other. What was at stake for the contenders was not simply political power but the rewards that went with it. Much of Essex's wealth came from the monopoly of sweet wines which the Queen had given him – as she had earlier given it to Leicester. The Cecils' wealth also derived from royal favour, though in this case it was the grant of offices rather than pensions or monopolies.

As Lord Treasurer and Master of the Wards, Lord Burghley was a key player in the distribution of the Crown's patronage, and he did very well out of it. He once protested that his official fees were insufficient even to cover the costs of his stable. This may well have been true, but he said nothing of his unoffical remuneration by way of 'gifts' from suitors who needed his assistance. His professions of poverty in the Crown's service have to be set against the fact that he built two magnificent palaces for himself – Burghley House, where his descendants still live, and Theobalds, which his son gave to James I. Significantly, Elizabeth undertook no major building operations. While her favourites and ministers competed to outshine each other in ostentatious display, she was economical to the point of niggardliness. The contrast tells us much about the true state of the royal finances in her reign.

Further reading

F. C. Dietz, *English Public Finance 1558–1641* (Frank Cass, 1964) – old but invaluable; still the basic work.

Roger Schofield, 'Taxation and the political limits of the Tudor state' in Claire Cross, David Loades and J. J. Scarisbrick (eds), *Law and Government under the Tudors* (Cambridge University Press, 1988).

R. W. Hoyle (ed.), *The Estates of the English Crown 1558–1640* (Cambridge University Press, 1992).

19 Elizabethan Parliaments

Time chart of Parliamentary sessions

1 **January–May 1559**

2 **January–April 1563; September 1566–January 1567**

3 **April–May 1571**

4 **May–June 1572; February–March 1576; January–March 1581**

5 **November 1584–March 1585**

6 **October 1586–March 1587**

7 **February–March 1589**

8 **February–April 1593**

9 **October 1597–February 1598**

10 **October–December 1601**

In an age that knew nothing of radio or television, Parliament was one of the principal means of communication between the Queen and her subjects. The representatives who assembled from time to time in the former royal palace of Westminster were a miniature version of the 'political nation' (*i.e.* the upper section of society that dominated politics). They informed the queen and her ministers of the wishes of their constituents. Then, after the session was over and they returned to their homes, they took with them news of what they had agreed upon. Bearing in mind that Elizabeth had no police or standing army to force her subjects into obedience, Parliament helped secure a wide measure of acceptance for her policies. It was, in Professor Elton's phrase, a 'point of contact' between the government and the governed.

The origins of Parliament went back to the Middle Ages, but its importance had increased markedly under Henry VIII, who used it to push through the break with Rome. Parliament was now virtually omnicompetent – there was no area of English life which was out of its jurisdiction. Nor were there any limits upon what it could do. Under Edward VI it was used to create a Protestant Church in England; under Mary to destroy it.

Frequent sessions of Parliament from 1529 onwards gave its members – particularly the Commons – an increased awareness of their own identity and importance. Indeed, it used to be thought that while the powerful and arrogant Henry VIII managed to dominate Parliament, it became increasingly difficult to control after his death. When so much depended upon the personality of the ruler, it was argued, a boy king and two queens were not strong enough to hold the Commons in check. This interpretation was linked with the so-called 'rise of the gentry' – the belief that the smaller landowners, whose influence and numbers had increased as they took over former monastic property, came to Westminster in order to flex their muscles and 'seize the initiative' from the Queen and her ministers. The history of Elizabethan parliaments, according to this view, was one of confrontation between an increasingly assertive House of Commons and an increasingly isolated and defensive queen.

In this chapter we shall look at what Parliament actually did and suggest other ways of interpreting its role.

Membership and meetings

The senior house of Parliament was the Lords, consisting of 26 bishops, or 'lords spiritual', and some 60 lay peers, or 'lords temporal'. This small body of less than a hundred persons comprised the top level of English society and in a deferential age its views carried great weight. The House of Lords was an active partner in the business of government, and those members of the Privy Council who were nobles were regular attenders. After 1571, when the Queen's chief minister, William Cecil, moved to the Upper House (the Lords) as Lord Burghley, its importance increased yet further.

The House of Commons consisted of county members, known as 'knights of the shire', and 'burgesses' who represented urban constituencies. The burgesses outnumbered the knights of the shire by four to one, and their strength was increased by 62 during Elizabeth's reign as she created new parliamentary boroughs. This did not mean that tradesmen and merchants were now flooding into the Lower House (the Commons). On the contrary, the pressure on the Queen to expand representation came from the country gentry who saw this as a way into Parliament. Boroughs were usually only too happy to elect local gentlemen who would serve at their own expense, but the consequence was that Parliament represented land rather than other forms of wealth.

The fact that gentlemen were so anxious to get into Parliament tells us something about the high prestige that institution enjoyed. Being an MP was not, of course, a full-time occupation. There were 13 parliamentary sessions under Elizabeth, but they lasted for a total of only 126 weeks.

This would give an average of three weeks for every year of the reign, but Parliament – as you can see from the time chart on page 166 – did not meet every year: in 26 out of the 44 years of the reign it did not meet at all.

The fact that Parliament was only an occasional body serves as a useful reminder that it was not the government then any more than it is today. The Elizabethan equivalent of the Prime Minister and Cabinet was the Queen and Privy Council. They did the governing, and they only summoned Parliament when they felt it could help them in this task.

Parliamentary business

What was the purpose of Parliament? It had three main functions:

1 *To act as a point of contact*, as described in the first paragraph of this chapter.

2 *To vote money*. Elizabethan governments asked for 'supply' from all parliaments except that of 1572, and in every case the Commons responded by voting it.

3 *To make law*. Most of the legislation put before Parliament was uncontentious and passed without difficulty. Major bills were introduced by the government, but many bills were 'private' – that is, they affected only a particular interest group. If a town wanted to raise money for a major building project or have its charter amended, it might well ask its MP to introduce a bill for this purpose. Where members found that their local concerns overlapped they could combine to produce a 'public' bill that would have the same effect as several private ones.

Opposition?

While the government could usually take the support of the Lords for granted, this was not the case with the Commons. The main reason for this was that the Commons consisted, by the end of the reign, of 462 members, and they were not disciplined by party whips as is the case today. A body as large as that could not operate effectively without guidance, and this was provided by those Privy Councillors who had been elected as MPs. In this extract from an account of proceedings in 1566 we see them at work:

> '*A motion was made by Mr Molineux for the reviving of the suit touching the declaration of a successor in case her Majesty should die without issue ... which motion was very well approved by the greater part of the said House ... Mr Secretary Cecil and Sir Francis Knollys, her Majesty's vice-chamberlain, declared unto the House that the Queen's Majesty was, by God's special providence, moved to marriage ... Sir Ambrose Cave, chancellor of the Duchy, and Sir Edward Rogers, controller of her Majesty's Household, affirmed the same, and thereupon persuaded and advised the House to see the sequel of that before they made further suit touching the declaration of a successor.*'

This extract tells us a great deal. The overwhelming majority of members of the Commons were alarmed at the prospect of what might happen if the Queen were to die. Since she was unmarried, there was no husband or heir to carry on the government, and the consequent confusion might give an opening to England's enemies. The Commons were therefore pressing her to name her successor, but Elizabeth had no intention of doing so. She could not go to the Commons in person to explain her position, but she used her Councillors as her mouthpiece. Their intervention was successful in the short run, and Mr Molineux's motion was not taken up by the House.

The extract is also misleading because of what it does *not* tell us. On this occasion, as on a number of others, the opposition to the Queen's policy extended well beyond the House of Commons, even into the Privy Council itself. Members of the Council – the governing body of Elizabethan England – shared the prevailing view that uncertainty about who would succeed to the throne in the event of the Queen's death was potentially dangerous. But they came up against the obstacle of Elizabeth herself, who did not care to contemplate her own demise. How could they persuade her to do what they felt to be essential? One way was to increase pressure on her by extending the debate into Parliament.

Councillors themselves could not risk openly criticising the queen, but they had many unofficial links with the members of the Commons, and it turns out that a number of prominent critics of crown policy in the Lower House were working in collusion with the Council. One of the most influential of the Council's 'men of business' was **Thomas Norton**.

The Council only 'prompted' the Commons into discussing a specific topic when it despaired of making the Queen change her mind. In 1563 and 1566 it did so on the question of the succession; in 1571 on reform of the Church; and in 1572–87 on the fate of Mary, Queen of Scots. It was

---

PROFILE: *Thomas Norton*

Norton was born about 1532, the son of a wealthy London citizen descended from a Bedfordshire yeoman family. He trained as a lawyer at the Inner Temple and demonstrated his Protestant commitment by marrying the daughter of Archbishop Cranmer. He sat in every one of Elizabeth's parliaments from 1558 to 1581, and such was his dedication to the Commons' business that fellow members called him 'Master Norton, the Parliament man'. The historian Sir John Neale described him as 'a radical Puritan' and 'a catalytic figure in the growth of persistent organised parliamentary opposition'. But more recently Michael Graves has demonstrated that Norton had close links with the government. When, in 1581, he was congratulated for the pains he had taken in drawing up Acts considered by the Commons, he insisted that 'there is none of [them] that I did draw and offer of my own first device, but all that I have done I did by commandment of the House, and specially of the Queen's Council there, and my chiefest care was in all things to be directed by the Council'. Thomas Norton died at the age of 52.

---

always risky to extend discussion in this way, because things could all too easily get out of hand. In 1571, for example, proposals for limited reform of the Church were hijacked by the puritan Walter Strickland, who put forward his own bill for radical reform of the Prayer Book – something which was anathema to Elizabeth.

Another outspoken puritan MP who constantly went beyond the limits that the Council felt obliged to maintain was Peter Wentworth. He took his stand in 1576 on the Commons' privilege of free speech which he claimed was 'granted by a special law, as that without which the Prince and state cannot be preserved or maintained':

> *'Two things do great hurt in this place, of the which I do mean to speak. The one is a rumour which runneth about the House, and this it is, "Take heed what you do; the Queen's Majesty liketh not such a matter; whosoever preferreth it, she will be offended with him": or the contrary, "Her Majesty liketh of such a matter; whosoever speaketh against it, she will be much offended with him" ... I would to God, Mr Speaker, that these two were buried in hell, I mean rumours and messages, for wicked undoubtedly they are; the reason is, the devil was the first author of them, from whom proceedeth nothing but wickedness.'*

KEY TERM:

Privileges

During the late medieval period the rulers of England had granted members of the House of Commons a number of **privileges** which were designed to make sure that their debates could go ahead smoothly and efficiently. They were, for instance, free from arrest for such things as debt while Parliament was in session. They were also free to speak their minds without fear of incurring royal displeasure. However, this privilege of free speech had never been given precise definition, and during Elizabeth's reign it became apparent that there was a wide difference of opinion over its exact nature and limits between the Queen and some of the more outspoken members.

If every member of the Commons had been like Peter Wentworth the Queen might well have despaired. Fortunately for her he was the exception. Indeed, the Commons were so shocked by his outburst in 1576 that they sent him to the Tower of London.

At the beginning of every Parliament the Speaker asked the Queen for confirmation of the Commons' **privileges**, including freedom of speech, and the Queen duly obliged (see Figure 19.1). But she insisted that this did not mean freedom to discuss anything at all. In 1593 the Lord Keeper, speaking on her behalf, laid down very precise limits:

> 'Her Majesty granteth you liberal, but not licentious speech. Liberty, therefore, but with due limitation. For even as there can be no good consultation where all freedom of advice is barred, so will there be no good conclusion where every man may speak what he listeth, without fit observation of persons, matters, times, places, and other needful circumstances ... For liberty of speech, her Majesty commandeth me to tell you that to say "Yea" or "No" to bills, God forbid that any man should be restrained or afraid to answer according to his best liking, with some short declaration of his reason therein, and therein to have a free voice, which is the very true liberty of the House; not, as some suppose, to speak there of all causes as him listeth, and to frame a form of religion or a state of government as to their idle brains shall seem meetest. She saith no king fit for his state will suffer such absurdities.'

The implied threat in the last part of this statement was no mere form of words, for Elizabeth was quite prepared to take action against members who had, in her view, gone beyond 'liberty' into 'license'. In 1593, to take one example, she sent the irrepressible Peter Wentworth back to the Tower, where he remained a prisoner until his death three years later.

Firm action of this sort was effective where the member in question was something of a maverick (someone who thinks and acts independently). However, in the last two parliaments of the reign there was widespread resentment about monopolies, and instead of trying to stifle debate Elizabeth intervened with a promise to take appropriate measures herself. By so doing she preserved her prerogative – that special authority which belonged to her as queen – and her independence. What is remarkable about the relationship between Elizabeth and her parliaments is the extent to which she managed to get her own way – sometimes

Figure 19.1
Elizabeth in Parliament with the Speaker and Commons at the bar

by stubbornly refusing to budge, sometimes by making a timely concession.

However, conflict was the exception, not the rule. In general the two important functions of voting money and passing laws went ahead smoothly. This was only partly a result of good management. The important thing to remember is that the Queen and members of Parliament, both Commons and Lords, shared the same objectives – namely defence of England and of the Protestant religion. They all profited from cooperation, and although in certain instances they might have differences of emphasis they were reluctant to treat these as matters of principle on which no compromise was possible.

One other, very important, factor was the personality of Elizabeth. Regarded at first as an inexperienced woman who needed manly guidance, she became a sort of icon or image, the personification of the country over which she reigned (see chapter 20). Although she was conscious of the majesty of her exalted position, and careful to maintain it, she knew how to charm. After the end of her last, stormy Parliament, in November 1601, she summoned the Commons to her palace of Whitehall and delivered what they christened her 'golden speech'. It ended with:

> 'I have ever used to set the last judgement day before mine eyes, and so to rule as I shall be judged to answer before a higher judge. To whose judgement seat I do appeal, that never thought was cherished in my heart that tended not to my people's good ... And though you have had and may have many princes more mighty and wise sitting in this seat, yet you never had or shall have any that will be more careful and loving ... And so I commit you all to your best fortunes and further counsels. And I pray you, Mr Controller, Mr Secretary, and you of my Council, that before these gentlemen depart into their countries [i.e. counties] you bring them all to kiss my hand.'

Task: note-taking

This note-taking exercise is slightly different from that in chapter 2. It involves picking out points from several chapters in order to construct a table. Sometimes it is worth putting your notes in the form of a table or diagram in order to make them more logical and easier to remember.

Use this chapter, as well as any relevant points from chapters 18, 23 and 26, to construct a table of the main occasions on which members of the House of Commons argued with Elizabeth, or tried to get her to change her policy. Head it like this:

Date of the Parliamentary session	Subject of the argument	Outcome

At the end of the table summarise briefly which you think were the most serious occasions on which queen and Parliament disagreed.

Further reading

G. R. Elton, *The Parliament of England 1559–1581* (Cambridge University Press, 1986).

M. A. R. Graves, *Elizabethan Parliaments 1559–1601*, Seminar Studies in History (Addison Wesley Longman, 2nd edn, 1996) – the best single-volume account, with an excellent bibliography.

M. A. R. Graves, *Thomas Norton: The Parliament Man* (Blackwell, Oxford, 1994).

Patrick Collinson, 'Puritans, Men of Business and Elizabethan Parliaments', *Parliamentary History* vol. 7 (1988).

D. M. Dean and N. L. Jones (eds), *The Parliaments of Elizabethan England* (Blackwell, 1990) – shows how Parliament actually worked.

20 The Tudor Court 2: the cult of monarchy

The Tudor cult of monarchy starts with Henry VIII and his carefully fostered new image of imperial kingship (see chapter 7). But after the period of weak monarchy which ended in 1558 there was a need for a fresh image to suit the times and to justify the accession of another female ruler. In a period of instability and potential unrest it was essential to raise the prestige of the new young monarch as a focus for popular feeling, especially as the destruction of so many of the beliefs and rituals of the old religion had left behind a vacuum in which people could easily become disoriented and lose their sense of belonging to the community. New verbal and visual images were required to attract the loyalty of a divided people.

This became even more crucial later in Elizabeth's reign, as it became clear that Catholic Europe under the leadership of the Pope and Spain was becoming increasingly hostile to Protestant England. As Frances Yates put it in her book *Astraea*: 'The lengths to which the cult of Elizabeth went are a measure of the sense of isolation which had at all costs to find a symbol strong enough to provide a feeling of spiritual security in face of the break with the rest of Christendom.' In other words, to defeat the Armada needed not only a powerful navy but also a powerful symbolism, strong enough to convince all Englishmen of the rightness of their cause.

An elaborate ritual was therefore created which aimed to present Elizabeth to her subjects as a ruler whose reign was bringing in a new golden age of peace and plenty. This cult was complex and many-sided, as suited the intellect of the queen herself, and also the Renaissance sophistication which was by now increasingly percolating through to England. There was a bewildering variety of symbols, mostly taken from classical antiquity, so that Elizabeth became at one and the same time: God's anointed and the guardian of the Gospel; a classical goddess returned to earth; the focus of knightly devotion and chivalry; a virgin queen; a subject for romantic love. In the art and literature of the day she was perpetually adulated, so much so that even she, who loved flattery, became bored at times. Once, at a tournament to celebrate her accession day, she said she would not have come if she had known there would be so much talk about her, and went to bed.

The following are some of the commonest names that writers and courtiers gave her:

1 Luna, Cynthia, Diana

These all refer to the moon, of which Diana, alias Cynthia, was the Roman goddess. This was perhaps the most popular comparison employed by Elizabeth's admirers. In the Middle Ages the moon had often been used as a symbol for the emperor, and the sun for the papacy, so the queen was 'a chaste moon goddess shedding the beam of pure religion from her royal throne'.

2 Gloriana

This was Edmund Spenser's name for her in his epic poem, 'The Faerie Queene' (first published in 1590). Gloriana held an annual 12-day feast during which knights appeared who had to undertake whatever task she gave them. The structure of the poem is based on the exploits of twelve of these knights.

3 Astraea

The Roman poet, Ovid, tells how, at the beginning of the world, things got steadily worse as the golden age was succeeded by ages of silver, bronze and finally iron, the age in which evil was unloosed and war and greed took over. At this stage the goddess Astraea, last of the immortals to remain on earth, abandoned it in disgust. However, one day she was to return and proclaim a new golden age.

4 Virgo

When Astraea reached heaven she turned into the constellation Virgo. With the coming of the new age of gold, Virgo would descend to the earth and rule mankind justly and wisely as the 'imperial virgin'. This symbol was linked, of course, with Elizabeth's decision not to marry. An early Christian interpretation of the Virgo story identifies Christ's mother, Mary, as this classical virgin. Elizabeth's courtiers were prepared to commit what was for the Catholics the ultimate blasphemy by comparing Elizabeth to the Virgin Mary, whose images had so recently been torn down from churches throughout the country:

She was, She is (what can there more be said?)
In earth the first, in heaven the second Maid.

Visual imagery

Visual images of, or relating to, Elizabeth could be seen everywhere, not only in the large numbers of portraits of her on canvas, but also in engravings, woodcuts, coins and medallions. However, generally the intention behind portraits of the queen was not to convey a recognisable likeness or to show the reality of her changing appearance as she grew older. In fact, painters were actively discouraged from trying to do this. Instead, they were expected to copy certain established patterns when it came to painting her face, so that even when she was quite elderly the portraits still show the 'mask of youth' which had been officially approved early in the reign. A proclamation written in 1563 explains this policy. This particular proclamation was never issued but it still shows the intentions of the Council.

'Therefore her Majesty ... commandeth all manner of persons to forbear from painting, graving, printing or making of any portrait of her Majesty until some special person that shall be by her allowed, shall have first finished a portraiture thereof, after which finished, her Majesty will be content that all other painters, printers or gravers shall and may at their pleasures follow the said patron [i.e. pattern] or first portraiture. And for that her Majesty perceiveth that a great number of her loving subjects are much grieved and take great offence with the errors and deformities already committed by sundry persons in this behalf, she straightly chargeth all her officers and ministers to see to the due observation hereof, and as soon as may be to reform the errors already committed, and in the meantime to forbid and prohibit the showing and publication of such as are apparently deformed, until they may be reformed which are reformable.'

KEY TERM:

Icons

The term refers to religious paintings, usually of Christ or a saint, which were themselves the object of veneration. Paradoxically, the Reformation in the West involved *iconoclasm* (i.e. the destruction of pictures and statues in churches) because it was thought that uneducated people might worship them. So the Elizabethans would very likely have been horrified to have portraits of their queen described as icons.

If portraits of the queen were not to show her likeness, what was their purpose? The answer is that these images were intended to be studied for the message their complex symbolism conveyed, and they were also **icons** for the viewer to revere.

Another point about Elizabethan portraiture is that it lacked the new techniques of painting which had been developed in the Italian Renaissance. The subtleties of perspective, or of careful modelling in light and shade, are missing. There is no attempt to combine a realistic background landscape with figures in the foreground, as was usual with contemporary Italian pictures. This may be partly owing to the lack of artistic education in England during this period – the only artist of international stature was the miniaturist, Nicholas Hilliard (see page 179) – but it is also because the painters were not trying to produce the illusion of real space enclosed within a picture frame, as were the Italian masters.

Two portraits

We look here at two examples of Elizabethan portraiture – one of Elizabeth herself, and the other connected with her – and try to analyse some of the symbolism behind them. The first is the 'Rainbow Portrait' (Figure 20.1), attributed to Marcus Gheeraerts and painted about 1600, in which an ageless but still beautiful Elizabeth – she was then actually 67 years old – stands holding a rainbow in her right hand.

Figure 20.1 'The Rainbow portrait' of Elizabeth I by Marcus Gheeraerts, c. 1600

Here the rainbow, with its motto, *Non sine sole iris* (No rainbow without the sun), signifies peace after storms; the queen is the sun who brings the promise of peace. The eyes, ears and mouths all over the queen's cloak symbolise her fame, spoken of by many mouths, seen or heard by many eyes and ears. Alternatively, they may represent the knowledge brought to her by her many servants and agents. The various pearls she is wearing, including in her necklace, stand for virginity. The strange head-dress contains an imperial crown, and a jewel shaped like a crescent moon – an allusion to the queen as Cynthia, the moon-goddess. The serpent on her left sleeve symbolises wisdom. Just above its head is a tiny armillary sphere, a model of the universe, and hanging from its mouth a red, heart-shaped jewel. This serpent is wise not only in things of the mind (the sphere), but also in those of the heart (the jewel). On her bodice is a pattern of spring flowers which refer to the myth of Astraea who was goddess of the golden age in which spring was eternal, making the point that with Elizabeth this age had now returned to the earth. And on the queen's ruff is a jewelled gauntlet, showing that she was the object of her knights' chivalry. So this picture gives us a composite vision of Elizabeth as monarch of wisdom and peace, the object of devotion, the just virgin of a golden age returned.

We might wonder how the artist imagined that the viewer could have picked up all these references, but one has to remember that at this time allegory and symbolism were much studied, and many educated people owned textbooks about them.

The second example is the miniature by Nicholas Hilliard, 'Young Man amongst Roses' (Figure 20.2), painted about 1587, which has been the subject of some detection work by the art historian, Roy Strong. It shows an elegantly dressed young man leaning against a tree and apparently standing in the middle of a clump of white roses.

To start with, these are not ordinary roses – they are single, white, five-petalled roses, known as eglantines, and they refer to the Queen. Elizabeth was connected with the white rose of York, and with the colour white, but in addition the eglantine was known as her particular flower, mentioned as such in many poems and pageants. The young man is clutching his heart, with the Queen's flowers all round him – this clearly tells us of his love for her. And, apart from some brown on his doublet, he is dressed entirely in black and white, which were Elizabeth's colours – white for virginity and black for constancy. The tree which he is leaning against has a fine, straight trunk, another symbol of constancy – he is constant and resolute in his love. Inscribed around the top is some Latin: *Dat poenas laudata fides* (a praised faith brings punishment). This implies that the young man's devotion is causing him some suffering. The

Figure 20.2 *'Young Man among Roses' – miniature by Nicholas Hilliard, c. 1587*

Courtly love

The Elizabethans, while in tune with the latest ideas from Renaissance Italy, were also much influenced by the culture of the Middle Ages. The **courtly love** tradition went back to the troubadours of Provence at the time of the Crusades, and formed part of the feudal code of chivalry. It involved elaborate rituals in which the female object of a knight's devotion provided the ostensible – but always unattainable – motive for romantic yearnings and deeds of daring. Elizabeth's supreme art was to use this tradition, turning the disability of her sex into a subtle and unique advantage.

Latin tag comes from a speech by a classical writer about the Roman general, Pompey, who became a military hero when he was only 23.

We now turn to the career of Elizabeth's brilliant young favourite, Robert Devereux, Earl of Essex. Essex was about 20 when this picture was made, and had just started to build his reputation as a dashing military leader by his prowess at the siege of Zutphen in the Netherlands, in 1587. He had also started his intense platonic affair with the elderly Elizabeth, a relationship which was to continue, with its violent ups and downs of acceptance and rejection, until his revolt and final execution for treason in 1601. Roy Strong argues convincingly that Essex must have commissioned Hilliard to paint this miniature of himself as a lovelorn swain, which he then presented to the Queen.

New festivals

Before the Reformation the calendar had contained many saints' days, in addition to the great religious festivals such as Corpus Christi and Whitsun. These had been swept away, but people's natural impulse to celebrate something was now partly satisfied by new annual festivals centred on Elizabeth. One feature of these new occasions was that they deliberately harked back to the old traditions of chivalry and **courtly love**, as descended from the fifteenth-century Burgundian court.

The most important of the new festivals was the anniversary of Elizabeth's accession, 17 November. This was celebrated throughout the land with bonfires, bell-ringing, entertainments, and sermons extolling the importance of the occasion for religion and the security of the realm. At Court there was a solemn tournament to which the public had access – everyone could see Gloriana receiving the homage of her knights.

Another feature of the Elizabethan year was the 'progresses' the Queen made every summer to various parts of southern and central England – she never crossed the river Severn or the river Trent. John Nichols, the nineteenth-century historian who edited a three-volume work, *The Progresses and Public Processions of Queen Elizabeth*, lists 241 places she visited for a night or more. She must have been seen by many thousands of her loyal subjects as she attended public ceremonies, listened politely to speeches from mayors and recorders, or travelled the country roads, along with the 400 carts and 2,400 pack-horses necessary to transport her Court – at the rate of 10–12 miles a day. All this concern for her public image contrasts sharply with the isolation of the Court during the reigns of her Stuart successors, an isolation which contributed to the unpopularity and eventual downfall of Charles I.

Elizabeth's court

Competition was the essence of a courtier's life; he was constantly seeking favours or promotion, either for himself or on behalf of some client who looked to him for patronage. Many failed, and suffered the penalties – humiliation, wasted expense and boredom – and even the fortunate courtiers often beggared themselves in the process of succeeding. The career of **Sir Christopher Hatton** who did just that – succeeded and became bankrupt – illustrates several features typical of the Elizabethan court, in particular that a successful courtier was expected to be an all-rounder, adept at whatever task he was set by his sovereign. Hatton was also a supreme exponent of the game of courtly love that anyone aspiring to be favoured by the Queen had to play.

PROFILE: *Sir Christopher Hatton*

Christopher Hatton was born in 1540, of a family of small Northamptonshire squires, and received a conventional education, ending up at one of the Inns of Court. When he was still a student he impressed Elizabeth with his ability to dance the galliard, a complicated affair involving much leaping in the air and other refinements. Even so his progress was gradual – in 1565 he joined the Gentleman Pensioners (honorary guards of high status), and a year after that got his first diplomatic appointment, accompanying the Earl of Bedford to Scotland for the christening of James Stuart. Two years later (1568) he was given some crown lands; in 1571 he was elected to the House of Commons; in 1572 he was appointed captain of the Gentlemen Pensioners.

Other important posts followed as Hatton became one of Elizabeth's most trusted and intimate servants. When absent from Court he wrote her what appear to our eyes as gushing love letters, but apparently these went down well. The Queen made him her Vice-Chamberlain, in charge of progresses and major ceremonies, and he played an important role as government spokesman in the Commons.

Finally, in 1587, he was appointed Lord Chancellor, in charge of the law courts, much to the envy of others better qualified in the law. By this time he had received more land, including the splendid London estate of the Bishop of Ely, in what is now called Hatton Garden. Nevertheless, he over-reached himself financially, spending enormous sums on a palatial house, Holdenby, in Northamptonshire, where he could entertain Elizabeth. He died in 1591, in debt to the tune of a massive £65,000, most of it to the Queen.

Elizabeth's Court was far more of a Renaissance court than her father's had been. The Court's elegance sent a message to gentry and noble households throughout the country. Elizabeth's patronage of learning, literature and music meant that all these became fashionable among the English upper classes, and the result was a great improvement in taste and refinement. Whereas even in the mid-century a nobleman might have measured his status by the number of armed retainers he could muster, by the end of the century the criteria were more likely to include a house containing a long gallery with family portraits, a library, and the capacity to stage allegorical masques or concerts. Thus, due largely to Elizabeth's personality and especially her unique capacity for self-advertisement, the Court played an important part in both the cultural and the political life of the nation. 'When she smiled', wrote Elizabeth's godson Harington, 'it was pure sunshine that everyone did choose to bask in if they could', but when a storm arose, 'the thunder fell in monstrous measure on all alike'.

Task: working with visual sources

Figure 20.3 Elizabeth gives an audience to Dutch ambassadors

In this chapter we have looked at some examples of the meaning and significance of Elizabethan portraiture and other images. In an age of

illiteracy, or semi-literacy, such as the sixteenth century, visual images were a most important means of communication, especially for the government. This can be seen from the way Elizabeth's advisers took such trouble to control and manipulate the production of portraits of the queen. Another example is the way such an effort was made at the Reformation to destroy all the images associated with the Catholic Church (see the diagrams of a church service before and after the Reformation on pages 20 and 155). So it is sometimes just as important for the historian to consider the significance of visual images as of written documents. Here are some questions to make you think about a few aspects of this topic:

1 Look at the seal of Mary and Philip on page 102. Suggest ways in which the artist who designed this seal tried to convey the status of the two sovereigns, and the nature of their relationship.

2 Look at the etching of the Queen in Parliament on page 172. What features of the picture emphasise Elizabeth's role and status in relationship to the members of her Parliament?

3 Look at the detail from the memorial painting of Sir Henry Unton on page 277. How far would you class this as a realistic scene? Comment on what the artist seems to be saying here about Unton, his guests and the troupe of actors playing a masque.

4 The opening paragraph of this chapter argues that the defeat of the Spanish Armada needed a powerful new symbolism as well as a good navy. What do you understand by this? Can you supply any twentieth-century parallels involving the deliberate manufacture of new symbols or images for comparable purposes? Think of political posters today or of the ways in which advertisers use an image to sell a product, without using words to argue why people should buy it. Television advertising is full of this kind of persuasion. How close do you think they are to the kind of messages you have been studying in this chapter?

Further reading

David Loades, *The Tudor Court*, New Appreciations in History No. 18 (Historical Association, 1989) – an excellent introduction.
David Loades, *The Tudor Court* (Batsford, 1986).
Frances A. Yates, *Astraea* (Penguin, 1977) – a fascinating study of the image of Elizabeth.
Roy Strong, *The Cult of Elizabeth* (Thames and Hudson, 1977) – a survey of the Queen's portraits.

21 Government and the governed

Tudor monarchs had no standing army or police force, nor did they have a massive civil service. Yet their governments were efficient by the standards of the day, and rebellions were rare and always unsuccessful. In this chapter we look at the institutions of government, both central and local. Before doing so it is worth asking the question 'Why did English people obey the orders of their government?'.

One answer to this is 'habit', for the English monarchy had hundreds of years of history behind it, and its authority was taken for granted. Another is 'deference'. English society was a carefully graded hierarchy in which everyone knew his or her place. Admittedly the Tudor period saw the lines of division between one grade and another becoming blurred as a result of economic changes, but society as a whole remained deferential, prepared to accept orders from above. 'Self-interest' is another. The top level of society – what we call 'the political nation' – was a minority, and its privileged position depended, like that of the Crown, upon the acquiescence of the mass of the population. What members of the political nation valued above all was stability, and it therefore made sense for them to cooperate with the royal government in the task of maintaining this.

The desire for stability was not confined to the political nation. Most people wanted a quiet life, and the best way of achieving this was to support the existing order. Tudor society, with its different grades or 'degrees', was the very opposite of egalitarian, but it seemed to work, and the only apparent alternative was chaos. Shakespeare put this point well in the speech he gave to Ulysses in *Troilus and Cressida*:

> *How could communities*
> *Degrees in schools, and brotherhoods in cities,*
> *Peaceful commerce from dividable shores.*
> *The primogenity and due of birth,*
> *Prerogative of age, crowns, sceptres, laurels,*
> *But by degree stand in authentic place?*
> *Take but degree away, untune that string,*
> *And hark what discord follows . . .*

The Privy Council

The Privy Council was the governing body, the 'cabinet', of Elizabethan England. In December 1601 its membership was recorded as follows:

1 *John Whitgift, Archbishop of Canterbury*
2 *Sir Thomas Egerton, Lord Keeper of the Great Seal*
3 *Sir Thomas Sackville, Lord High Treasurer*
4 *The Earl of Nottingham, Lord High Admiral*
5 *The Earl of Shrewsbury*
6 *The Earl of Worcester, Master of the Horse*
7 *Lord Hunsdon, Chamberlain of the Household*
8 *Sir William Knollys, Comptroller of the Household*
9 *Sir John Stanhope, Treasurer of the Chamber*
10 *Sir Robert Cecil, the Queen's principal Secretary, and Master of the Wards*
11 *Sir John Fortescue, Chancellor of the Exchequer*
12 *Sir John Popham, Chief Justice of the Queen's Bench*
13 *John Herbert, Secretary to the Queen*

The first thing to note about this body is its size. At its first recorded meeting in 1540 the Privy Council consisted of 19 members, but numbers gradually increased, particularly under Mary. At Elizabeth's accession there were once again 19 Councillors, but she steadily reduced the number, which at one stage fell to 11.

Prior to the break with Rome, churchmen played a major role in the King's Council, but by 1540 there were only three bishops on it. As you can see from the above list, Elizabeth reduced this figure to one, the Archbishop of Canterbury. More prominent were holders of great offices of state such as the Lord Treasurer and his second-in-command, the Chancellor of the Exchequer; the Lord Chancellor (or, as in the case of Egerton, Lord Keeper: the same office but a slightly lesser title); and the Lord Admiral. Robert Cecil held the newer post of principal Secretary, but had succeeded his father (William Cecil) as the Queen's principal adviser. Two lay peers, Shrewsbury and Worcester, were on the Council partly on account of their rank but mainly because they had shown themselves to be loyal servants of the Queen. The remaining members, apart from the Chief Justice, held key offices in the royal household.

Not all members of the Council were present at every meeting. This was particularly the case when Elizabeth was on progress during the summer, moving from one great country house to another. A handful of Councillors would be in attendance on her, making sure her wishes were known, even though she rarely attended Council meetings. It was this handful of Councillors that did most of the routine business of administration, but as the range and complexity of government increased, so did the workload. By the end of the reign the Council was meeting virtually every day. It drew up proclamations which were issued in the Queen's name and had the force of law. It also sent letters to local authorities, transmitting the orders of the government.

The Star Chamber

'There is yet in England another court, of the which ... there is not the like in any other country. In the term time ... every week once at the least ... the Lord Chancellor and the lords and other of the Privy Council ... [and] the two chief judges, from nine of the clock till it be eleven do sit in a place which is called the Star Chamber.'

Sir Thomas Smith, *De Republica Anglorum* (c.1565).

In modern states it is customary to draw a line between administration and justice. But this was not the case in Tudor England, where administrators were also judges, and judges administrators. Royal Councillors had long had the duty, as the King's representatives, to provide justice where it was lacking, and had set aside certain times for this purpose. Under Wolsey, who had a passion for justice, this particular function expanded to such an extent that the Council sitting in Star Chamber turned into a separate court. Its membership under Wolsey was the same as that of the Council, but after the creation of the much smaller Privy Council in the late 1530s there was a difference: the two chief justices, who had been members of the old Council but were not appointed to the new, retained their place in Star Chamber.

The Court of Star Chamber dealt with riots and other threats to the queen's peace. It also acted in cases where the common law courts had been either ineffective or browbeaten. Star Chamber had the right to impose fines or imprisonment – though not capital punishment – and because its judges were the most important men in the realm, its justice was swift and effective. This appealed to private suitors, who made increasing use of Star Chamber, and although it acquired a reputation for harshness under the Stuarts it was apparently a popular court in the Tudor period.

Regional councils

In an age of poor communications the effectiveness of government action diminished the further it got from London. For this reason, special councils were set up to enforce the law and maintain order in the north of England (the **Council of the North**). A similar council, based at Ludlow, administered the turbulent marcher lands of the Welsh border. There was also, for a brief period, a Council of the West, set up by Henry VIII in 1539 to cover Cornwall, Devon, Somerset and Dorset.

The common law courts

The two most important common law courts were both medieval creations – namely Queen's (or King's) Bench and Common Pleas. Queen's Bench dealt with criminal cases and Common Pleas with civil, though there was no hard and fast line between the two. Judges, appointed by the monarch, had received their legal education in one of the Inns of Court that still survive in London. They were experts in the common law which had grown out of precedents extending back into the Middle Ages, and in the statute law made by Parliament. Twice a year the common law judges set out on **assizes** which took them round the whole of the kingdom.

Local government

Although appointed on an annual basis, most Justices of the Peace served for a long period. They were drawn from the leading families of the shire and they commanded respect as much for their social position as for the fact that they were the Queen's officers. Their main responsibilities were summarised in their oath of office:

> 'Ye shall swear that . . . in all articles in the Queen's Commission to you directed, ye shall do equal right to the poor and to the rich after your cunning, wit and power, and after the laws and customs of the realm and statutes thereof made; and ye shall not be of counsel with any quarrel hanging before you; and that ye hold your sessions after the form of statutes thereof made.'

The language may be old fashioned, but the meaning is plain: JPs were to uphold the law for all the Queen's subjects without prejudice. This was a

KEY TERMS:

Council of the North

The **Council of the North**, based at York, had its origins under Richard III. It was given its final form by Thomas Cromwell in 1537 and became the principal institution of government in the area beyond the river Trent. After the suppression of the 1569 revolt of the northern earls, Elizabeth appointed her cousin, the Earl of Huntingdon, as president of the Council, in 1572, and he stayed in office for nearly a quarter of a century. As a result of his capable rule, the north gave no further trouble to Elizabeth.

Assizes

The main job of the common law judges was to try persons accused of serious crimes, but in the 1590s they were briefed, before setting out, by the Lord Chancellor or Keeper. He called their attention to specific problems with which the queen and her ministers were concerned and reminded them that an important part of their task was to make sure that local government was working properly. In this way the judges acted as a link between the Council and the Justices of the Peace (see key term on page 63).

high ideal, and one which in practice was often breached, but in general JPs had a good reputation. The Justices of every county came together four times a year in Quarter Sessions, to deal with offenders presented to them by the grand jury of the shire. They punished most of those they found guilty, but passed on the more serious cases to the assize judges. However, as with most Tudor officials, their duties were not solely judicial. At Quarter Sessions they also supervised the entire administration of the county, including poor relief, the repair of roads and bridges, the licensing of alehouses, and the guardianship of illegitimate children (as well as the punishment of their parents for imposing this burden upon the local community).

Until the second half of Elizabeth's reign the JPs were supreme in their shires. But in the 1580s, as the war clouds gathered, the Privy Council decided that the military organisation of the country must be improved. All able-bodied adult men were under an obligation to serve in their county's militia – a sort of Home Guard – but they were often poorly trained and inadequately provided with arms. From 1585, therefore, leading noblemen and councillors were appointed as Lords Lieutenant, with instructions to take charge of the counties and organise the militia. They were assisted in this task by senior JPs who were known as Deputy-Lieutenants.

The smallest unit in local government was the parish, and its principal officials – appointed by, and responsible to, the JPs – were the constables and the overseers of the poor. The parish constable was the Queen's representative, charged with the duty of maintaining peace, enforcing the law, and arresting offenders. But the office, which was unpaid, was far from popular, and persons of character and ability did their best to wriggle out of it. The oath which constables had to take set high standards:

> 'You shall see and cause her Majesty's peace to be well and truly kept and preserved according to your power ... You shall do your best endeavour that the watch in and about your town be duly kept for the apprehending of rogues, vagabonds ... such as go armed, and the like; and that hue and cries be duly raised and pursued ... against murderers, thieves and other felons.'

But there was often a big contrast between theory and practice. In *Much Ado About Nothing* Shakespeare's Constable Dogberry is a figure of fun, but many Elizabethans must have recognised this character at the same time as they laughed at him. In the following extract Dogberry is instructing the persons chosen to act as watchmen:

> DOGBERRY: *This is your charge: you shall comprehend all vagrom [i.e. vagrant] men. You are to bid any man stand, in the Prince's name.*
> SECOND WATCHMAN: *How if a' will not stand?*
> DOGBERRY: *Why then, take no note of him but let him go. And presently call the rest of the watch together and thank God you are rid of a knave … If you meet a thief you may suspect him, by virtue of your office, to be no true man, and for such kind of men, the less you meddle or make with them, why the more is for your honesty.*
> FIRST WATCHMAN: *If we know him to be a thief, shall we not lay hands on him?*
> DOGBERRY: *Truly, by your office you may. But I think … the most peaceable way for you, if you do take a thief, is to let him show what he is and steal out of your company.*

Church courts

The Church had had its own courts since the early Middle Ages, and they survived the break with Rome and the establishment of Protestantism. Every diocese had what was called a consistory court, presided over by the bishop or his deputy, as well as a number of lesser courts run by the archdeacons. Persons who felt that justice had been denied them could appeal to the courts established in the provinces of Canterbury and York, under the supervision of the two archbishops.

Church courts had originally been set up to discipline the clergy, who claimed immunity from secular jurisdiction, and to settle disputes between clergy and laity – many of which concerned tithes. But over the course of time these courts had come to specialise in moral issues, such as adultery, breach of promise, perjury and defamation. They also had a major role in anything to do with marriage, and in the probate of wills. They had very limited powers of punishment, however – the most important being excommunication (see key term, page 53) – and in practice their judgements were often ignored.

The Court of High Commission

See also chapter 17. Elizabeth's accession to the throne was followed by the Act of Supremacy, which recognised her as supreme governor over the Church of England. The Act also confirmed her right to appoint commissioners to exercise the royal supremacy, and this she did in 1559. The list of commissioners began with the Archbishop of Canterbury and the Bishop of London, but the remaining 17, with the exception of the queen's almoner, were all laymen, mainly lawyers. They were instructed to search out:

> *heretical opinions, seditious books, contempts, conspiracies, false rumours, tales, seditions, misbehaviours, slanderous words or showings, published, invented or set forth ... by any person or persons against us or contrary or against any the laws or statutes of this our realm, or against the quiet governance and rule of our people ... [They were also to punish] disturbances and misbehaviours done and committed ... in any church or chapel, or against any divine service or the minister or ministers of the same, contrary to the laws and statutes of this realm: and also to enquire of, search out and to order, correct and reform all such persons as hereafter shall or will obstinately absent themselves from church and such divine service as by the laws and statutes of this realm is appointed.*

This was in effect the origin of a new court, the Court of High Commission, which played a prominent role during Elizabeth's reign in maintaining the infant Church of England against puritan assaults. Unlike the other church courts, it had the right to fine and imprison, and was therefore far more effective. Puritans, of course, feared and hated it, as did many common lawyers who believed it was trespassing on their territory. But they could do nothing while Elizabeth was on the throne, because she strongly approved of the High Commission and gave it her full support.

Task: essay-writing

'The Elizabethan government was an essentially amateur system which found it difficult to enforce its will on the country.' Discuss.

This type of question poses two problems in deciding what kind of answer is required: first, there are the 'key words' (or phrases) of the question – words and phrases which you will have to define and on which your answer will focus. In this case they are 'amateur' and 'difficult to enforce its will'. 'Amateur' here is the opposite of professional, implying that Elizabethan government relied on people who were untrained or part time. Second, this is an 'Aunt Sally' question: a statement is made which you are invited to attack, or support. In fact, you must do both; you will never totally agree or disagree. It is really a question of 'How far is the statement true?'

For hints on essay-writing look at the end of chapter 10. Points relevant to this question may be found in chapters 18, 19, 21 and 28.

Don't forget, too, that the main index at the end of the book may be helpful if you want to pursue a particular topic.

Further reading

G. R. Elton, *The Tudor Constitution* (Cambridge University Press, 2nd edn, 1982).

A. G. R. Smith, *The Government of Elizabethan England* (Arnold, 1967) – a clear, succinct overall account.

P. Williams, *The Tudor Regime* (Clarendon Press, 1979) – good on the relationship of government to society.

P. Williams, *The Later Tudors: England 1547–1603*, New Oxford History of England (Clarendon Press, 1995).

A. G. R. Smith, *Tudor Government*, New Appreciations in History No. 20 (Historical Association, 1990) – the best introduction to the subject.

22 Foreign policy 2: Anglo-Spanish hostility

Time chart

1562–3: Unsuccessful English intervention in France on behalf of Huguenots leads to humiliating withdrawal from Le Havre

1566: Protestant revolt in Netherlands against Philip II's rule

1567: Spanish army led by Duke of Alva sent to suppress revolt

1568: **May** Mary, Queen of Scots, escapes to England, where she is imprisoned

September On his third trading voyage to the Indies John Hawkins is attacked by Spanish at St John of Ulua (survivors return to Plymouth in January 1569)

November Elizabeth confiscates Spanish silver en route to pay Alva's troops

1570: **February** Pope Pius V issues Bull of excommunication against Elizabeth

1571: **August** Discovery of Ridolfi plot against Elizabeth's life
October Spanish defeat Turkish fleet at Lepanto

1572: **April** England makes defensive alliance with France – Treaty of Blois

August Massacre of St Bartholomew restarts religious war in France

1578: Duke of Parma takes charge of Spanish forces in Netherlands

1578–81: Francis, Duke of Alençon, offered sovereignty of the Netherlands, and visits England (in 1578 and 1581) to further courtship of Elizabeth

1580: **August** Spanish army captures Lisbon to implement Philip's claim to Portuguese throne

September Drake returns with Spanish bullion after successful voyage round the world, and is knighted by Elizabeth on board *Golden Hind*

1584: **May** Alençon's death, which makes Protestant Henry of Navarre heir to French throne, leads to Treaty of Joinville between Catholic League and Philip (December)
July Assassination of William of Orange

1585: **August** Fall of Antwerp to Parma's troops. Elizabeth concludes Treaty of Nonsuch with Dutch rebels, and sends Leicester with army to Netherlands

September Drake sets off on successful expedition against ports in Spain and Spanish America

October Philip starts planning invasion of England

First quarrels with Spain

At the start of Elizabeth's reign Spain was England's ally in a war against France, and on Mary's death Philip II of Spain even proposed marriage to Elizabeth, a suggestion which was politely but firmly declined. Yet within a decade the two nations were at loggerheads, and although the 1570s saw some improvement in their relationship there was renewed hostility in the early 1580s, leading to a war which was to occupy the remainder of Elizabeth's reign. This chapter looks at the factors behind this fluctuating relationship, and at the causes of the war of 1585.

During the first decade of the reign the tradition of Anglo-Habsburg friendship, which had dominated English foreign policy since Henry VII signed the Treaty of Medina del Campo in 1489, continued. Both sides saw peace as important to compensate for the threat of France, and Philip for his part twice dissuaded the Pope from excommunicating Elizabeth. However, between 1568 and 1572 relations deteriorated sharply, due to the following factors:

1 Alva and the Spanish silver

Events in the Netherlands were the main cause of the breakdown in Anglo-Spanish relations. Under Charles V the Dutch provinces and cities had been allowed a large degree of self-government, but Philip tried to impose Catholic orthodoxy as well as a more centralised rule. When a revolt broke out he despatched a powerful Spanish army from Italy under the Duke of Alva to suppress it. By the end of 1568 Alva had achieved considerable success, and the presence of his experienced troops so close to the English coastline was threatening. Once he had subdued the Netherlands there would be little to stop him crossing the Channel and invading England.

Elizabeth had few options open to counteract this danger, but one unexpected opportunity did suddenly present itself. In November 1568, five Spanish ships carrying a consignment of silver to pay Alva's troops took refuge in English ports, to avoid French privateers. Although the Spanish ambassador explained that the money belonged to Philip, who had been lent it by Genoese bankers, Elizabeth nevertheless ordered it to be taken to the Tower of London. Philip retaliated by seizing English property in Spain and the Netherlands and freezing all trade with England.

2 St John of Ulua

Spain's claim to a monopoly of trade with the American continent stemmed from a decision of the papacy set out in the Treaty of Tordesillas of 1494, which divided all new lands, discovered or to be discovered, between Spain and Portugal. This monopoly was still largely intact at Philip's accession. But in 1562 the Plymouth merchant, John Hawkins, made a voyage to take cloth and slaves to the Indies, returning with hides and sugar. He repeated this on a larger scale in 1564–5 and again in 1567. On this third voyage he had ten ships, including two belonging to Elizabeth. All went well until they were caught in a storm when preparing to come home and were forced to shelter in the small Mexican port of St John of Ulua. By sheer bad luck they encountered a Spanish fleet bringing the newly-appointed viceroy of Mexico. A furious fight inside the harbour led to the capture of most of Hawkins's squadron, including the Queen's ship, the *Jesus*. Hawkins himself escaped and managed to straggle back to Plymouth, arriving in January 1569, but most of his men were killed or captured.

3 The Ridolfi plot

One reason why Philip had maintained a fairly correct and neutral relationship with Elizabeth during the first decade of her reign was that he preferred her to her potential successor. If anything happened to Elizabeth there was a good chance that her cousin, Mary, Queen of Scots, would succeed her. Mary was closely associated with France, and Philip preferred a heretic on the English throne to a French takeover. However, Mary's involvement in the death of her husband, her deposition by Scottish nobles, and her flight to England in 1568 greatly lowered her status and meant that she no longer received support from France (see chapter 23). Furthermore, Elizabeth's imprisonment of Mary shocked the Catholic world and was one of the reasons why the Pope excommunicated Elizabeth and started to urge Philip to invade England.

Against his better judgement, Philip was drawn into the complex Ridolfi plot. Masterminded by the Spanish ambassador in London, the aim was to assassinate Elizabeth and have Alva invade England, protected while crossing the Channel by a fleet despatched from Spain. It was, in other words, a dry-run for the Armada plan of 1588. When the go-between, a Florentine banker named Roberto Ridolfi, fell into the hands of the English government and revealed all under torture, Elizabeth grasped that Philip had tried to have her killed, and her attitude towards him was never the same again. Even after the plot's discovery, in August 1571, Philip continued to urge Alva to invade England. For him this was the optimum moment for such an enterprise, as the Netherlands appeared relatively subdued and he had just defeated his Turkish enemies in the naval battle of Lepanto.

4 The Treaty of Blois

These three factors led to England's increasing hostility towards Spain, and this in turn implied the need for a better relationship with France. However, the last thing that Elizabeth and her leading minister, William Cecil, wanted was to increase French power. French control over the Dutch coast would be just as dangerous as Spanish control. So Elizabeth had to try to cooperate with the French in a strictly limited way. The upshot was the Treaty of Blois, a defensive alliance providing for mutual support if either country were attacked. At the same time, Elizabeth allowed some discussion to take place about the possibility of her marrying Henry, Duke of Anjou, the brother of the French king (and soon to succeed to the throne himself, as Henry III). In the event, all this diplomacy hardly mattered because the massacre of Huguenots that took place a few months later, on St Bartholemew's Day, 24 August 1572, meant that France was plunged into another round of religious war and ceased to play much part in international affairs for some time.

Hostile neutrality

In spite of these events, Spain and England did not come to blows, and in fact, after 1572, relations between them improved. Neither Philip nor Elizabeth was ready for war. Philip's hands were full with the Turkish counter-attack after Lepanto, and with continuing resistance by the Dutch. As for Elizabeth, she was content that the struggle in the Netherlands should continue, but she resisted pressure from her council to intervene in it. Over the next decade her policy involved allowing English volunteers to join the Dutch, but stopped short of sending royal troops. She continued to encourage the French to support the revolt, although seeking to prevent them acquiring any real power in the Netherlands, and to this end she allowed Henry III's younger brother, **Francis, Duke of Alençon**, to seek her hand in marriage at the same time as he was involving himself in the Netherlands struggle.

During this period Elizabeth's caution in not becoming involved was criticised by many of her contemporaries, including Leicester and Walsingham, who wanted her to support the Protestant cause more

PROFILE: *Francis, Duke of Alençon*

Francis was born in 1554. He was the youngest son of Catherine de Medici. When his brother, Henry, became king in 1574, Francis succeeded to Henry's title of Duke of Anjou, but it is probably less confusing to continue to refer to him as Alençon – especially as both brothers courted Elizabeth at different times!

Alençon became involved in the Netherlands struggle when, in 1578, he accepted the offer of the Brussels States-General to be their 'Protector' against Spain. Elizabeth hoped to keep him under control by offering him her hand in a diplomatic marriage, and for the next three years this project was pursued in a leisurely style, Alençon visiting England twice to further his courtship. The Queen, now in her mid-forties, was possibly amused by the attentions of Alençon, whom she nicknamed her 'little frog', but it is unlikely she took him too seriously. After all, he was, according to historian R. B. Wernham, 'an unprepossessing, undersized, pockmarked little prince'. He failed to achieve anything substantial in the Netherlands, quarrelling with his sponsors, the States-General, and attempting in vain to occupy Antwerp and other Dutch cities with his French troops. He quitted the Netherlands in disgrace in 1583 and died a year later.

overtly. They argued that the international Catholic threat must be stopped in the Netherlands, before it became strong enough to attack England. But Elizabeth did not see it that way, and she had her reasons for non-intervention, among which were:

1 She remembered the failure of her pro-Huguenot intervention in 1562–3.

2 She tended never to sympathise with those who rebelled against their rightful sovereign.

3 She disliked the uncompromising Calvinism of many of the rebels.

4 She had to consider the enormous financial cost of a military campaign on the continent.

The road to war

In the early 1580s new hostility developed between England and Spain, a hostility which this time was to lead to war. The following factors contributed:

1 Drake's circumnavigation

During the 1570s the Queen tolerated – and sometimes even encouraged – privateering expeditions against Spanish interests. Between 1572 and 1577 there were 11 English expeditions to Spanish America, starting with Drake's daring exploit of 1572, when he cooperated with rebel black slaves, sacked Nombre de Dios, and seized a major treasure convoy. But the most provoking expedition of all was Drake's round-the-world voyage of 1577–80 during which he sacked several Spanish ports, returning home with 100 tons of Spanish silver and 100 tons of gold. Added insult came when Elizabeth knighted him on the deck of his flag-ship, the *Golden Hind*. Philip was much angered by all this, although it was not in itself a cause of war. For one thing he needed to build up a powerful enough ocean-going navy before he could consider mounting an invasion of England. Much of the Spanish fleet at this time consisted of oared galleys, suitable for the Mediterranean but not designed to cope with Atlantic storms.

2 Portuguese galleons

In 1580 Philip suddenly acquired the means to attack England. The last legitimate male heir to the throne of Portugal died in that year, leaving Philip, whose mother had been a Portuguese princess, as next-of-kin. There were other claimants, but Philip alone had the power to enforce his claim, and after an effective combined operation by land and sea, a Spanish army commanded by Alva entered Lisbon, and Philip was

Figure 22.2 *'Queen Elizabeth leading the Dutch Cow': Philip II is riding the cow and the Duke of Alva is milking it, while William of Orange holds it by the horns and the Duke of Alençon tries to pull it backwards.*

proclaimed king of Portugal. This meant that he acquired a new empire – in Brazil, Africa and Asia – as well as a new navy, including 12 large, ocean-going galleons, which could be used as the nucleus round which to build an armada against England.

3 The Treaty of Joinville

The death of Alençon in 1584 produced a crisis in France which was much to Elizabeth's disadvantage. The heir to the French throne was now the Protestant leader, Henry of Navarre, who was totally unacceptable to the Catholic faction led by Henry, Duke of Guise (the son of Francis, Duke of Guise, who had been assassinated earlier in the French religious wars). The Catholics now formed a paramilitary organisation known as the League, and made an alliance with Spain. In the Treaty of Joinville both sides pledged mutual assistance to the Catholic cause in France and the Netherlands, Philip promising to subsidise the League. The danger to Elizabeth was acute, because the treaty meant that Philip need no longer worry about the claims of Mary, Queen of Scots, rivalling his own, as they were now in the same camp. Nor was there any longer the potential power of France to check Spanish ambitions. The development added fuel to the arguments of those such as Walsingham who wanted Elizabeth to intervene directly in the Netherlands.

4 Parma's victories

Since 1578 and the appearance of the **Duke of Parma**, the war in the Netherlands had been going badly from Elizabeth's point of view. In 1581 Parma launched a new strategy which involved the piecemeal conquest of the rich cities of Flanders and Brabant by a combination of bribery and military force. Bruges and Ghent fell in the summer of 1584, and Parma then began the siege of Antwerp, the best fortified of all, by building a huge barrage across the river Scheldt near its mouth so as to cut off the city's trade. In spite of attempts to relieve it, Antwerp was clearly doomed, especially after the assassination of William of Orange, the capable Dutch commander, which left the rebels without an experienced leader. The city fell in August, and Elizabeth was now faced with the prospect of the whole of the Netherlands coming under Spanish control, with the invasion of England clearly on the cards.

The coming of war

Under these circumstances even Elizabeth grasped that underhand aid to the Dutch and unofficial Caribbean piracy were no longer enough, and that England's security required more decisive action against the power of Spain. In August 1585, she concluded the Treaty of Nonsuch (named

PROFILE: *Duke of Parma*

Alexander Farnese (1546–92) was one of the most gifted military commanders of the entire century. He was only 32 when he was appointed to lead the Spanish armies in the Netherlands in 1578, but he was an ideal choice. As Philip's nephew – his mother was Philip's illegitimate elder sister – his royal blood and experience of the Spanish Court meant that he had the status required to lead the touchy Spanish officers, but he was also a tough and professional soldier with military experience, including that of the Lepanto campaign. As the ruler of the large Italian state of Parma he was wealthy enough to maintain his own spy network, and to provide what the Dutch called his 'golden bullets' – the bribes paid out to Dutch leaders to make them betray their cities to the Spanish.

By the summer of 1585 Parma had captured Antwerp, and now had only the maritime provinces of Holland and Zealand (see Figure 22.3) to subdue. He joined in reluctantly with Philip's 'Enterprise of England' of 1588, probably aware from the outset that the Armada plan was unworkable. From 1590 he was forced to divert his armies to France in order to counteract Henry IV's military success. Consequently, by the time of his death in 1592, he had failed to complete his ambition, the final conquest of the Netherlands.

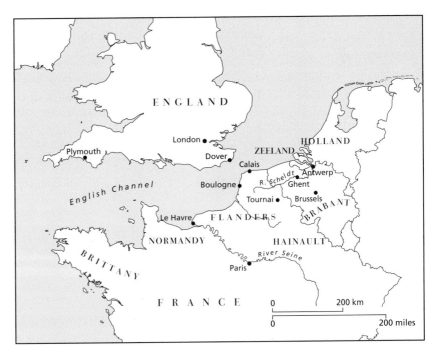

Figure 22.3 *France and the Netherlands*

after a royal palace, now destroyed) with a delegation from the Dutch rebels, whereby she promised to send 1,000 cavalry and 6,000 infantry to fight against Spain, to grant the rebels subsidies worth £126,000 a year, and to provide a governor-general to direct the war. The troops were quickly collected and dispatched, and just before Christmas the new governor-general – Elizabeth's favourite, Robert Dudley, Earl of Leicester – arrived.

At the same time the Queen issued another direct challenge to Philip by despatching an expedition under Drake to release English ships that had been detained in Spanish ports, and to raid the ports and shipping of the Caribbean. This was a major undertaking involving 25 ships, two of them belonging to the Queen, and 1,900 men. It sailed from Plymouth in September, attacked Vigo and Bayonne in Spain, followed by Santiago in the Cape Verde Isles and finally Santo Domingo, the capital of Spain's oldest Caribbean possession, Hispaniola.

Everyone now understood that England had challenged Spain to war. To send an army officially into another ruler's dominions to assist rebels was an action that no sovereign could ignore, and Philip reacted predictably by starting to plan a highly ambitious but (given his enormous resources) quite achievable project – the invasion of England. In the three decades since the death of Mary Tudor, relations between England and Spain had come full circle, from a marriage alliance to full-scale war.

Task: class discussion

Work together in groups to consider the causes of the Anglo-Spanish war. Different groups might look at the diplomatic developments in this period from different vantage points. For instance:

1 What were the international aims and priorities of Philip II during the 1570s and early 1580s?

2 What were those of the 'puritan' faction on Elizabeth's Council, including Walsingham and Leicester?

3 What was the point of view of Elizabeth herself?

Further reading

Susan Doran, *England and Europe 1485–1603*, Seminar Studies in History (Addison Wesley Longman, 2nd edn, 1996) – the best brief survey, with a comprehensive bibliography.

R. B. Wernham, *The Making of Elizabethan Foreign Policy 1558–1603* (University of California Press, 1980) – a full and detailed account.

23 What problems did Mary, Queen of Scots, pose for Elizabeth?

Mary Stuart, Queen of Scots (Figure 23.1), was the daughter of James V of Scotland and Mary of Guise. She was born in 1542, nine years after Elizabeth, and she spent most of her early life in France. However, on the death of her husband, Francis II, king of France, she was advised by her

Figure 23.1 Mary, Queen of Scots

Guise relations to leave France, and she arrived in Scotland in the summer of 1561, not yet 19.

Elizabeth already had good cause to distrust Mary, who had failed to ratify the Treaty of Edinburgh (see chapter 15), and who herself claimed the English throne through her grandmother, Margaret, the sister of Henry VIII. Elizabeth refused to recognise her as her heir, knowing, as she put it, 'the inconstancy of the people of England, how they ever mislike the present government and have their eyes fixed upon that person who is next to succeed'. There then arose the question of whom Mary was to marry, and here an even greater threat posed itself – the possibility that she would pick a foreign prince, such as the Archduke Charles, or Philip II's son, Don Carlos, or even her brother-in-law, King Charles IX of France. None of these matches would have been in England's interests, and so Elizabeth suggested an Englishman, no less than her own favourite, Robert Dudley, the newly created Earl of Leicester. The proposal was that if Mary agreed to marry Leicester, Elizabeth might consider recognising her officially as heir to the English throne. However, Dudley himself cold-shouldered the plan as he still had hopes of marrying Elizabeth. Furthermore, Mary's eye had lighted on someone for whom she felt more attraction, **Lord Darnley**.

Before Darnley's death Mary had fallen in love with another unsavoury

---

PROFILE: *Lord Darnley*

Henry Stewart, **Lord Darnley**, was a handsome 19-year-old when he married Mary in 1565. He was not a popular choice from Elizabeth's point of view because he was a Catholic and because he had a claim to the English throne equal to Mary's, as he was also a grandchild of Margaret Tudor, through her second marriage (see family tree on page 129). What became apparent after they were married was that Darnley was an obstinate, arrogant character, and a thoroughly unpleasant husband, drunken, uncouth and spiteful. When Mary became pregnant Darnley was persuaded to believe that the father was her confidential secretary, David Riccio, and he took part in a plot to murder Riccio, who was dragged screaming from Mary's supper table and stabbed to death. Mary bided her time for revenge; a year later, in February 1567, the house in which Darnley was staying was blown up, and his body found strangled outside the ruins. Mary's behaviour at the time points to her complicity in the murder. Darnley's main contribution to English history is that he – almost certainly – was the father of Mary's child, later to succeed Elizabeth as James I (see Figure 23.2).

character, the Earl of Bothwell. After the redundant husband had been disposed of, Bothwell arranged to abduct her and carry her off to Dunbar Castle where, according to her account, he raped her and then she went through a Protestant form of marriage with him. This marriage, together with the suspicion that she had planned Darnley's murder, ruined Mary's reputation for good. The Pope declared that she was quite as bad as the heretic Elizabeth, and in Edinburgh placards appeared depicting her as a naked mermaid, meaning a prostitute. The rebellious Protestant lords, led by the Earl of Moray, rose up against her. She was taken prisoner and lodged in the island castle of Lochleven, while Bothwell fled to Denmark. She was forced to abdicate the throne of Scotland in favour of James, her son from the Darnley marriage, with Moray assuming the regency.

Elizabeth's dilemma

In May 1568, after nearly a year as a prisoner, Mary managed to escape

Figure 23.2 Contemporary sketch, sent to Cecil in London, of the scene after the murder of Darnley at Kirk-o'-Field in February 1567. Note: the figure of the infant James (son of Darnley and Mary) in his cradle with the legend 'Judge and avenge my cause, O Lord' (top left); the quadrangle of houses with the house in which Darnley stayed reduced to a heap of rubble; the body of Darnley is carried away (bottom right); Darnley and his servant lie in the garden, with a chair, cloak and dagger beside them (top right).

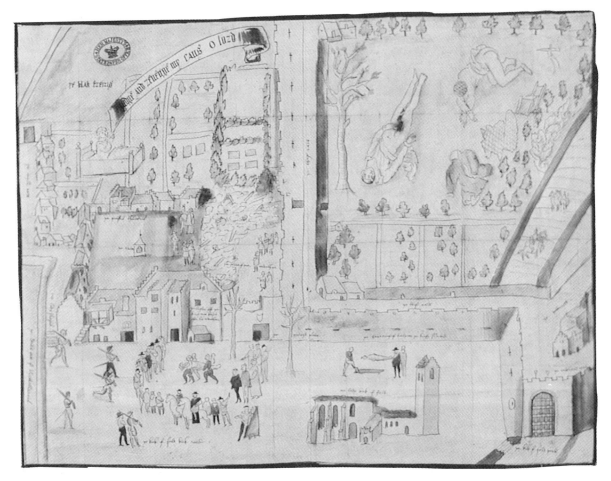

from Lochleven. She called her supporters to arms, but was defeated at Langside, and made her way across the Solway Firth to England, where she threw herself on the mercy of Elizabeth. She was lodged in semi-captivity at Carlisle Castle while Elizabeth decided what to do with her. Meanwhile, Sir Francis Knollys, a trusted member of the Council, together with Lord Scrope, was sent to interview her. The following extracts are from letters sent to Elizabeth towards the end of May by Mary herself, and by Scrope and Knollys. They show how difficult it was to decide between the various options. Should Mary:

- Be given freedom of movement within England, and perhaps be invited to meet Elizabeth?
- Be sent back over the border, either alone or with an English army to help her against Moray?
- Be kept a prisoner in Carlisle, or moved further south?
- Be allowed to travel to France?
- Be put on trial for the murder of Darnley?

a Mary to Elizabeth, 28 May 1568 (in French):

'I have now sent Lord Herrys, my faithful and well-loved subject, to inform you of all matters whereof I learn by Messieurs Scrope and Knollys you are in doubt. Praying you to credit him as myself, and answer at once by writing, and if it please you I come to you without ceremony or in private I will tell you the truth against all the lies [of my enemies] – and meantime assure me you will adopt my just cause till I am restored, as all princes should do for each other. I also send my cousin, Lord Flemyng, a faithful subject, to France (if assured by you), to thank the king for his good offices. If for any reason I cannot come to you, seeing I have freely come to throw myself in your arms, you will I am sure permit me to ask assistance of my other allies – for thank God I am not destitute of some. I find it strange that, coming so frankly without condition but trust in your amity, I have been kept as if a prisoner in your castle 15 days, and on your councillors' coming not allowed to go to you only to declare the truth of my grievances. Consider the importance to me of this long delay, and act like my good cousin and sworn friend.'

b Scrope and Knollys to Elizabeth, 29 May 1568:

'We arrived here at Carlisle yesterday at 6 of the clock after noon, and by the way my Lord Harris met us six miles from this town, and after he had discoursed of the lamentable estate of the Queen of Scots his mistress, inveighing much against the treasonable cruelty of her enemies, and also saying as much as he could for the innocence of his mistress touching the murder of her husband, the which he said would be easily proved if the Queen his mistress might be heard to speak for herself in your Highness presence. And affirming that he trusted your Highness would either give her aid to the chastening of her subjects for her relief and comfort, or else that your Highness would give her leave to pass through your country into France to seek relief other ways.

'Whereunto we answered that your Highness could in no wise like her seeking aid in France, thereby to bring Frenchmen into Scotland; and we doubted whether your Highness could think it meet to receive her

so honourably into your presence as your desirous affection and good will towards her did wish, until your Highness might be well instructed and satisfied by probable reasons that she was clear and innocent of the said murder, by some such wise man as he that might set forth the same manifestly. Whereupon, and through other conferences private with me the Lord Scrope, he seemed to determine to ride towards your Highness for that intent within a day or twain: which was the thing that we specially sought for.

'And after this, repairing into the castle, we found the Queen of Scots in her chamber of presence ready to receive us ... and we found her in her answers to have an eloquent tongue, and a discreet head; and it seemeth by her doings she hath stout courage and liberal heart adjoined thereunto; and after our delivery of your Highness letters, she fell into some passion with the water in her eyes, and ... complained unto us for that your Highness did not answer her expectation for the admitting her into your presence forthwith; that upon good declaration of her innocence your Highness would either without delay give her aid yourself to the subduing of her enemies, or else being now come of good will and not of necessity into your Highness hands (for a good and greatest part of her subjects, said she, do remain fast unto her still) your Highness would at the least forthwith give her passage through your country into France to seek aid at other princes' hands; not doubting but both the French King and the King of Spain would give her relief in that behalf to her satisfaction ...

'And therefore I, the Vice-Chamberlain, do refer to your Highness' better consideration, whether it were not honourable for you in the sight of your subjects and of all foreign princes to put her grace to the choice whether she will depart freely back into her country without your Highness' impeachment, or whether she will remain at your Highness' devotion within your realm here ... And yet I think it is likely that if she had so her own choice she would not go back into her own realm presently, nor until she might look for succors of men out of France to join with her there ... And on the other side she cannot be kept so rigorously as a prisoner with your Highness' honour (in mine opinion), but with devices of towels or toys at her chamber window, or elsewhere in the night, a body of her agility and spirit may escape soon, being so near the border. And surely to have her carried far into the realm is the high way to a dangerous sedition as I suppose.'

Plots and counter-plots

Elizabeth had a low opinion of Mary as a person, but a high opinion of her rank as a queen, and she thought it might reflect on her own dignity if Mary was humiliated in any way. However, she was warned by Cecil against receiving her at Court, which might imply official recognition of her as heir to the English throne. The solution was to keep Mary in secure but comfortable accommodation, but to use the suspicion of her complicity in the Darnley murder as an excuse for not allowing a personal meeting until her name had been cleared. Therefore an inquiry was held – the word 'trial' was avoided – and both sides invited to produce their evidence, although Mary herself was not allowed to attend. The proceedings, first held at York and then moved to Westminster, were fairly muddled, and Mary's agents withdrew at an early stage, before Moray had produced the famous **Casket letters**.

Casket letters

The commission investigating Mary's guilt were shown 'a small gilded coffer not fully one foot [30 cm] long' containing eight letters and some love poems said to have been written by Mary to Bothwell and to reveal their mutual complicity in Darnley's murder. Unfortunately, these letters disappeared soon afterwards and have not been seen since, so it has never been possible to decide their authenticity by the crucial test of handwriting. Going by the copies made by the commission, most historians have concluded that the letters were wholly or partly forged. Some passages may have been by Mary to Bothwell, but other parts clearly were not, and the commissioners themselves obviously were not convinced, or they would hardly have returned an inconclusive verdict.

The inquiry ended inconclusively, but Mary, although no charges against her had been 'sufficiently proven', was kept in confinement, and still not allowed to see Elizabeth. For the next 19 years she was to be shuffled around from castle to castle, with her lifestyle becoming steadily less like a queen's and more like that of a prisoner. This increasingly severe treatment was the result of a series of plots in which she was involved, to a greater or lesser extent. The sequence starts with a scheme for Mary to marry the **Duke of Norfolk**.

The fiasco of the Norfolk marriage project was hardly Mary's fault, because she had always made it plain that Elizabeth's backing was a necessary pre-condition. Nor was she personally involved in the badly-organised northern rising, under the Catholic earls of Northumberland and Westmorland, which took place in the autumn of the same year. This was mainly an attempt by the two earls to restore the Catholic religion, as well as their own feudal influence, in the North. Unfortunately for Mary, one of their stated objectives was to rescue her from captivity and make her queen of England instead of Elizabeth. When the rebellion failed, therefore, it had the effect of making the majority of English people more hostile to Mary. This was compounded by the papal bull of 1570 excommunicating Elizabeth, which declared that English Catholics were released from their loyalty to her, hence widening the gap between the Catholics and the rest of the population.

Shortly afterwards Mary became entangled in the Ridolfi plot, in which an Italian banker, Roberto Ridolfi, together with Mary's official agent in London, John Leslie, Bishop of Ross, plotted to replace Elizabeth by Mary, assisted by a Spanish army from the Netherlands. When the plot was uncovered Elizabeth was under great pressure from Parliament to execute not only Norfolk, which she did, but also this 'monstrous dragon', as one member described Mary. By now Elizabeth's reluctance to execute her royal cousin was the one obstacle which stood between Mary and the block. 'Can I put to death the bird that, to escape the pursuit of the hawk, has fled to my feet for protection?', she asked the Privy Council. 'Honour and conscience forbid.'

In 1583 yet another plot against Elizabeth's life was uncovered. A young English Catholic, Francis Throckmorton, confessed on the rack that an invasion of England was planned, and that Mary, Queen of Scots was implicated. Again, largely due to Elizabeth, no action was taken against Mary, except to guard her even more closely and restrict all contact with the outside world. The main result of the uncovering of the Throckmorton plot was that the Privy Council drew up a Bond of Association whereby, if Elizabeth were assassinated, they undertook to destroy anyone in whose interests the crime was committed. The Bond,

---

PROFILE: *Duke of Norfolk*

Thomas Howard, England's only duke, was a widower of 33 in 1569. He was not an especially glamorous figure. Mary never, in fact, met him, but the suggestion that they should marry received much support, including from many of Elizabeth's councillors, who at this time were opposed to the influence of William Cecil and especially to his anti-Spanish policies (see chapter 14). They banked on this marriage leading to a realignment in English policy.

Norfolk probably had visions not only of Mary and himself on the Scottish throne, but also of their succeeding to the English throne as well. He hoped that Elizabeth would agree to the marriage, but he was too frightened to put her in the picture for some time. When she finally did find out, in September 1569, her rage was extreme, and Norfolk found himself in the Tower. He was released a year later, only to become involved in the Ridolfi plot. He was imprisoned once more, and this time was found guilty of treason and executed, in 1572.

---

which was obviously directed against Mary, was widely distributed and signed by thousands of Elizabeth's loyal subjects.

Three years later, details began to emerge of yet another large-scale plot against Elizabeth. This time the evidence for Mary's involvement was so clear that even Elizabeth would be unable to resist the pressure to have her executed. The Babington plot was different from the others because it was practically the creation of Elizabeth's minister in charge of counter-espionage, Francis Walsingham. By this time Mary was under the supervision, not of the Earl of Shrewsbury – who had been in charge of her for 15 years and who had treated her in a relatively civilised way – but of the extreme puritan, Sir Amyas Paulet, a strict gaoler and entirely immune to Mary's famous charm. Paulet watched Mary so closely that she was unable to communicate with anyone outside her household. Walsingham instructed the gaoler to allow her secret letters to be taken out of the house in a waterproof bag inside a beer barrel, and letters for her to be smuggled in similarly. The letters were then to be extracted, decoded by Walsingham's cryptographers, resealed and sent on. In this way, Walsingham finally got the proof he was looking for, in the shape of a letter by Mary approving of the details of the plot, including Elizabeth's assassination. Mary was taken to Fotheringhay Castle in Northamptonshire, where in October 1586 she was put on trial before a commission of over 30 peers, councillors and judges, and found guilty of 'imagining and encompassing her Majesty's death'.

The end of Mary

The final act in the story involves Elizabeth's last-minute reluctance to approve the execution. At the end of 1586 a delegation from both Houses of Parliament went to see her at Richmond to insist that she sign a warrant for the execution. Elizabeth's speech to them was a masterpiece of prevarication, ending with a statement so opaque that most of the delegates must have come away completely in the dark as to her decision.

> 'If I should say I would not do what you request, it might peradventure be more than I thought, and to say I would do it might perhaps breed peril of that you labour to preserve, being more than in your own wisdom and discretions would seem convenient, circumstances of place and time being duly considered. As for your petition, your judgement I condemn not ... but pray you to accept my thankfulness, excuse my doubtfulness, and take in good part my answer answerless.'

Nevertheless, the warrant was eventually signed, though Elizabeth called back William Davison, the secretary who was given it, to ask if even now it might not be possible to find someone to murder Mary quietly, so that her signature on the warrant would not be required. But there was nobody, and Davison hurried it to Fotheringhay where, three days later, on 8 February 1587, the victim was beheaded (see Figure 23.3). When Elizabeth heard the news she flew into a tantrum, claiming that she had never intended the warrant to be sent. Davison became a scapegoat, losing his position and spending some time in the Tower. But Mary's death, although it caused outrage in Europe, affected the course of English policy surprisingly little as she had long since ceased to play a significant role.

Task: source evaluation

1 Read the letters from Mary, and from Scrope and Knollys, to Elizabeth, in May 1568 (pages 204–205). What impression of Mary's character is derived from:
   a her own letter
   b the comments about her made by Scrope and Knollys?

2 What are the various objections mentioned by Scrope and Knollys to:
   a allowing Mary to proceed to France?
   b allowing her to meet Elizabeth?
   c keeping her a prisoner?

Figure 23.3 The execution of Mary, Queen of Scots, at Fotheringhay Castle in 1587

3 In your opinion, was Mary's execution politically, legally and ethically justifiable?

Further reading

Antonia Fraser, *Mary, Queen of Scots* (Weidenfeld and Nicolson, 1969).

Michael Lynch (ed.), *Mary Stuart: Queen in Three Kingdoms* (Oxford, 1988).

Jenny Wormald, *Mary, Queen of Scots: a study in failure* (George Philip, 1988) – the best available biography.

24 Why did the Armada fail?

After Leicester's expedition to the Netherlands, Philip II started to plan the invasion of England (see chapter 22). The idea was to land a Spanish army in Kent, and threaten, if not occupy, London. Philip believed – realistically – that this would force the English government to come to terms. After all, Spanish troops were the best in Europe, and England, without a regular army, had only the militia with which to oppose them. In these circumstances his minimum conditions for peace would have been: toleration for English Catholics, the withdrawal of English forces from the Netherlands, and perhaps the payment of an indemnity. Philip did not envisage actually deposing Elizabeth and adding England to the Spanish Empire – even the most optimistic of his advisers thought this outcome unlikely.

The problem was that, as things stood, an invasion could hardly be mounted from the Netherlands because Parma's army needed naval support before it could risk crossing the Channel. After much thought, Philip decided on a scheme which turned out to be fundamentally unsound. It involved the despatch of a large fleet from Spain carrying 19,000 soldiers and a siege train. This was to rendezvous with Parma and reinforce his army of 30,000 which would be waiting at the Flemish ports, and the whole force would then cross the Channel to Kent.

Unfortunately, Philip had neglected to solve the crucial question of how the Armada was actually to meet up with Parma. The sea off Holland and Zealand was too shallow for the big Armada galleons, and if Parma's invasion force had tried to row out to the fleet they would have been easy prey for the Dutch, who controlled the shallow waters with their small manoeuvrable fly-boats. For the plan to work, Spain needed a deep-water port, and the only one large enough was Flushing, which was in the hands of the rebels. Nevertheless, in spite of contrary advice – including Parma's – Philip insisted on pressing ahead, and during 1586 preparations were under way. It was, for the time, a massively ambitious project – comparable perhaps to putting a human on the moon in today's world – and its costs took up over two-thirds of the entire revenue of Philip's empire. In April 1587, the arrangements were set back by Drake's pre-emptive raid, in which he destroyed or captured 35 ships in Cadiz harbour. However, by July 1588 all was finally complete, and the great Armada set out under the command of the **Duke of Medina Sidonia**.

PROFILE: *Duke of Medina Sidonia*

When Spain's most experienced admiral, the Marquis of Santa Cruz, died, in January 1588, Philip chose to replace him as commander of the Armada, **Don Alonso Perez de Guzman, seventh duke of Medina Sidonia** (?1549–88). Although Medina Sidonia had no practical naval experience and was not a particularly charismatic personality, he proved to be the right person for the job. In the first place, he was the head of one of Spain's most aristocratic families, and none of the Armada's proud and touchy captains could feel any resentment at serving under him. Secondly, he had already proved to be a first-class administrator, and now his tireless attention to detail brought order out of the chaos which hitherto had surrounded the preparations. Nevertheless, he begged Philip to cancel the appointment, and made no secret of his pessimism about the chances of success.

During the campaign, Medina Sidonia showed himself an excellent commander, demonstrating personal bravery as well as strategic skill, and the ultimate failure was not his fault. He also managed to get the shattered remnants of the Armada back to Spain, and then he retired as soon as possible back to his orange groves. As one of his captains said, 'Even our enemies will admit, although it may grieve them, that no commander in the world has done more than this one.'

The fleets compared

Even if Philip's plan had not been flawed, the Armada would still have had a good chance of being defeated, owing to the advantages possessed by the English. But this was far from evident to Drake and Hawkins when they first saw the 130 ships of the Spanish fleet off Plymouth on the morning of 30 July. It must have been a terrifying sight – the largest fleet ever gathered in northern waters, with its disciplined, tightly-knit formation. In the week that followed, and especially during the key battle off Gravelines on 8 August (see Figures 24.1–24.4 on pages 214–215), the differences between the two sides became apparent, and they were much to England's advantage:

1 The Spanish ships were on the whole much slower and less manoeuvrable than the English. This was partly because the Armada included many merchant ships, commandeered to carry the necessary stores and equipment. Among them were some enormous, slow-moving hulks normally used to bring corn from the Baltic. It was also because, since the 1560s, the English under John Hawkins had developed a new type of fighting galleon – faster, with a lower superstructure, and hence more 'weatherly' (*i.e.* they could sail closer to the wind) than any in the Spanish fleet.

2 Another advantage enjoyed by the English was the number and quality of their seamen. The Armada carried about 19,000 soldiers as well as other supernumeraries such as Catholic priests, all of whom took no part in actually sailing the ships. Also, many of the sailors came from Mediterranean ports like Venice or Valencia, and had little or no experience of Atlantic waters. On the English ships everyone on board was capable of participating.

3 The whole of Catholic Europe contributed to the Armada. Consequently there were not only far too many different types and sizes of gun, but also a range of nationalities among the crews, which must have made coordination in seamanship and in battle much harder. As the contemporary Italian observer, Ubaldino, commented, 'Among the artillery it had been absolutely decided by the English that all should be of one nationality, one language, and therefore one constant disposition to serve well, and we cannot consider that this was at all so among the enemy.'

4 The Armada overall probably had rather less fire-power than the English fleet, but an even more crucial point is that it did not make the most of the guns it had. Recent research on Armada wrecks sunk off Ireland has shown that it is not true – as used to be thought – that the Spanish ships ran out of powder and shot. It was just that their rate of fire during battle was far lower than the English rate. This may have been due to the following factors:

- A lack of training in the technique of continuous firing and reloading. In battle the Spanish expected to deliver one massive broadside and then get near enough to the enemy to grapple and board – something the English never allowed them to do.

- Many of the Spanish cannons, cast in a hurry just before the Armada sailed, turned out to be defective. Some even exploded on use.

- The type of gun-mounting used for their larger guns was clumsy, making reloading very difficult; whereas the English four-wheeled truck carriages proved most effective in battle and 'might well be regarded as England's decisive secret weapon in 1588' (Martin and Parker).

Diary of the campaign

29 July
Armada sighted off the Scillies. That night the English fleet leaves Plymouth harbour and succeeds in getting to windward of the Spanish.

30 July–1 August
Armada in crescent-shaped battle order proceeds up the Channel under a south-westerly wind, closely followed by English who try to 'pluck their feathers' (*i.e.* pick off stragglers). Two Armada ships are disabled due to accidents and captured; otherwise little damage.

2–3 August
Inconclusive engagements off Portland Bill and Isle of Wight. English demonstrate superior mobility but cause only minor damage. English fleet is now divided into four squadrons, under Howard, Drake, Frobisher and Hawkins. Medina Sidonia sends stream of messages to Parma warning him to be ready, but no reply received. English pressure forces Armada past Isle of Wight, giving no opportunity for landing.

4–6 August
More inconclusive skirmishes, in which both sides use up large quantities of ammunition. Little wind. Armada continues slowly towards Calais.

6 August
In the evening Armada anchors off Calais. Seymour's squadron from the Downs joins main English fleet shadowing Armada. No word from Parma.

7 August
Medina Sidonia receives news that Parma will not be ready for a fortnight. He decides to wait, although Calais anchorage is dangerous and exposed. That night English send fireships in amongst the Spanish ships, causing many to cut their anchors and disperse.

8 August
At dawn, seeing Armada formation is broken at last, English attack immediately. In battle off Gravelines, which lasts whole day, English fire-power does much damage at close range.

9 August
Many Spaniards almost driven onto shoals off the Zealand coast, but are saved by wind shifting to south, allowing them to regroup and sail north. But they cannot now return to Calais to meet Parma. Their only option is to continue northwards and try to return home by rounding Scotland and Ireland.

10–12 August
English follow Armada northwards to Firth of Forth, but then break off contact and return home due to extreme shortage of food and ammunition.

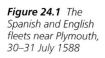

Figure 24.1 *The Spanish and English fleets near Plymouth, 30–31 July 1588*

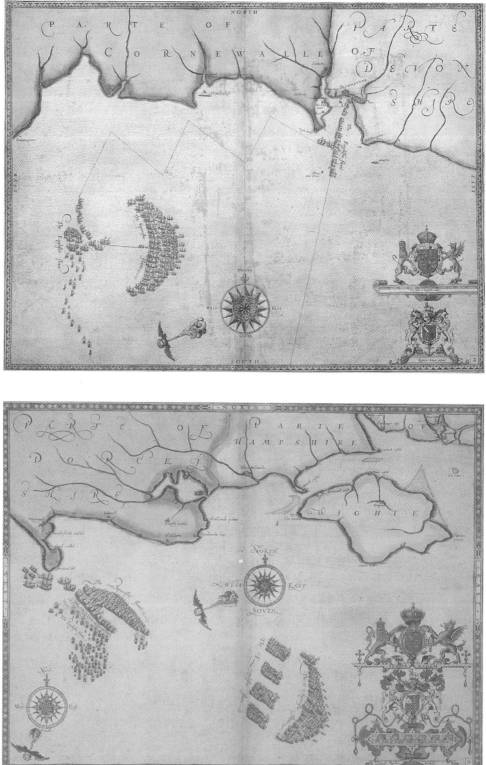

Figure 24.2 *The engagement between Portland Bill and the Isle of Wight*

Figure 24.3 *The fireship attack, 7 August*

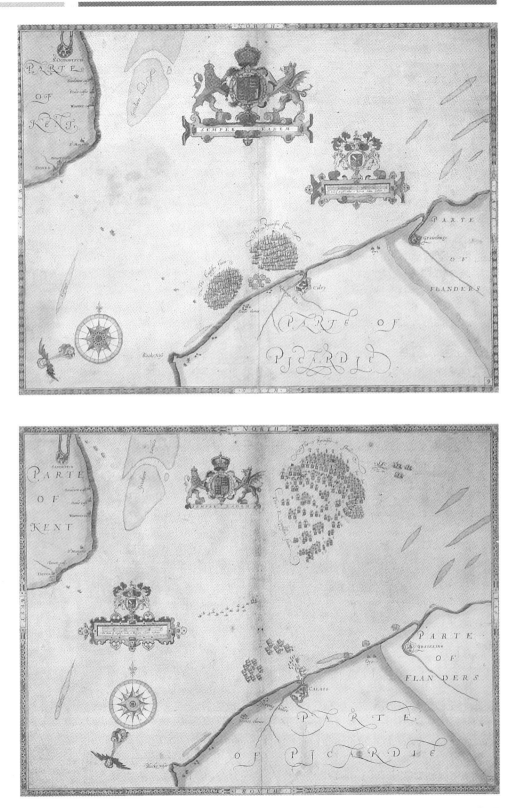

Figure 24.4 *The battle off Gravelines, France, 8 August*

Hawkins' report

Two days after Gravelines, John Hawkins, from on board ship, snatched time to describe to Walsingham, Secretary of State, what had happened, and to outline the position as he saw it. In this section of his report he reveals the anxieties felt even at this date about the continuing strength of the enemy and about the deficiencies of the English fleet:

> 'Our ships, God be thanked, have received little hurt, and are of great force to accompany them, and of such advantage that, with some continuance at the seas, and sufficiently provided of shot and powder, we shall be able with God's favour to weary them out of the sea and confound them ...
>
> 'The men have been long unpaid and need relief. I pray your lordship that the money that should have gone to Plymouth may now be sent to Dover. August now cometh in, and this cost will spend ground tackle, cordage, canvas and victuals, all which would be sent to Dover in good plenty. With these things and God's blessing our kingdom may be preserved, which being neglected great hazard may come.'

After the battle

After Gravelines the Spanish Armada faced the long voyage home. Many of the ships were badly damaged, with heavy casualties, and few had sufficient food or water for the journey. Exhausted by days of fighting they sailed northwards and then westwards, into the autumn gales of the North Atlantic. Those ships that stuck with Medina Sidonia's flagship, the *San Martin*, mostly managed to struggle home to Spain, although many of their crews were dead, or near dead, and they continued dying for weeks after the ships made port. Others failed to make it, and were wrecked on the rugged Irish coast, where the survivors were generally massacred by the natives, or handed over to the English to be executed. Several Armada wrecks have recently been located and investigated, with the odd result that we now know more about the equipment and armament of the Spanish fleet than we do about the English.

Contemporaries saw in the rout of the Armada the hand of God, thus contributing to the 'providential' version of history, the view that God was always on the look-out and determining events, and in particular that he was protecting his favourite nation, Protestant England. On the medal struck to commemorate the victory were the words, 'God blew and they were dispersed'. Undoubtedly, the outcome boosted English pride and nationalism, as well as the prestige of England's Queen. The war against Spain was now seen, not merely in religious terms – Protestants against Catholics – but principally as the defence of England against her aggressive enemies.

However, the Armada was only the start of the war, which went on until 1604. Philip dispatched two further armadas, in 1596 and 1597, but both had to turn back owing to storms. Nevertheless, Spain after 1588 developed a powerful Atlantic fleet, and this, together with the strengthening of her defences in the New World, contributed to the lack of success of future English naval expeditions. More important was the fact that in 1589 the character of the war changed because Philip sent a Spanish army into France to aid the Catholic League against Henry of Navarre. This in turn caused Elizabeth to commit troops and money to France as well as the Netherlands, so that war on land started to take precedence over war at sea.

The Armada failed perhaps because it was a project beyond the capacity of any sixteenth-century state, even one with the resources of Philip II's empire. Yet one has to admire the immense planning and patience which went into creating this fleet, which was unlike any the world had seen before. No doubt the Armada failed, too, because Philip's plan was unworkable and he was too stubborn to take the advice of his leading commanders and call the whole thing off. If he had put all his resources into conquering the Netherlands before he attacked England, he might have stood a better chance. Then again, the Armada suffered from the various deficiencies in ships and guns mentioned above. It is an astonishing fact that England's navy was better trained and equipped than that of Spain, even though Elizabeth's annual income was not much more than a tenth of Philip's.

In spite of all this, if the Armada had had better luck it might have succeeded. If, for instance, Howard had just once allowed the Spanish ships to get close enough to board, so that they could deploy their soldiers. Or if Medina Sidonia had abandoned his orders and attempted a landing on the Isle of Wight, or in Kent. Or if the wind had changed after Gravelines, allowing another attempt at a meeting with Parma. This, of course, was precisely what concerned Hawkins when he compiled his report of 10 August. In all these cases the results might have been very different.

Further reading

Colin Martin and Geoffrey Parker, *The Spanish Armada* (Penguin, 1989) – full of information about guns, ships and crews.
Simon Adams, *The Armada Campaign of 1588*, New Appreciations in History no. 13 (Historical Association, 1988) – an excellent introduction to the subject.
David Loades, *The Tudor Navy: An administrative, political and military history* (Scolar Press, 1992).

25 The problem of Ireland

The Irish problem, as far as the rulers of England were concerned, can be summed up quite simply. Ireland was too close to ignore, but too large to conquer. It could not simply be left to go its own way, because the enemies of England might use it as a base from which to infiltrate or attack the mainland. But any attempt to annex it to the kingdom of England, as Edward I had done with Wales, would be enormously costly and quite likely to fail.

In the twelfth century Henry II led an expedition to Ireland and forced the native rulers to acknowledge him as their overlord. A number of Anglo-Norman adventurers who had gone with him stayed on and settled themselves and their families on the large tracts of land which they had seized from the native Irish. Their descendants became known

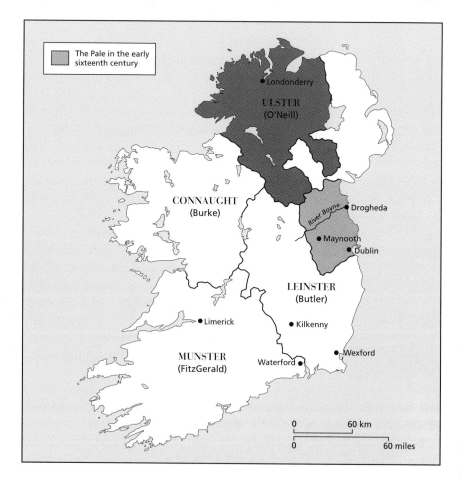

Figure 25.1 *Tudor Ireland*

as the Old English, but as the years passed and one generation succeeded another, they became more and more like their Irish neighbours.

Henry VII

The English kings had managed to retain Dublin and a strip of land known as the Pale, stretching northwards for some 50 miles, and 20 miles inland. Dublin Castle was the seat of the King's governor or Deputy, but he had little control of events 'beyond the Pale'. The remainder of Ireland, apart from a number of walled towns, was dominated by the chiefs of Gaelic-speaking clans and the Old English, of whom the most powerful were the Butlers, earls of Ormond, and the Fitzgeralds or Geraldines, earls of Kildare. Henry VII appointed as his Deputy the eighth Earl of Kildare, who had held the same office under the Yorkists, but his trust was betrayed when, in 1487, Kildare acknowledged the pretender Lambert Simnel as King. After Henry had crushed Simnel's revolt he sent a small force to Ireland to re-assert his authority. Kildare confessed his error and was allowed to stay on as Lord Deputy. Henry in fact had little choice, for his authority in Ireland was only nominal. It needed a great landowner with acknowledged prestige to uphold it, and these were thin on the ground.

Henry was forced to reconsider his policy towards Ireland when, in 1491, another pretender – Perkin Warbeck – appeared on the scene, for Kildare once again wavered in his loyalty. Henry now decided to break with the Old English magnates and impose direct rule upon Ireland. He nominated his baby son, the future Henry VIII, Lieutenant of Ireland, and appointed **Sir Edward Poynings** to govern in the prince's name. Poynings had

---

PROFILE: *Sir Edward Poynings*

Poynings was among those who chose exile in order to join Henry Tudor in France before his triumphant return to England in 1485. Like others of Henry's 'new men', he was rewarded by appointment to the royal council. In 1494 he was sent as Lord Deputy to Ireland. There he arrested and sent back to England the rebel Earl of Kildare. The parliament which he summoned passed 'Poynings' Law' which stated that in future the Irish parliament was to do nothing without the prior consent of the English government. Poynings continued to serve both Henry VII and his son, Henry VIII. In 1512, as Warden of the Cinque Ports, he was responsible for raising forces against a threat of French invasion. He died in 1521 at the age of 62.

instructions to fill all the key posts in the Irish administration with Englishmen, and was given an army of one thousand men to enforce his commands. Poynings did as he was told, and in December 1494 he crowned his achievements by persuading the Irish Parliament to accept 'Poynings' Law' which took away its independence.

In one respect, Poynings' mission was a failure. Henry had instructed him to reform Irish finances in such a way that they would meet the entire costs of the English administration there, including the maintenance of an army. This proved to be impossible, and Henry therefore had to face the perennial problem of whether to embark on a full-scale conquest or revert to indirect rule. He chose the cheaper option and recalled Poynings. His place as Lord Deputy was taken, yet again, by Kildare.

Henry VIII

Following the death of the eighth Earl of Kildare in 1513, his son, the ninth Earl, was appointed Deputy. Although charged with maintaining peace and good order, one of his principal concerns was the struggle for supremacy over the Butlers. Civil war between the two major Old English families produced widespread anarchy, and in 1520 Wolsey persuaded Henry VIII to dismiss Kildare from office and send over Thomas Howard, Earl of Surrey, as his Lieutenant. It looked as though direct rule was once again to be imposed, but Surrey's report made plain just how expensive this would be:

> '*After my poor opinion, this land shall never be brought to good order and due subjection but ... by conquest ... The least number [of soldiers] that your Grace must occupy can be no less than 2,500; for it is not to be doubted that whensoever the Irishmen shall know that your Grace intendeth a conquest, they will all combine together and withstand the same to the best of their power ... And if your Grace will, in more brief time, have your purpose brought to pass, and to set upon the conquest in divers places at one time, then ... 6,000 men is the least number that your Grace must occupy. But to advertise your Grace in how many years either the one number or the other should accomplish and perfect the conquest, the matter is so high and uncertain that I dare not meddle therewith.*'

The Earl of Surrey to Henry VIII (June 1521).

Henry VIII was no more willing than his father to pour money into the bottomless pit of Ireland, so Kildare was restored to office. But Henry's rejection of Catherine of Aragon – the aunt of the Emperor Charles V – and the subsequent break with Rome, transformed the situation. Charles, who was also King of Spain, had already been in contact with the native Irish leaders and offered to assist them if they rebelled against Henry.

The security of England demanded that Ireland should be brought under much closer control, but how was this to be done? Kildare was untrustworthy as well as ineffective, so the only alternative seemed to be a reversion to direct rule. This was the policy embraced by Henry's chief minister, Thomas Cromwell, and in order to start implementing it he summoned Kildare to London in 1534. After an examination by the Privy Council, Kildare was sent prisoner to the Tower, but he was already a sick man and he died there in September. Cromwell now hoped, as Henry VII had done before him, that Ireland could be made to pay for its own government. But this was a mirage, and Ireland remained a drain on the English Exchequer, costing the King some £4,000 a year. Henry had better things to spend his money on, and after the fall of Cromwell in 1540 he changed course yet again.

Henry had already been declared head of the Church in Ireland in 1536, but in order to assert his independence of the Pope and papal authority it was essential for him to take the further step of becoming king of Ireland. In June 1541, therefore, the Irish Parliament formally conferred the royal title upon him. This transformed the legal position of the inhabitants of Ireland. No longer were they savage creatures, 'beyond the Pale' of civilisation and liable to be treated as vermin. They were now the king's subjects, entitled to the protection of his laws in the same way as his English subjects.

Henry acknowledged the change of status by inviting the Irish chieftains to become English-style landowners. This they could do by surrendering their lands to him and having them regranted. They would now be tenants-in-chief of the Crown, with the same rights and obligations as their equivalents in England. In order to integrate them yet further into the English system they were given titles of nobility.

The newly-ennobled chieftains were expected to abandon their former lifestyles. Con O'Neill, for example, who received the title Earl of Tyrone, promised to 'utterly forsake the name of O'Neill' and to wear English-style clothes and use the English language insofar as he and his followers understood it.

It looked as though Henry VIII had at last solved the Irish problem, for in 1545 the Council in Ireland reported that the Irish 'recognise and acknowledge your Majesty to be King of this realm, and be more conformable to your Majesty ... than ever we knew them in our times'. Henry's religious changes were not particularly divisive, and most of the bishops, as well as leading figures among the laity, had accepted the Act of Supremacy which made him head of the Church in Ireland.

However, the imposition of Protestantism under Edward VI was far less acceptable, particularly the attack upon images and relics. Protestant bishops and clergy were only effective in English-speaking areas. There was no systematic attempt to provide services or sermons in Gaelic. As a result, the mass of the Irish-speaking population became increasingly detached from the official church and clung instead to the familiar Catholic beliefs and rituals. In other words, just as the English were defining their national identity in Protestant terms, so the Irish were adopting Catholicism as their national creed.

Elizabethan Ireland

Mary's reign was too brief to bridge the widening gap between the Protestant English and the Catholic Irish, and by the time Elizabeth came to the throne in 1558 it looked as though Ireland was slipping out of English control. Yet the danger of foreign intervention, first from France and later from Spain, had never been greater. It was therefore decided that the whole of Ireland should be divided into counties, on the English pattern, with Presidents appointed to rule over Munster and Connaught. Until then the greater part of Ireland – which lay outside the Pale – had had its own language, law and customs. Now it was to have English patterns forced on it. The result, as might have been expected, was rebellion.

The first uprising came in Munster in 1569 and was led by James FitzMaurice. He appealed for support to both Spain and the Papacy, but none was forthcoming and the rebellion collapsed. FitzMaurice escaped to the continent where he collected an army together and brought it back to Ireland in July 1579. He was accompanied by a prominent English Jesuit and proclaimed that 'this war is undertaken for the defence of the Catholic faith against the heretics'. This was only partly true, for FitzMaurice had also been spurred on by hatred of his rivals for power in Munster, the Butler family. Another clan, the Burkes, remained loyal to Elizabeth and killed FitzMaurice in a skirmish.

A later uprising in Ireland, in 1598, threatened to be more dangerous. **Hugh O'Neill**, the Earl of Tyrone, led his group of men in an organised and disciplined way. They virtually wiped out an English army at the Battle of the Yellow Ford. O'Neill then hoodwinked Elizabeth's commander, the Earl of Essex, in the peace negotiations which followed.

PROFILE: *Hugh O'Neill*

As the heir to the earldom of Tyrone, **Hugh O'Neill** was brought to England in 1562 at the age of 22 in the hope that an education at Court would ensure his loyalty. For some time after his return to Ireland in 1585, having succeeded to the title, he behaved as expected, but in 1595 his outrage at the way in which his fellow Irishmen were being treated prompted him to outright rebellion. He proved to be one of the few Irish leaders capable of organising and leading an army. In 1598 he scored his greatest success when he annihilated an English army at the Battle of the Yellow Ford. However, Tyrone was defeated in 1601 while he was attempting to link up with a Spanish expeditionary force sent to aid the rebels. By 1603 he had given up the struggle and submitted to James I, who pardoned and re-instated him. In 1607, however, he left Ireland for good and went to Rome, where he died in 1616.

However, the Earl of Tyrone was subsequently defeated by Essex's successor, Mountjoy, at Kinsale in 1601 while he was attempting to link up with a Spanish expeditionary force sent to aid the Irish rebels.

> ### Edmund Spenser's account of Munster after FitzMaurice's rebellion
>
> *'Notwithstanding that the same was a most rich and plentiful country, full of corn and cattle ... yet ere one year and a half they were brought to such wretchedness as that any stony heart would have rued the same. Out of every corner of the woods and glens they came creeping forth upon their hands, for their legs could not bear them. They looked like anatomies of death. They spake like ghosts crying out of their graves. They did eat of the dead carrions ... insomuch as the very carcasses they spared not to scrape out of their graves ... In short space there were none almost left, and a most populous and plentiful country suddenly made void of man and beast.'*

KEY TERMS:

Plantation

Following the suppression of FitzMaurice's rebellion, Elizabeth's government decided on a policy known as '**plantation**'. Enormous tracts of land were confiscated and handed over to newly-arrived English settlers. The former Irish owners of the land became tenants, if they were lucky, or otherwise were evicted and forced to find somewhere else to live. Ireland became, in effect, an English colony.

The 'New English' colonisers, unlike the Old English, had little understanding of the native Irish. They looked down on them as an inferior breed, sunk in barbarism, and they despised them for clinging so obstinately to the Catholic faith which the New English regarded as primitive superstition. As **plantation** got under way, so the English and the Irish drew further apart. Even the Irish chieftains, who held English titles and had earlier been seen as agents of civilisation on the English model, were driven to make common cause with their fellow Irishmen.

By the end of the Tudor period, then, the Irish problem had apparently been solved. At great expense, Ireland had been conquered, and the plantation policy, which was now extended to Ulster, meant that an English landowning class would be imposed upon the top of Irish society, firmly holding it in place. The cost of the conquest is difficult to estimate but cannot have been far short of a million pounds: it put a strain upon the royal finances that was seriously to weaken the Stuart monarchy.

Yet Elizabeth's success was, in a sense, a mirage. The fact that the Irish problem is still with us means that conquest was not a final answer. The major weakness of the English position in Ireland was the lack of consent of the native Irish. Their sense of their own separate identity was reinforced by their stubborn commitment to the Roman Catholic faith which England had abandoned. The suppression of this faith by the English rulers merely intensified Irish resentment.

Ireland in 1589: a Spanish view

'These people call themselves Christians. Mass is said among them, and regulated according to the orders of the Church of Rome. The great majority of their churches, monasteries and hermitages have been demolished by the hands of the English ... and of those natives who have joined them and are as bad as they. In short, in this kingdom there is neither justice nor right, and everyone does what he pleases.'

Task: class discussion

1 Working in groups, discuss the effects of the following developments, and their impact on English–Irish relations.
  a the eighth Earl of Kildare's support for Perkin Warbeck
  b Henry VIII's assumption of the title of king of Ireland
  c the English Reformation
  d Elizabeth's relations with Spain
  e the policy of 'plantation'
  f Hugh O'Neill's rebellion.

2 Discuss and draw up an essay plan to answer the question:
  'Why was Ireland a continuing problem for the Tudor monarchs?'

Further reading

Brendan Bradshaw, *The Irish Constitutional Revolution of the Sixteenth Century* (Cambridge University Press, 1979) – mainly focuses on Henry VIII's reign.

Nicholas P. Canny, *The Elizabethan Conquest of Ireland: A Pattern Established 1565–76* (Harvester Press, 1976) – particularly good on the colonisation of Ireland.

S. G. Ellis, *Tudor Ireland: Crown, Community and the Conflict of Cultures, 1470–1603* (Addison Wesley Longman, 1985) – the best single-volume survey.

26 Who were the Puritans?

Time chart

1559: Acts of Supremacy and Uniformity establish Protestant Church in England

1563: Puritan demands for further reform presented to Convocation

1565: Archbishop Parker issues *Book of Advertisements*

1570: Cartwright delivers lectures attacking episcopal government of Church

1571: Strickland introduces bill to reform Prayer Book. John Field produces *Admonition to Parliament*

1575: Grindal is appointed Archbishop of Canterbury

1576: Elizabeth orders Grindal to suppress 'prophesyings'

1577: Grindal refuses and is suspended from office

1583: Whitgift is appointed Archbishop of Canterbury

1584–5: Cartwright and Travers publish *Book of Discipline*

1587: Cope introduces bill to replace Prayer Book

1588: Death of Field and Earl of Leicester. Publication of '**Marprelate Letters**'

1593: Act against seditious sectaries (see page 231)

KEY TERM:

Marprelate Letters

These anonymous attacks on the bishops, written in a bitterly satirical manner, were meant to reinforce the puritan campaign. But their language was so unbalanced that they produced a backlash in the bishops' favour. They also prompted the government to take a much harder line against radical puritans.

The question 'When did England become Protestant?' may seem an easy one to answer. Henry VIII broke with Rome; under Edward VI the nation became temporarily Protestant; Mary made it Catholic once again, but the accession of Elizabeth marked the point at which it became irrevocably Protestant. The answer, then, is 1558.

It is, of course, true that Elizabeth's accession was followed by the establishment of a non-Catholic Church of England which remains to this day the official state church. But 'non-Catholic' does not necessarily equal 'Protestant'. The problem for the historian is that in Elizabeth's reign, as later, there was no agreement on what Protestantism meant. Disputes arose over the following issues:

■ Could a Church which retained bishops and the traditional ecclesiastical hierarchy be truly Protestant?

■ Was the Prayer Book sufficiently purged of popish remnants?

◼ Were the clergy of the Church of England really committed to rooting out Catholicism and implanting Protestant beliefs, or were they content to do the minimum necessary to retain their positions?

◼ Were the people as a whole embracing Protestantism with their hearts and souls, or merely conforming outwardly?

The vestments controversy

Many of Elizabeth's subjects, particularly those who had recently returned from exile on the Continent, regarded the settlement of 1559 only as a beginning. They pressed for further 'purification' of the Church, and for this reason the name of 'puritan' was applied to them. Puritans covered a wide spectrum, from hard-liners who demanded immediate reform to moderates who were content to wait. They were to be found at all levels in the Church hierarchy and also among lay men and women. Generally speaking, they wanted four things:

1 A complete break with the Catholic past. This involved abandoning all the ceremonies and vestments associated with the former Catholic Church.

2 The removal of pictures, statues and any other 'visual aids' to devotion, which in their view were not aids at all but barriers and blind alleys.

3 The primacy of the Bible, to be expounded from the pulpit and closely studied at home.

4 An *active* faith – one involving ministers and laity alike. Christianity, for them, was not a matter for Sundays and holy days only, nor was it merely a moral code or a pattern of behaviour. It was a living faith which people should absorb within themselves so that it affected and transformed every aspect of their lives.

Unfortunately for the Puritans, the head of the established Church was the Queen, who was far more conservative than they were. She valued set forms of service, and distrusted extempore preaching, which might well go beyond what she regarded as fit bounds. As for an educated ministry, she once told her archbishop that 'my meaning is not you should make choice of learned ministers only, for they are not to be found, but of honest, sober and wise men, and such as can read the scriptures and homilies well unto the people'. In other words, she was content with maintaining a minimum standard, whereas the Puritans wanted to press ahead with a campaign of evangelisation to produce the maximum results.

Homilies

Homilies were sermons specially appointed by the government to be read in churches, and therefore in accordance with the official viewpoint. A printed *Book of Homilies* was issued in 1563.

It was at the Queen's insistence that in 1566 Archbishop Parker drew up a *Book of Advertisements* prescribing instructions for the clergy. These included the following:

> II.2   *That no parson or curate not admitted by the bishop of the diocese to preach, do expound ... any scripture or matter of doctrine ... but only study to read gravely and aptly, without any glossing of the same or any additions, the **homilies** already set out ... for the quiet instruction and edification of the people.*
>
> II.6   *That every minister saying any public prayers or ministering the sacraments or other rites of the church shall wear a comely surplice with sleeves.*
>
> IV.4   *That ... all ecclesiastical persons ... do wear the cap appointed by the* Injunctions *[of 1559].*

On the face of it, Parker's *Advertisements* are not very provocative, but more than 30 London ministers resigned rather than accept them, and there was opposition too from the laity. Some hard-liners, fearing the Church would never change itself, began coming together in private groups at which they used the Calvinist form of service deriving from Geneva. They had no intention at this stage of breaking with the established Church, but they found Prayer-Book services insufficient for their spiritual needs.

Prominent puritans

Archbishop Grindal

Puritan hopes of further reformation in the Church of England rose at the end of 1575 when the Queen appointed Edmund Grindal as Archbishop of Canterbury (Figure 26.1). Grindal had gone into exile in Mary's reign and was a conforming Puritan. Recognising the key role of ministers in promoting Protestantism, he supported schemes for improving their educational standards, in particular the Bible-study meetings known as 'Prophesyings'.

Prophesyings

Groups of ministers would come together in a market town or some other convenient place where a learned preacher would expound a passage from the Bible. The other ministers would make notes and join in discussion, thereby increasing their knowledge of the holy scriptures. **Prophesyings** often took place before an audience of lay people, who profited in the same way.

Many of the leading preachers were of puritan persuasion, and the Queen feared that prophesyings were a means of undermining the established Church rather than strengthening it. In December 1576 she instructed Grindal to put an end to them. Grindal's reply is self-explanatory:

Figure 26.1 *Edmund Grindal*

'I am forced with all humility, and yet plainly, to profess that I cannot, with safe conscience and without the offence of the majesty of God, give my consent to the suppressing of the said exercises. Much less can I send out any injunction for the utter and universal suppression of the same … Bear with me, I beseech you, Madam, if I choose rather to offend your earthly majesty than to offend the heavenly majesty of God.'

Elizabeth responded by suspending Grindal from office and issuing orders direct to the bishops requiring them to put an end to these 'disputations' on the grounds that:

'great numbers of our people, specially the vulgar sort, meet [i.e. fitted] to be otherwise occupied with honest labour for their living, are brought to idleness and seduced and in a manner schismatically divided amongst themselves into variety of dangerous opinions.'

The puritan appeal to parliament

In the early years of Elizabeth's reign, those people who wanted further reform of the Church looked to the bishops, many of whom shared their opinions. But disillusionment set in when they realised that the bishops, who were under the queen's authority, could not bring about change. From their point of view **Thomas Cartwright's** denunciation of episcopacy came just at the right moment – which was why the government regarded him as dangerous. But rather than openly attacking episcopacy, the Puritans now appealed to Parliament to accomplish what the bishops had failed to do.

John Field acted as the link between the puritan movement outside Parliament and sympathetic MPs. It was one of these MPs, Walter Strickland, who in 1571 introduced a bill to amend the Prayer Book. The

---

PROFILE: *Thomas Cartwright*

Thomas Cartwright, born in 1535, came to prominence in 1570 when, as Professor of Divinity at Cambridge University, he gave a series of lectures denouncing episcopacy as unscriptural and advocating a Presbyterian system. For this he was expelled, and took refuge in Geneva. Returning to England in 1572 he became embroiled in the quarrel over the *Admonition to Parliament* in which he supported John Field. Forced into exile once again, he was only able to return in 1585 because of the patronage of Elizabeth's favourite, the Earl of Leicester. Following Leicester's death in 1588 Cartwright was accused of nonconformity by the High Commission and briefly imprisoned. He died at Warwick in 1603.

PROFILE: *John Field*

John Field, educated at Oxford, made a name for himself as a puritan preacher, though he never held a living. In 1572 he drew up the *Admonition to Parliament*, for which he spent a year in prison. On his release, he was chosen by a London parish to act as their 'lecturer' or official preacher. Subsequently the Bishop of London, John Aylmer, accused him of teaching 'God knows what' and withdrew his permission to preach. He now took to translating the works of foreign theologians, but kept in touch with the puritan leaders and remained a thorn in the side of the ecclesiastical authorities until his death in 1588.

Queen and her Privy Councillors promptly intervened, and the bill went no further. Field therefore set to work to whip up public opinion by drafting *An Admonition to the Parliament* designed to give a 'view of popish abuses yet remaining in the English Church'. This followed Cartwright by attacking not simply individual bishops but the whole system of episcopacy:

> '*The names of archbishops, archdeacons, lord bishops ... etc. are drawn out of the Pope's shop, together with their offices. So the government which they use ... is antichristian and devilish, and contrary to the scriptures. And as safely may we, by the warrant of God's word, subscribe to allow the dominion of the Pope universally to rule over the word of God, as of an archbishop over a whole province, or a lord bishop over a diocese.*'

Field also criticised the Prayer Book, which he described as 'an unperfect book, culled and picked out of that popish dunghill, the ... mass-book, full of all abominations'. Elizabeth responded with a proclamation, issued in 1573, strongly defending the Prayer Book, 'wherein is nothing contained but the scripture of God and that which is consonant unto it'. She warned its critics and those who did not conform to its provisions that the full force of the law would be brought to bear on them. One consequence of this was that the ecclesiastical Court of High Commission (see chapter 21) summoned Cartwright to appear before it – a summons which prompted him once again to flee the country.

The 'classical' movement

The suspension of Grindal as archbishop was a blow to the puritans, but they suffered an even heavier one when, following his death in 1583, the Queen appointed **John Whitgift** to replace him.

Whitgift's hard-line approach towards nonconformists drove some Puritans in the direction of separation from the established Church. In parts of south and south-east England ministers who felt strongly on the matter began meeting privately and forming something like a Presbyterian cell or, to use the Latin name, *classis*. In fact, by 1587 a rudimentary Presbyterian organisation was functioning alongside the established Church in Northamptonshire.

Presbyterians hoped to achieve through Parliament what they had been unable to obtain by other means, and in readiness for the 1587 session John Field drew up a survey of clergy in and around London. This

KEY TERM:

Presbyterianism

This was a non-episcopal system of Church government pioneered by John Calvin and established at Geneva. Pastors or ministers elected by the congregation were to concentrate on preaching and administering the sacraments. Discipline was to be the responsibility of elected presbyters or elders. An English version of this system was provided by Thomas Cartwright and Walter Travers in their *Book of Discipline* published in 1586. The basic unit, or presbytery, consisted of a minister and elders. Representatives from a number of presbyteries constituted a 'classis', and the 'classes' would, in turn, send delegates to provincial synods. From these would be chosen the members of a national synod which would act as the ultimate governor of the Presbyterian Church.

PROFILE: *John Whitgift*

Born at Grimsby in Lincolnshire about 1530, **John Whitgift** took holy orders after the accession of Elizabeth, and became Professor of Divinity in the University of Cambridge. While a Calvinist in his religious beliefs, he rejected **Presbyterianism** and engineered the expulsion of Cartwright for advocating it. In a vigorous pamphlet campaign against both Cartwright and Field he stoutly defended the existing structure and government of the Church of England. In 1577 he was appointed Bishop of Worcester, and in 1583, Archbishop of Canterbury. He made it his principal task to enforce discipline and conformity in the Church, using the Court of High Commission as his principal instrument. This aroused considerable criticism, but Whitgift, who was appointed to the Privy Council in 1586, always retained the support of the Queen, since his views on Church government were so close to her own. He died not long after Elizabeth, in February 1604.

revealed a large number of non-resident 'pluralists' (*i.e.* ministers holding more than one living) as well as low standards of learning and morality. Field's survey was not, of course, impartial, but it was close enough to the truth to provide ammunition for the Church's critics. It was against this background that in February 1587 Anthony Cope introduced a bill into the Commons designed to sweep away the existing episcopal government of the established Church and to replace the Prayer Book with the Geneva form of service.

The Speaker, knowing what the Queen would think of Cope's bill, tried to block discussion of it. But this brought the radical Peter Wentworth to his feet to insist that the House was free to discuss whatever it thought fit. Elizabeth responded by sending Cope and Wentworth to the Tower and ordering the Speaker to block discussion of any topic that fell within her sphere as supreme governor of the Church.

The Puritans had, for the time being, reached the end of the road. 1588 saw the death of Field and of Elizabeth's favourite, the Earl of Leicester, who had been the patron and protector of Cartwright and other prominent puritans. Public opinion was now swinging away from the Puritans – or at least from the Presbyterians. This was shown when, in 1593, Parliament passed an act outlawing 'the wicked and dangerous practices of seditious sectaries'. Under its provisions, any person refusing to attend his parish church or participating in a puritan service was to go into exile. If he returned without permission he was guilty of a felony and liable to be hanged.

The Elizabethan Church of England

We have been looking closely at the attitude of the puritan critics of the established Church, but this can give a misleading impression, for three reasons:

1 Presbyterians and radical puritans were always a minority, even among ministers.

2 While the Church may have begun as a compromise which satisfied nobody, it struck deep roots as the reign went on.

3 Elizabeth was on the throne for more than 40 years, during which time the Church of England underwent a process of steady improvement.

In its early days the Elizabethan Church had been so short of clergy that it had ordained men who had little or no educational qualification. But as the reign progressed, so Oxford and Cambridge turned out an increasing number of graduate clergy who took their place in the parishes. An educated ministry was of key importance to the new Church, since Protestantism was based on Bible knowledge rather than forms and ceremonies. It was a 'religion of the word', and understanding of the Word of God demanded learning and application. By the time Elizabeth died, not only were many of her clergy graduates, but also many of her lay subjects, particularly the wealthier ones, possessed their own copies of the Bible and often other religious works with a Protestant bias.

The effects of all these changes are summed up by Christopher Haigh:

'In the 1580s England was fast becoming a Protestant nation. The religious rhetoric of its leaders was Protestant, as was the public tone of its ruling order. Convinced Protestants dominated Court and parliament, and controlled the government of the Church. The administration of the law, by judges, lawyers and Justices of the Peace, was not yet exclusively Protestant; but in many parts of the country there were vigorous Protestant magistrates who backed Protestant preaching and demanded Protestant social discipline. The parish clergy included ... more and more educated evangelists, men who preached a Reformed gospel and expected informed commitment from their congregations ... It now, and only now, becomes appropriate to identify a true Protestant Reformation: now "Protestant" because it involved real changes in personal belief, not merely shifts in ecclesiastical policy.'

Christopher Haigh, *English Reformations: Religion, Politics and Society under the Tudors* (1993).

Task: class discussion

This topic is often difficult to come to terms with because of confusion over who exactly the Puritans were, and what they wanted. These discussion points are intended to help you talk through these problems.

1 Look at the wording of the *Book of Advertisements*, and also at the arguments over 'prophesyings'. How did the Queen see the role of **a** the clergy and **b** the laity in the Church?

2 In what ways did the puritans challenge Elizabeth's view of her role and prerogative (for 'prerogative' see chapter 14)?

3 a Look at the four points of dispute on the opening page of this chapter. What were the Puritans' objectives in each case?
  b How far, by the end of Elizabeth's reign, had the Puritans succeeded in achieving their objectives?

Further reading

Patrick Collinson, *English Puritanism*, Pamphlet G.106 (Historical Association, 1983) – an introduction to this complex topic by the acknowledged expert. See the same author's *The Religion of Protestants: The Church in English Society 1559–1625* (Clarendon Press, 1982) – a survey of the established Church; *The Birthpangs of Protestant England: Religious and Cultural Change in the Sixteenth and Seventeenth Centuries* (Macmillan, 1989) – a collection of essays; particularly enlightening on the role of towns.

Christopher Haigh, *English Reformations: Religion, Politics and Society under the Tudors* (Clarendon Press, 1993).

Diarmaid MacCulloch, *The Later Reformation in England 1547–1603* (Macmillan, 1990) – a brilliant brief account. See the same author's *Building a Godly Realm. The Establishment of English Protestantism 1558–1603*, New Appreciations in History No. 27 (Historical Association, 1992).

J. J. Scarisbrick, *The Reformation and the English People* (Blackwell, 1984) – emphasises that the Protestant triumph was not inevitable.

27 What became of English Catholicism?

Time chart

1559: Acts of Supremacy and Uniformity establish Protestant Church in England

1569: Rebellion of the Northern Earls

1570: Papal bull of excommunication against Elizabeth

1571: Act against bringing in papal bulls

1574: First seminary priests arrive in England

1580: Jesuits arrive in England to join Catholic mission

1581: Act to retain queen's subjects in due obedience

1585: Act against Jesuits and seminary priests

1593: Act against popish recusants

One of the ways in which our interpretation of the English Reformation has changed over recent years is in giving much greater prominence to the Catholics. It used to be taken more or less for granted that English Catholicism was doomed and the triumph of Protestantism inevitable. But the revaluation of the Catholic revival under Mary suggests something quite different – namely, that only the sudden and early death of both Mary and Cardinal Pole prevented Catholicism taking root once again. In 1558 Elizabeth became queen of what was in effect a Catholic nation, and this accounts in part for the cautious nature of the Elizabethan religious settlement. Yet 40 years later England was undoubtedly Protestant and the Catholics had shrunk to a tiny minority. In this chapter we shall consider how and why this came about.

Getting over the shock

The sudden change of monarch, and therefore of religious orientation, left the Catholics at sea. Their natural leaders were the bishops, but these had failed in their attempt to prevent the passage of the Acts of Supremacy and Uniformity and they subsequently resigned – with the single exception of the Bishop of Llandaff. Many holders of lesser offices also left the Church, but only some 300 parish clergy – about 5 per cent.

Priests who had left or been deprived of their livings frequently continued to say Mass in private houses and thereby keep the old faith alive. In parts of England, the north-west in particular, they were aided by parish priests who had come to terms with the new regime but were in no sense Protestant. The services laid down in the Elizabethan Prayer Book – as the Puritans constantly complained – showed evident traces of their Catholic ancestry, and were not, therefore, totally unacceptable to those who clung to the old forms.

In general, Catholic laity continued going to church. For one thing, the church was the centre of the life of the parish, and gentlemen had a social obligation to appear there. And for another, it seemed short-sighted to retreat into isolation when nobody knew how long the new religious settlement would last. The Tudors were not a long-lived dynasty, and there was no reason to assume that Elizabeth would reign for as long as she did. If the Queen died, the Elizabethan settlement would die with her, and nobody could be sure what would happen after that.

When Catholics argued along these lines in order to justify their outward conformity, they were not indulging in wishful thinking. Protestants also were aware of the possibility of the Queen's death and what might follow it. Hence the parliamentary pressure for her to marry, or at least name a successor. As the Commons' petition of January 1563 put it:

'We fear a faction of heretics in your realm, contentious and malicious Papists . . . most unnaturally against their country, most madly against their own safety, and most treacherously against your Highness, not only hope for the woeful day of your death, but also lay in wait to advance some title under which they may revive their late unspeakable cruelty . . . We see nothing to withstand their desire but your only life.'

The Bull of Excommunication

There were too many Catholics, including nobles and gentry, for the government to attempt to coerce them. Instead it resorted to a policy of benign neglect, hoping that as the years passed the majority of Catholics would come to accept the Church of England. This policy might have worked if it had been given time. The Papacy shared the fear that English Catholicism would die out unless steps were taken to revive it. In particular, it accepted the need to give guidance to Catholics. Were they to put their loyalty to Elizabeth before their commitment to the international Catholic Church? Were they to continue conforming, or should they stand aloof from the Church of England and the community ties and obligations that went with it?

These questions acquired a sudden urgency with the outbreak of the Northern Rebellion in 1569. Many Catholics in the North supported this and welcomed the fact that after the rebel army occupied Durham, Mass was celebrated once again in the cathedral. But there was no general rising of Catholics against the Queen's government. Loyalty to Elizabeth, abhorrence of rebellion, fears for personal safety – all these were factors determining the Catholics' attitude. Another, highly important, factor was uncertainty: how should English Catholics behave when there was an apparent conflict between their secular and religious commitments?

The answer – or at least an answer – to this question was given in 1570 when Pope Pius V issued the bull *Regnans in Excelsis*.

'He that reigneth on high, to whom is given all power in heaven and earth, has committed one holy Catholic and apostolic Church, outside of which there is no salvation, to one alone upon earth, namely to Peter, the first of the apostles, and to Peter's successor, the pope of Rome, to be by him governed in fullness of power ... Therefore, resting upon the authority of Him whose pleasure it was to place us (though unequal to such a burden) upon this supreme justice-seat, we do out of the fullness of our apostolic power declare [Queen] Elizabeth to be a heretic and favourer of heretics, and ... to have incurred the sentence of excommunication and to be cut off from the unity of the body of Christ.

'And moreover [we declare] her to be deprived of her pretended title to the aforesaid crown ... and also [declare] the nobles, subjects and people of the said realm, and all others who have in any way sworn oaths to her, to be forever absolved from such an oath ... We charge and command all and singular the nobles, subjects, peoples and others aforesaid that they do not dare obey her orders, mandates and laws. Those who shall act to the contrary we include in the like sentence of excommunication.'

This bull, coming as it did immediately after the Northern Rebellion (the first serious challenge to the Elizabethan regime) alarmed the government since it implied that all Catholics were potential traitors. The official response came with the 1571 Act 'against the bringing in and putting in execution of bulls and other instruments from the see of Rome'. At the same time Elizabeth informed Parliament that as long as Catholics observed her laws and did not 'wilfully and manifestly break them by their open acts, her Majesty's meaning is not to have any of them molested by an inquisition or examination of their consciences in causes of religion'.

The seminary priests

Elizabeth was still hoping that English Catholicism would gradually die out. This was indeed likely, for the simple reason that as time passed the number of Catholic priests would diminish. Catholics were dependent upon properly consecrated priests for saying Mass and administering the sacraments, for these were functions beyond the capacity of any lay person. Where there were no priests there was no Mass; and where there was no Mass there was no Catholicism.

KEY TERM:

Jesuits

One of the ways in which the Roman Catholic Church and the Papacy responded to the challenge thrown down by the Protestant reformers was through the formation of new religious orders – groups of men and women who put themselves under a strict discipline so that they could combat heresy and spread what they believed to be the true faith. One of the most successful of these new orders was the Society of Jesus, founded by the Spaniard, Ignatius Loyola, in 1540. Initially designed for missionary activities in Asia and America, the **Jesuits** – as the members of the Society were known – also worked to turn back the Protestant tide in those parts of Europe which had been lost to Catholicism.

William Allen was not thinking in terms of sending missionaries to England when he first set up his seminary at Douai. He assumed that in God's good time England would return to the Catholic fold. But the young men who came over from England were not prepared to wait. They had seen what was happening at home and feared that unless immediate action was taken to revive the Catholic priesthood there, England would become irrevocably Protestant. It was this sense of urgency that transformed the college in Douai into a centre of missionary activity. The first seminary priests from Douai landed in England in 1574, and by 1580 about a hundred were at work there. Some indication of their impact comes in a report from the Bishop of London in 1577 that 'the papists marvellously increase both in numbers and in obstinate withdrawal of themselves from the Church and services of God'.

The English mission

The English college at Rome had passed under the control of the **Jesuits**, and at Allen's suggestion they now turned their attention closer to home. In 1580 the first Jesuit missionaries, Robert Parsons and Edmund

KEY TERM:

Recusants

In the early years of Elizabeth's reign many Catholics continued to attend their local parish churches despite the fact that the 1559 Prayer Book prescribed Protestant services. They did so partly out of a sense of social obligation, and partly because they hoped that the Protestant interlude would be short lived. But the Catholic missionaries encouraged English Catholics to stand firm in the old faith and refuse to attend the new services. Since the Latin word for 'refuse' is *recusare*, those who now stayed away from church became known as **recusants**. Their fellow Catholics who continued to attend were called 'church papists'.

Campion, arrived secretly in England. Though always fewer in number than the seminary priests, the Jesuits played a key role in organising the mission. By the late 1580s Henry Garnet was moving around the country, knitting the Catholic outposts together, while his fellow Jesuit, Robert Southwell, remained in London to welcome and shelter new arrivals. In 1596 Garnet described how:

> *'When the priests first arrive from the seminaries we give them every help we can. The greater part of them, as opportunity offers, we place in fixed residences. This is done in a very large number of families, through our offices. The result now is that many persons who saw a seminary priest hardly once a year now have one all the time, and most eagerly welcome any others, no matter where they come from.'*

Persecution

As the seminary priests and Jesuits moved secretly from one Catholic household to another they created a sense of Catholic identity that had earlier been lacking. They also encouraged Catholics to refuse to attend Anglican services, and as a consequence the number of **recusants** increased substantially. This alarmed the government because it put an end to hopes that English Catholicism would quietly wither away. Another cause for alarm came from the deterioration of relations with Spain, because Philip II had made himself the secular champion of Catholicism. Could English Catholics be relied upon to remain loyal to their queen and country if the Pope and the King of Spain called on them to rise up against her? Some members of the government, and many members of Parliament, felt that the answer to this question was No.

In 1581 Parliament responded to what it saw as the Catholic threat by raising the fine for recusancy from one shilling per week to £20 a month. This was a huge increase and threatened financial ruin for those who still refused to conform. The 1581 Act also laid down that:

> *'all persons whatsoever which ... practise to absolve, persuade or withdraw any of the Queen's Majesty's subjects ... from their natural obedience to her Majesty, or to withdraw them for that intent from the religion now by her Highness' authority established ... shall be to all intents adjudged to be traitors and ... shall have judgement, suffer and forfeit as in case of high treason.'*

This was no mean threat, since the penalty for treason was a painful and lingering death by hanging, drawing and quartering. Four years later, in 1585, came a further Act, this time aimed against 'Jesuits, seminary priests and such other like disobedient persons'. They were accused of working not only 'to withdraw her Highness' subjects from their due obedience to her Majesty, but also to stir up and move sedition, rebellion and open hostility within her Highness' realms and dominions, to the great dangering of the safety of her most royal person and to the utter ruin, desolation and overthrow of the whole realm.'

Jesuits and seminary priests were now forbidden to enter or remain in England. If they did so, they would be liable to execution as traitors, while those who sheltered them would risk being put to death as felons. It was also made an offence to send children abroad without royal licence or to provide funds 'for the maintenance or relief of any college of Jesuits or seminary ... in any foreign parts'. The first seminary priest to be executed was Cuthbert Mayne, in 1577. A second execution took place in the following year, and by 1585 27 priests and 8 laymen had been put to death. Thereafter repression intensified. Between 1586 and 1592, 69 priests were executed and 28 laity.

Was the English mission successful?

No one can doubt the courage of the missionary priests nor of the Catholic lay men and women who provided shelter for them. But Christopher Haigh, in particular, has argued that the resources of the mission were too narrowly focused. Catholicism had been a genuinely popular faith in Lancashire and other parts of the North and West, but the missionaries concentrated their attention on the relatively barren soil of the South and East.

This was partly for geographical reasons: Essex and Kent provided easy access from the Continent, and were close to London, the operating centre of the mission. Also, gentry houses were thick on the ground in the southern counties but diminished in number as the distance from London increased. There was little alternative to reliance on the Catholic gentry, because they provided not only the 'safe houses' for the priests but also the funding without which the mission could not have functioned. In general, the seminary priests, like the Jesuits, were recruited from the upper sections of English society and were therefore more at ease with their fellow gentry than they would have been with, say, Catholic villagers. They could also argue, with reason, that the gentry and nobles were key figures not simply at local but also at national level. If they were won for Catholicism it would not be long before the rest of society followed suit.

For a variety of reasons, then, the English mission was narrowed down in practice to the Catholic gentry of the South and East. There were priests at work among ordinary people in the North, but they were few in number and distinctly lacking in glamour. As a consequence, popular Catholicism gradually died out. The English Catholic community came to be defined in terms of its gentry adherents and the hard core of recusants. By the time Elizabeth died, this community probably numbered no more than 40,000, or 1 per cent of the population. In less than half a century the Catholics in England had declined from a mainstream majority into a relatively insignificant sect.

Task: essay-writing

'Account for the nature of the threat the English Catholics represented to the Elizabethan state.'

(See suggestions for essay-writing at the end of chapters 10 and 21.)

Hints: Do not write a narrative account, but plan the essay in topics. Deal with the topics in chronological order, where possible. Each topic does not necessarily need a separate paragraph – this depends on its length, and on whether it can be suitably combined with another. The following topics could be brought into this essay:

- Elizabeth's headship of the church
- the need for conformity in religion
- the North of England – the northern earls
- Mary, Queen of Scots
- the Pope and the Counter-Reformation
- the growing threat from Spain
- Ireland
- the seminary priests – agents of a foreign power?
- the English government's reaction

Apart from this chapter, you may find useful chapters 17, 23, 25 and 32 and the suggestions for further reading that they contain.

Further reading

John Bossy, *The English Catholic Community 1570–1850* (Darton, Longman and Todd, 1976).

Alan Dures, *English Catholicism 1558–1642*, Seminar Studies in History (Addison Wesley Longman, 1983) – the best brief account of the topic.

Christopher Haigh, 'The Continuity of Catholicism in the English Reformation' in his collection of essays, *The English Reformation Revised* (Cambridge University Press, 1987). See the same author's 'From Monopoly to Minority: Catholicism in Early Modern England' in *Transactions of the Royal Historical Society* vol. 31 (1981) – these present the revisionist view.

Part Three Culture, society and the economy

28 Poverty and vagrancy

Time chart

1495: Act against vagabonds and beggars

1531: Act concerning punishment of beggars and vagabonds

1535: Act for punishment of sturdy vagabonds and beggars

1547: Act for punishment of vagabonds and for relief of poor and impotent persons

1563: Act for relief of the poor
Act of artificers and apprentices

1572: Act for punishment of vagabonds and relief of the poor and impotent

1576: Act for setting the poor on work and for avoiding of idleness

1598: Act for relief of the poor
Act for punishment of rogues, vagabonds and sturdy beggars
Act for erecting hospitals or abiding and working houses for the poor

1601: Act for relief of the poor

Poverty and vagrancy in the sixteenth century were cause and effect. Men and women who could find no means of livelihood in the places where they had been born or were resident took to the roads. The authorities, both central and local, were alarmed by this phenomenon, because the hierarchical Tudor society was based upon the assumption that people knew their own place – both socially and geographically – and stayed there. Vagabondage was a powerful solvent that threatened to dissolve the slender bonds that held society together. Hence the need to find ways to combat and control it.

The causes of poverty

There was nothing new about poverty, and increasing evidence of it in the Tudor period may be due as much to the invention of printing – which has left a great deal of written material for historians to analyse – as to changes in society and the economy. But other factors can be identified.

Population increase

When Henry VII came to the throne there were some 2 million people living in England and Wales, but by the time Elizabeth died this figure had doubled to 4 million. Tudor England was still mainly an agricultural society, and since the amount of land available could not be increased significantly there were few opportunities for new jobs. In fact, the demand for cloth had led many landowners to switch from arable to sheep farming, which employed fewer men, and there were widespread complaints that labourers' houses and sometimes whole villages had been pulled down and their inhabitants evicted.

Landowners would often enclose their fields with hedges, to keep their sheep from straying, but this would limit the grazing space for the rest of the villagers (see chapter 29). Communal rights were also threatened when landowners increased the number of sheep and cattle they pastured on the common fields. Not only did this squeeze out the live-stock of lesser men; it also led to the eviction of 'squatters' – the poorest members of the community who had built their hovels there.

Discharged soldiers and sailors

The restoration of law and order under the Tudors meant that there were fewer employment opportunities for soldiers or for liveried retainers. Although the Tudor monarchs were from time to time engaged in war – against France, Scotland and Spain – they never attempted to create a permanent army. Soldiers were raised for a campaign and disbanded once it was over. The navy was on a more permanent footing, but even so it made little provision for its sick and wounded, other than licensing them to beg.

The cloth trade

The most important industry in England was the production of woollen cloth (see chapter 30). Evidence of the great wealth of the clothiers – the men who organised the making and marketing of cloth – is to be seen in villages such as Lavenham in Suffolk and small towns like Bradford-on-Avon in Wiltshire. The prosperity of the cloth merchants was in sharp contrast to the precarious condition of the men, women and children who spent long hours spinning and weaving the raw material, usually at home. As long as the trade flourished they could be sure of an income, but the sixteenth century saw periods of boom followed by slumps in which textile workers were laid off. One contemporary recorded how:

'infinite numbers of spinners, carders [and] pickers of wool are turned to begging, with no small store of poor children who, driven with necessity (that hath no law), both come idly about to beg, to the oppression of the poor husbandmen, and rob their hedges of linen, steal pig, goose and capon ... steal fruit and corn in the harvest time, and rob barns in the winter time.'

Inflation

See chapter 16. Because of inflation, many wage-earners found that the money they were paid was not enough to live on. Labourers' wages were worth only half as much at the end of the sixteenth century as they had been at the beginning. Their situation became particularly bad when, as in the mid 1540s and late 1590s, the harvest failed for several years in succession. This drove up the cost of basic foodstuffs beyond the level they could afford. Shortage of food, if not actual starvation, was responsible for the high death toll at such times.

Poor relief

Charity

There was a well-established tradition of charitable bequests in England, particularly among the merchant communities in the major towns. Before the Reformation much of this charity had been directed towards the Church, but subsequently the bulk of it went to the relief of poverty. It seems unlikely that merchants were, by nature, more charitably inclined than other sections of society, yet they were responsible for some 60 per cent of sixteenth-century philanthropy. Perhaps they had uneasy consciences, for money-making and the acquisition of material goods tended to be condemned by the Church, both before and after the Reformation. No doubt they also valued the maintenance of good order, for trade cannot flourish where there is civil unrest, and acute poverty was a known cause of disturbances.

In his pioneering study, *Philanthropy in England* (published in 1959), W. K. Jordan produced figures which apparently proved that merchant charity was far more important than the actions of local and central government in relieving poverty. However, he neglected to take account of inflation, and subsequent revision of his statistics in order to do so produces a somewhat different picture. Even so, charitable giving by merchants was clearly of great significance, not simply for the immediate relief of poverty but also for the provision of funds with which unemployed or debt-ridden artisans could set themselves up in business on a sound financial basis. Helping the poor to help themselves was an ideal calculated to appeal to merchants, who were often self-made men (or liked to believe they were). The social historian, John Pound, describes their achievement in these words:

> *'The merchants were virtual pioneers in the field of social rehabilitation ... In the middle years of the [sixteenth] century they provided three-quarters of the funds, and during Elizabeth's reign their share rose to just under 87 per cent. In the process they made available six times as much capital as they had done during the years 1541 to 1560, a significant increase even when full allowance has been made for inflation ... By any standards, their contribution was impressive and a worthwhile and important supplement to their interest in poor relief.'*
>
> John Pound, *Poverty and Vagrancy in Tudor England* (1986).

Although merchants as a group were far and away the major philanthropists of Tudor England, the charitable impulse was not confined to them. At all levels of society we can find men and women, often themselves of limited means, making contributions towards the relief of poverty. Without this substantial and continuous private giving, the lot of the poor would have been a good deal worse.

Local initiatives

Many of those who were driven by poverty to quit their place of residence and take to the roads made their way to London and other major towns. This was particularly the case after the dislocation caused by the mid-Tudor crisis (see chapter 13). The immediate reaction of the urban authorities was to try to keep out the unwelcome newcomers. Vagabonds were whipped, and sometimes branded, before being sent back to their native parishes (see Figure 28.1).

Such measures were difficult to enforce, however, and they did not solve the problem of poor townspeople. By the time Elizabeth came to the throne many towns had built up corn stocks at the public expense to feed those who were too poor to feed themselves. They also started surveys of the poor, and licensed those whom they permitted to beg. Sometimes they took over medieval hospital buildings and used them to house the poor. In London, St Bartholomew's and St Thomas's were turned into hostels for the 'impotent' poor – that is, those who, because of age or illness, were incapable of fending for themselves. 'Sturdy beggars' who were deemed to be capable of work were set to hard labour in the

Figure 28.1 A beggar being
whipped

Bridewell. Similar measures were taken in other towns, such as Norwich, Ipswich and York.

Poor relief of this sort inevitably costs money. The authorities at first relied on the citizens' charity, with house-to-house collections. However, as the scale of the problem increased so did the need for greater funding, and in 1547 London led the way in instituting a compulsory poor rate.

Early Tudor governments and the poor

Poor relief did not come high on the agenda of Tudor governments, but they were forced to take action at times of crisis. One such was in the late 1520s, when the interruption of the cloth trade with the Netherlands, brought about for political reasons, aroused fears of unemployment and consequent unrest. The government responded with the Act of 1531, which drew a distinction between 'aged, poor and impotent persons' who were unfit to work and were therefore to be licensed to beg, and 'persons being whole and mighty in body and able to labour'. Anyone who fell into the second category was to be: 'tied to the end of a cart, naked, and be beaten with whips ... till his body be bloody by reason of such whipping, and after ... shall be enjoined upon his oath to return forthwith without delay ... to the place where he was born, or where he last dwelled ... and there put himself to labour like as a true man oweth to do.'

The weakness of the 1531 Act derived from the erroneous assumption that work was readily available for all those who wanted it. The circle of humanists around Thomas Cromwell recognised the need to provide work at public expense. They drew up an Act to bring this about, but opposition from the majority of landowners in the 1536 Parliament led to it being watered down.

The hard-line attitude of Members of Parliament was demonstrated even more clearly in the crisis years of the mid-century. The danger of political unrest following the accession of the boy-king Edward VI in 1547, and fear that bands of vagabonds might become involved in insurrection, led to the notorious 1547 Act which prescribed that vagabonds were to be branded and enslaved for two years. If they subsequently attempted to escape from their masters, they were to be enslaved for life or executed.

This Act was counter-productive, for the savagery of its provisions made it unacceptable to the JPs and others who would have had to implement it. It was repealed in 1550, and there is no evidence that it was ever put into effect.

The Elizabethan poor law

When Elizabeth came to the throne in 1558, the money required for poor relief was still being raised by voluntary subscriptions, except in places like London, Norwich and Ipswich where compulsion had been introduced. It was the effectiveness of these local measures that persuaded the government to follow suit in 1563 with an Act requiring all local authorities to appoint special collectors of alms. These were to:

'gently ask and demand of every man and woman what they of their charity will be contented to give weekly towards the relief of the poor. [Those refusing to contribute were to be brought before the bishop or JPs, who] shall have authority ... to commit the said obstinate person to prison ... [and] to cess, tax and limit upon every such obstinate person so refusing, according to their good discretions, what sum the said obstinate person shall pay.'

In practice, Elizabethan governments were not powerful enough to create the highly regulated society envisaged in the **Statute of Artificers**, and nothing of this sort was ever attempted again. In the disturbed period following the rebellion of the northern earls in late 1569 the government resorted to more traditional remedies. The 1572 Act made provision for the punishment of 'rogues, vagabonds and sturdy beggars' who were accused of being responsible for 'horrible murders, thefts and other great

KEY TERM:

Statute of Artificers

Passed in 1563, the **Statute of Artificers and Apprentices,** was part of the government's attempt to deal with poverty and vagrancy. All males between the ages of 12 and 60 below the rank of gentleman (see key term definition, page 75) were placed under a legal obligation to find employment and not to move from it without permission. In a further attempt to control the market, maximum wages were to be set by JPs in every locality, and it was made an offence to pay more than they prescribed.

outrages'. They were to be 'grievously whipped and burnt through the gristle of the right ear with a hot iron'. Repetition of the offence of vagrancy was defined as a felony, which rendered the offender liable to the death penalty.

A more constructive approach, once again modelled on local initiatives, was taken by the 1576 Act 'for the setting of the poor on work, and for the avoiding of idleness'. Town corporations were required to supply the poor with raw materials to keep them profitably employed. Every county was instructed to set up 'houses of correction' where sturdy beggars could be set to work. The government actively encouraged local communities to lay in corn stocks to provide for the poor when harvests failed. In many places such measures had already been taken, but the period from the mid 1560s to the mid 1590s was one of relative prosperity, with generally good harvests. Disaster struck in 1594 with four successive harvest failures. The price of grain rose so high that there were food riots in many areas. A Somerset JP, Edward Hext, wrote to Lord Burghley to warn him that the situation was getting out of hand:

> '*I do not see how it is possible for the poor countryman to bear the burthens ... laid upon him ... There be [some] that stick not to say boldly they must not starve, they will not starve. And this year there assembled 80 in a company and took a whole cartload of cheese from one driving it to a fair, and dispersed it amongst them ... which may grow dangerous by the aid of such numbers as are abroad, especially in this time of dearth [i.e. scarcity].*'

It was against this background that the government brought in the Act of 1598, confirmed with slight modifications in 1601, which gave final shape to the Tudor poor law. It ordered every parish to appoint 'overseers of the poor', with power to raise:

> '*... by taxation of every inhabitant and every occupier of lands in the said parish ... a convenient stock of flax, hemp, wool, thread, iron and other stuff to set the poor on work, and also competent sums of money for the necessary relief of the lame, impotent, old, blind and such other among them being poor and not able to work ... And to the intent that necessary places of habitation may more conveniently be provided for such poor impotent people ... it shall be lawful ... to erect ... at the general charges of the parish ... convenient houses of dwelling for the said impotent poor ...*'

While the community as a whole accepted the responsibility for relieving the poverty of those who could not fend for themselves, no such charity was applied to 'rogues, vagabonds and sturdy beggars'. There was a widespread fear of robber bands, making the roads unsafe and terrorising the countryside. Edward Hext told Burghley that:

> *'of these sort of wandering idle people there are three or four hundred in a shire, and though they go by two or three in a company, yet all or the most part in a shire do meet either at fair or market, or in some alehouse, once a week … And they grow the more dangerous in that they find they have bred that fear in Justices [of the Peace] and other inferior officers that no man dares to call them into question.'*

There is some evidence that organised bands of vagrants were in operation in certain areas at certain times, but the fear they generated was out of all proportion to their numbers. Elizabethan governments were concerned with social control and therefore wanted to limit mobility, particularly among the lower levels of society. Hence the harshness with which they responded to the problem of vagrancy. Under the terms of the 1598 Act anyone convicted of this offence was to be whipped and then returned to the parish where he or she had been born, with a possible ultimate threat of banishment from the realm.

Was poor relief effective?

By the time Elizabeth died, a coherent system of poor relief had been established and was to remain in effect for more than 200 years. But while private charitable giving went on all the time, intervention by central government – or even by local authorities – tended to be sporadic. At times of political unrest, when the need to maintain law and order became imperative, the governors of Tudor England were galvanised into action. The same was true of periods of harvest failure, for as Edward Hext's letter shows, starving men and women might well be driven into acts of violence that threatened social stability. Most people most of the time were prepared to accept the hierarchical structure of the society in which they lived, because the benefits they derived from it – however small in our eyes – were better than nothing. But starvation was worse than nothing. Hence the recognition by those at the top of Tudor society that it was in their own best interest to make sure that the poor did not starve and that the worst symptoms of poverty were alleviated. However, their readiness to intervene was generally confined to brief periods of crisis. For most of the time they intervened as little as possible.

In short, by the second half of the sixteenth century the 'impotent poor' were reasonably cared for by a combination of public and private charity. The rest, except when disaster threatened, were generally left to fend for themselves. Tudor England was a long way from being a welfare state.

Task: examination-style source questions

We end this chapter with some examination-type questions on sources. Before you tackle them, re-read the suggestions on how such questions might be approached which you will find at the end of chapter 3. As with the questions there, and at the end of chapter 17, remember to:

■ Read the document carefully first, working out the meaning of all the words.
■ Look at the provenance of each source – in this instance, note that documents 2 and 3 are fictional.
■ Note the number of marks available and tailor the length of your answer accordingly.
■ Make sure you are clear what each question is looking for.

Note that question **c** expects you to use your own knowledge.

Hints on answering the questions here:

1 Question **a** is testing the skill of comprehension. It is really asking how well you understand document 1.

2 Question **b** is quite different, and more demanding. The words 'compare and contrast' ask you to look at all three documents and show the similarities and differences between them. However, you are not asked here about the content but about 'tone and use of language'. How are the attitudes of the three authors reflected in the kind of words they use? You should give several examples of the points you make, either by quoting from the text, or by giving the line references.

3 Question **c** makes two statements about the problem and asks you to comment on them, using information from the documents, as well as other points which you already knew. It is really asking for a mini-essay, so your answer should be reasonably long, will probably be divided into paragraphs, and ought to reach a specific conclusion directed at the question.

Examination question:
The problem of beggars and vagrants in Tudor England

Read the following documents, and then answer questions **a** to **c** which follow.

Document 1

A Declaration of the Citizens of London to the Privy Council (1552)

'And first, may it please your honors to understand, that it was too evident to all men that beggary and thievery did abound. And we remembering how many statutes from time to time have been made for the redress of the same, and little amendment hath hitherto followed, thought to search the cause hereof, and after due examination had, we evidently perceived that the cause of all this misery and beggary was idleness: and the means and remedy to cure the same must be by its contrary, which is labour. And it hath been a speech used by all men, to say unto the idle, work! work! even as though they would have said, the means to reform beggary is to fall to work.

'And we considered also that the greatest number of beggars fallen into misery by lewd and evil service, by wars, by sickness, or other adverse fortune, have so utterly lost their credit, that though they would shew themselves willing to labour, yet are they so suspected and feared of all men, that few or none dare, or will receive them to work: wherefore we saw that there could be no means to amend this miserable sort, but by making some general provision of work, wherewith the willing poor may be exercised; and whereby the froward, strong and sturdy vagabond may be compelled to live profitably to the commonwealth.'

Document 2

Utopia, by Thomas More (1516)

'... make a law that they which plucked down farms and towns of husbandry shall re-edify them, or else yield and uprender the possession thereof to such as will go to the cost of building them anew. Suffer not these rich men to buy up all to engross and forestall, and with their monopoly to keep the market alone as please them. Let not so many be brought up in idleness; let husbandry and tillage be restored; let clothworking be renewed, that there may be honest labours for this idle sort to pass their time in profitably, which hitherto either poverty hath caused to be thieves, or else now be either vagabonds or idle serving men, and shortly will be thieves.'

Document 3

'Alms Houses', a poem by Rev. Robert Crowley (1550)

A Merchant, that long time had been in strange lands,
Returned to his country which in Europe stands,
And in his return, his way lay to pass
By a Spittlehouse, not far from where his dwelling was.
He looked for this hospital, but none could he see;
For a lordly house was built where the hospital should be.
Then, by the wayside, him chanced to see
A poor man that craved of him for charity.
Why (said this Merchant) what meaneth this thing?
Do ye beg by the way, and have a house for a king?
Alas! sir (said the poor man) we are all turned out,
And lie and die in corners, here and there about.
Men of great riches have bought our dwelling place,
And when we crave of them, they turn away their face.
Lord God (said this Merchant) in Turkey have I been,
Yet among the heathen none such cruelty have I seen.
The vengeance of God must fall, no remedy,
Upon these wicked men, and that very shortly.

Questions

a Look at Document 1. What, according to this extract, were the reasons for 'beggary'?

4 marks

b Look at all three documents. Compare and contrast the tone and use of language in these extracts, suggesting words or phrases which best indicate the attitude of the respective authors towards beggars and vagabonds.

7 marks

c 'The problem of beggars and vagrancy in Tudor England was both long-term and caused by factors largely outside the control of beggars and vagrants themselves.' Using the evidence of these documents, as well as your own knowledge, comment on the appropriateness of this judgement.

9 marks

Further reading

A. L. Beier, *The Problem of the Poor in Tudor and Stuart England*, Lancaster Pamphlets (Routledge, 1983).

A. L. Beier, *Masterless Men. The Vagrancy Problem in England 1560–1640* (Methuen, 1985) – the best single-volume survey.

Clark, Peter and Paul Slack (eds), *Crisis and Order in English Towns 1500–1700* (Routledge, 1972).

John Pound, *Poverty and Vagrancy in Tudor England*, Seminar Studies in History (Addison Wesley Longman, 2nd edition, 1986).

29 Why was enclosure seen as a problem?

Agriculture was by far the most crucial economic activity in Tudor England, and the fluctuating quality of annual harvests has been described by D. M. Palliser in *The Age of Elizabeth* as the heartbeat of the economy. The vast majority of the working population was employed on the land, and even those who were not farmers often used the products of farming, such as wool or leather, in their industry.

However, it is difficult to generalise about methods and changes in agriculture because of the wide variations between different parts of the country. It is possible to make a three-fold classification of types of region, so long as one remembers that there was much variation within regions. The highland zone was north and west of a line drawn between the Tees estuary and Weymouth on the south coast. Here, open pasture was the norm and the emphasis was on the raising of sheep or cattle. The lowland zone, to the south and east of this line, can be divided into regions of 'wood pasture', where woodland, meadow and pasture predominated, and regions of 'mixed farming', where there was a combination of arable and animal husbandry. Figure 29.1 shows these three categories.

The open field system

The regions of mixed farming, and in particular the Midlands, were where the open field, or champion, method was practised. This was a system suited for subsistence, rather than commercial, farming. It was relatively democratic, in that arable, meadow and pasture were distributed among the community. Usually, the villagers lived centrally, surrounded by the open fields as well as by the common or waste land belonging to the village. Two, three or more large fields were divided into patches, or 'furlongs', which were in turn divided into unfenced strips, and each strip allocated to a member of the community. These were often, though not always, farmed according to an annual three-field rotation, whereby one field was sown with spring corn, one with autumn corn, and one left fallow. Meadow land was also divided into strips, and after the hay harvest it was used for common grazing, as was the stubble of the arable fields after the corn harvest. The common lands were not divided, though a stint was sometimes imposed limiting the number of cattle or sheep each villager might graze on them.

Figure 29.1 Farming regions in England and Wales, 1500–1640

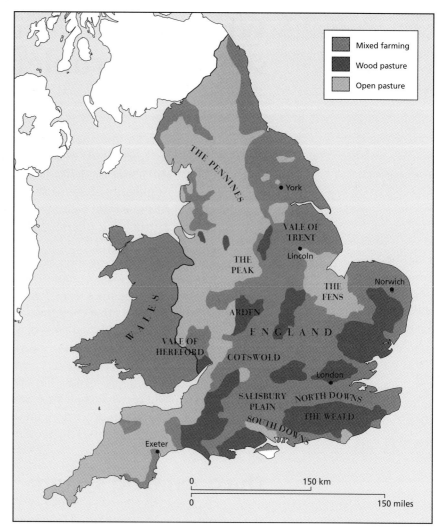

The system demanded a high degree of cooperation. This was enforced through the manorial courts, where fines could be imposed for offences such as allowing one's animals to stray, or failing to perform communal duties. It was also a highly conservative and not especially effective system, which is why attempts were sometimes made to increase productivity through enclosure. Most of the enclosures which attracted comment took place in areas of open field mixed farming, and not in the wood pasture or open pasture districts.

Enclosures

The problem of enclosures bulks very large in the propaganda and legislation of the period. Many laws were passed against enclosures, and many pamphlets written and sermons preached about them, usually condemning them. But it is by no means certain that they were as important as contemporaries thought; enclosing landowners, like usurers (money-lenders), forestallers and regraters (see chapter 16), were convenient scapegoats when things seemed to be going wrong.

There were various kinds of enclosure. Firstly, a landowner might put fences or hedges around his land so as to protect his livestock or crops more effectively, or to try out new methods. Secondly, if his lands were held in widely separated strips the landowner might try to 'engross' them, to form a consolidated land-holding. This could be achieved through an amicable exchange of lands with neighbours, but it might require threats or financial pressures. Thirdly, the landowner might find some excuse to annex part, or all, of the common land of the village, and deny its use to others. Then there was the question of how the landowner proceeded to exploit his newly enclosed holding. He might, for instance, find he needed to employ less labour than he had previously, and he might find it convenient to knock down unnecessary houses standing on his enclosed fields. This was much more likely if he was converting from arable to pasture, since looking after sheep needed fewer men than growing corn.

Consequently, contemporaries did not condemn all enclosures indiscriminately, but made a distinction between good and bad ones. As John Hales (see profile on page 95) wrote in 1548, in his instructions to the commissioners appointed to enquire into recent enclosures:

> 'But first, to declare unto you what is meant by this word inclosures. *It is not taken when a man doth enclose and hedge in his own proper ground, where no man hath commons. For such inclosure is very beneficial to the commonwealth; it is a cause of great increase of wood: but it is meant thereby, when any man hath taken away and enclosed any other mens' commons, or hath pulled down houses of husbandry, and converted the lands from tillage to pasture. This is the meaning of this word, and so we pray you to remember it.'*

During the first half of the century the main motive for enclosure was sheep farming, as the demand for woollen cloth rose steadily, approximately doubling by the mid-century (see next chapter). However, after 1551 the cloth industry ceased to be quite so attractive, and the new motive for enclosure was now to produce more food. Not only was the population increasing overall, but also more people were moving to the towns, especially London. This meant that farmers who were in a

KEY TERM:

Copyholders

The rules under which land was held by tenants were complicated, and varied according to region, but about two-thirds of all tenants were **copyholders**, or – which often came to the same thing – held their land 'subject to the custom of the manor'. Theoretically, copyholders held a copy of the entry in the manorial roll which stated their particular rights. A number of copyholds were by inheritance, which gave some security of tenure; some were for life – or for the lives of more than one person; others were 'by the will of the lord', the least secure category. The problem of establishing a legal right to one's tenure was often a key issue in enclosure disputes.

position to transport their products to a large town, especially those within striking distance of London, had a major incentive to cater for the urban market rather than merely for local subsistence, as had been the case under the open field system.

The rights of tenants

The landowner who wanted to enclose had often to begin by dispossessing the sitting tenants. If these were freeholders he could proceed only with their agreement. However, **copyholders** were more vulnerable. In many cases it was possible for the landlord either to get rid of them altogether, or at least to make them pay more for their tenancies.

Even if the copyholder's tenure was secure, the question might arise of whether his payments to his landlord were fixed or uncertain. Many fortunate tenants paid rents which had been fixed at an earlier date and were now quite out of step with inflation. However, in other cases it was possible for the landlord to 'rack-rent', that is, increase rents enormously, either so as to force the tenant to quit, or merely to obtain a higher income from his land. Then again, copyholders had to pay fines, which were charges due whenever a tenancy changed hands, and raising fines could have the same effect as raising rents. Only the minority of copyholders who could prove a sound title, held their tenure by inheritance, and had fixed rents and fines, were completely safe. Others might be liable to dispossession when their landlord wanted to enclose, and they were also subject to rack-renting, arbitrary fines, and the invasion of their rights on the common land.

The attitude of the government

The problem of enclosures preoccupied Tudor governments throughout the century, and numerous anti-enclosure acts were passed, starting in 1489 and ending in 1597. Two major commissions of enquiry were also set up, one by Wolsey in 1517, and one under Somerset in 1548. The first produced information from a wide area, but Somerset's enquiry, masterminded by John Hales, only involved the Midlands, and its main effect seems to have been to stimulate local rioting. In general, it is unlikely that much positive emerged from all these efforts. The government's motives for opposing enclosure, which were probably shared by the majority of the population, were as follows:

1 Grievances over enclosures were seen to lead to popular unrest, either in the shape of local riots – see the document at the end of this chapter (pages 258–9) – or as a contribution to some of the major rebellions of the century. Ket's rising of 1549 in Norfolk was mainly due to agrarian unrest, and the destruction of hedges and fences accompanied both the Pilgrimage of Grace (1536) and the Western Rebellion (1549).

2 The military factor was also important. Conversion from arable land to pasture was opposed because it was generally held that shepherds made poor soldiers as compared to ploughmen, and any depopulation was thought to endanger contributions to the militia, as this account shows:

> '... there was in Seaton Delavale town [near Alnmouth, Northumberland] 12 tenements, whereon there dwelt 12 able men, sufficiently furnished with horse and furniture to serve her Majesty at all times when they were called upon ... who paid 46s 8d rent yearly apiece, or thereabouts. All the said tenants and their successors, saving 5, the said Robert Delavale [lord of the manor] either thrust out of their fermoulds [holdings], or wearied them by taking excessive fines, increasing of their rents unto £3 apiece, and withdrawing part of their best land and meadow from their tenements ... So that where there was 12 tenants with sufficient horse and furniture able to serve, they are now brought to 5 ... who have not one serviceable horse amongst them all for the causes aforesaid.
>
> John Hales's account from the 1590s of an enclosure in Northumberland, quoted in H. H. E. Craster, *A History of Northumberland*, vol. IX (1909)

3 There were also more idealistic motives. The authorities believed in maintaining the social structure of the nation, which entailed protecting peasants as well as landowners in the status in which God had placed them. In the mid-century especially, preachers such as Hugh Latimer, as well as the layman, John Hales, eloquently denounced greedy landlords, and demanded justice for the poor. This group, sometimes known as the 'Commonwealth school', influenced the policies of Protector Somerset. Its voice can be heard in the wording of this prayer, from Cranmer's 1552 Prayer Book:

> 'The earth is thine (O Lord), and all that is contained therein; notwithstanding thou hast given the possession thereof unto the children of men, to pass over the time of their short pilgrimage in this vale of misery: We heartily pray thee, to send thy holy Spirit into the hearts of them that possess the grounds, pastures, and dwelling places of the earth,

that they, remembering themselves to be thy tenants, may not rack and stretch out the rents of their houses and lands, nor yet take unreasonable fines and incomes after the manner of covetous worldlings, but so let them out to others, that the inhabitants thereof may both be able to pay the rents, and also honestly to live, to nourish their families, and to relieve the poor: give them grace also to consider, that they are but strangers and pilgrims in this world, having here no dwelling place, but seeking one to come; that they, remembering the short continuance of their life, may be content with that that is sufficient, and not join house to house, nor couple land to land, to the impoverishment of other, but so behave themselves in letting out their tenements, lands, and pastures, that after this life they may be received into everlasting dwelling places: through Jesus Christ our Lord. Amen.'

A Star Chamber case

In 1516 a dispute arose between some of the inhabitants of Draycote and Stoke Gifford, in Somerset, and their manorial lord, Sir John Rodney. It started with an affray in which, according to Sir John, 'riotous and evil disposed persons to the number of seven score', armed with 'bats and staves and other weapons', started to pull down a recently erected fence on Stoke Moor. When Sir John himself appeared on the scene they gave him 'many despiteful words', and one of them 'with a pike fork struck two times at the said Sir John intending to have slain him', so he beat a retreat and left them to it. The following are from the account of events leading to the riot which each side gave before the court of Star Chamber.

I Articles of complaint by the inhabitants of Draycote and Stoke Gifford v. Sir John Rodney

Where the said inhabitants and their ancestors ... by reason of their holds and tenures in the same towns and villages have used time out of mind to have common of pasture for their beasts in a moor within your said county, called Stoke Moor, which moor the said Sir John hath now of late enclosed in to his park of Stoke and taken as his several [private ownership] contrary to right justice and good conscience, by reason whereof your said subjects must leave their tenures and holds, which is to their utter undoing ... Also the said Sir John hath stopped the common way which your said subjects and all other persons inhabitants with the said towns and villages by reason of their tenures there have used to have to their said common.

Also the said Sir John at sundry and divers times at his courts holden within the said manors of Stoke Gifford and Draycote compelleth such of your said subjects as be his tenants to show him their writings that they have of their said holds, and when he hath them in his hands, some of the said writings he [e]razeth, and delivereth the same so razed to his said tenants again, by colour whereof he daily troubleth and menaceth them to put them from their said holds and tenures contrary to all right and good conscience.

II   The answer of Sir John Rodney Knight to the bill of articles of complaint

The said Sir John sayeth that before the time of the enclosure supposed in the said articles he was, and yet is, fully seized [in legal possession] of the manor of Stoke ... whereof divers of the said complainants be tenants to the said Sir John for term of life by copy of Court Roll after custom of the said manor, and some be tenants for term of life by deed, and some occupieth by sufferance and at pleasure and will of the said Sir John without having any copy or deed, and some of the said complainants be no tenants nor occupiers of any land in the said lordships of Stoke or Draycott, so that the said persons which be no tenants make their complaint of pure malice without any ground or cause.

And as [for] the foresaid persons which be tenants for term of life by deed, copy, or by sufferance of the said Sir John, [he] sayeth that they ought not, nor may by the common law, prescribe to have common against [him], owner of the said manor whereof they be tenants, and ... [he] sayeth that it is lawful for him that is their lord and owner of the said manor ... to empower himself in his own ground, leaving to his said tenants sufficient common there ... in which land called Stoke Moor is more pasture than his said tenants been [are] able to occupy, without that the said tenants or inhabitants of Draycott ought to have any common in the same moor called Stoke Moor ...

Also as to the article wherein is contained [alleged] that the said Sir John should raze the deeds of his tenants, [he] sayeth that he never razed any deed of any of his tenants. And forasmuch as that article is very slanderous and uncertain, [he] prayeth that the said complainants may be compelled to express the names of such persons whose deeds by their surmise should be so razed, and he shall make more precise answer thereunto ...

Tudor Economic Documents I

Public opinion in the sixteenth century was very concerned about enclosures, but this should not lead us to exaggerate the amount that took place. It has been estimated that even in those Midland counties most affected, such as Leicestershire, less than 5 per cent of the arable land was enclosed during the century. Enclosure was only one of the remedies open to an enterprising landowner who wanted to take advantage of higher wool or food prices. Another technique open to him was to force or persuade his copyhold tenants to exchange their copyholds for lease-holds. Short-term leases made it possible for the landlord to adjust rents and fines upwards every time a lease fell in, in order to keep up with, or beat, inflation.

Conclusion

To sum up, some enclosures, especially when the aim was to substitute pasture for arable, undoubtedly led to suffering on the part of the expl-oited and the dispossessed. The other side of the coin is that, overall, enclosures benefited the economy. Unlike on the Continent, there were no major famines in England after the sixteenth century. The changes we have been discussing certainly contributed to this.

Task: source evaluation

1 With regard to the Star Chamber case:
   a Give the meaning of the following phrases:
      i 'show him their writings'
      ii 'to empower himself in his own ground'.
   b Express in your own words Sir John's answers to the following charges:
      i that he had enclosed the Commons
      ii that he had destroyed certain documents proving tenants' rights.
   c Do you think that Sir John's actions come into the definition of enclosure as stated by John Hales (page 257)?

2 Comment on the style and vocabulary of
   a the account of events in Seaton Delavale
   b the 1552 Prayer Book.
   In these two extracts how do the words used reveal the attitudes of the two authors towards enclosure?

Further reading

D. M. Palliser, *The Age of Elizabeth, 1547–1603* (Addison Wesley Longman, 2nd edn, 1992).
Joan Thirsk, *Tudor Enclosures*, Pamphlet G.41 (Historical Association, 1959) – a good introduction to the subject. See the same author's chapter on enclosures in *The Agrarian History of England and Wales*, vol. IV 1550–1640 (Cambridge University Press, 1967).

30 How did the pattern of English trade change during the century?

This chapter is mainly about overseas trade, which historians have tended to concentrate on, rather than internal trade between different parts of the country. Trade with foreign countries is much better documented, through port books, and accounts kept by customs officials. However, it has been estimated that the internal market may have been at least ten times as large. Much was carried by water, either by navigable rivers or along the coast. For instance, Newcastle exported thousands of tons of coal annually to London and other east-coast ports. There was also considerable transport of goods by road, although this was far more expensive. The costs of land-carriage ranged from 4d [1.5p] to 12d [5p] per ton-mile, as compared with 1d or less by water. Therefore cities such as York, Gloucester, Exeter and Norwich utilised their rivers to carry much of their trade in small ships to the coastal ports.

Roads cannot have been all that bad, as the accounts of merchants and shopkeepers indicate that they traded widely throughout the country. For example, those of William Wray, a mercer from the small North Yorkshire town of Ripon, show that in the 1580s he regularly bought goods wholesale from York, Beverley, Coventry and Norwich. Packhorses were the main method of road transport early in the century, but the first horse-drawn passenger coach appeared in 1555, and the first long, four-wheeled goods wagon shortly afterwards. Undoubtedly, too, internal trade increased, as agriculture became more specialised and commercial during the second half of the century.

The cloth trade

Throughout the Tudor period England's exports were dominated by one commodity – woollen cloth. In earlier centuries the main export had been raw wool, which was sold through Calais by the 'merchants of the Staple', but the wool trade was in decline, partly due to over-taxation. In 1485 the English customs duty on wool amounted to nearly one-third of its value, whereas that on cloth was about 3 per cent. The loss of Calais in 1558 was a further blow to the wool trade.

Woollen cloth was exported in rolls of 24 yards (22 metres) or more in length, known as 'cloths'. It was mostly undyed, because English cloth-finishing and dyeing was not as technically advanced as on the Continent. The cloths came from many parts of the kingdom, but the best known were the heavy west-country broadcloths, from Gloucester, Somerset and Wiltshire, and the lighter kerseys from Berkshire, as well as from the West Riding and from Devon. By the end of Henry VII's reign 82,000 cloths were being shipped abroad annually, a figure which rose to a record 133,000 in 1550.

The cloth trade was entirely in the hands of the **Merchant Adventurers**. It was also increasingly focused on London. By the close of Henry VIII's reign about 88 per cent of cloth exports were shipped from London – although some of these might have originated from the 'outports', as other English ports were called. The 'mart' or 'staple' for the cloth was Antwerp (see Figure 30.1), which by this date had become the commercial and financial capital of western Europe, and was easily reachable from London. Antwerp was a truly international city, in which there were permanent colonies of foreign merchants. It was also a banking centre, so that an English merchant could not only find there an Italian, German or Spanish buyer for his cloth, but might also obtain credit, or change his money into a foreign currency.

Figure 30.1 *The port of Antwerp in the early sixteenth century*

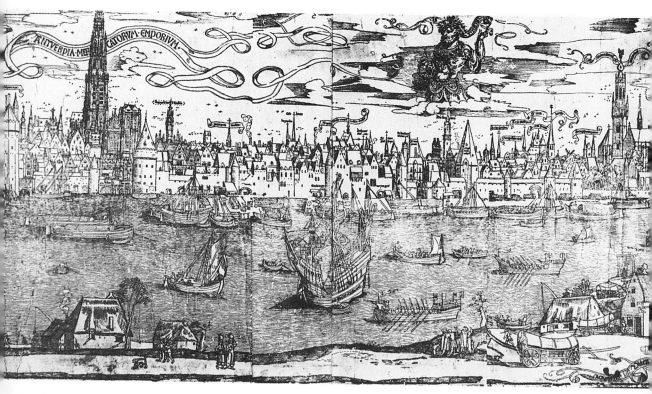

Merchant Adventurers

The **Merchant Adventurers** were a regulated company, meaning that they were a group of merchants trading individually but under an agreed set of regulations. They shipped their cloths jointly in periodic fleets, and displayed them together at Antwerp on specified days. But each merchant kept his own balance sheet; if he went bankrupt he could not expect help from the company.

The Adventurers were far from living up to their name. They pursued a safety-first policy of easy profits in an established market, and they did not – at least until after the decline of Antwerp – try to find new markets. Their business methods were conservative; one of their main objectives was to stop 'interlopers' challenging their monopoly. This highly concentrated trade was therefore very vulnerable to any crisis which might hit the single market.

The Antwerp trade was all the more important for England's economy because other export markets had declined for various reasons. For instance, Henry VIII's breach with Rome had led to some victimisation of English merchants in Seville, and consequently Anglo-Spanish trade had suffered. Again, by the early sixteenth century English ships in the Mediterranean were coming under increasing attack from Turkish galleys, or from their allies, the Moslem pirates who operated from bases along the coast of North Africa. Thirdly, England's important Baltic trade, which involved commodities such as timber, tar and hemp – all vital for shipbuilding – had been for some time under the control of the powerful Hanseatic League of North German cities.

All this meant that by the middle of the sixteenth century there was a quite unhealthy reliance on the narrowly-based cloth trade through Antwerp, to finance the variety of goods which England needed to import from abroad. The welfare of this trade was, too, an important factor behind Tudor foreign policy, which, from Henry VII's reign until well into Elizabeth's, tended always to try to maintain friendship with the Habsburgs, who controlled the Netherlands, rather than with other powers such as France or the German Protestant princes.

Decline

Cloth continued to be England's main export throughout the century, but the Antwerp trade suffered a series of setbacks which resulted in some diversification of trade, and particularly in a search for new markets during the second half of the century.

1 Successive debasements of the English coinage, especially after 1543, led to an artificial boom in cloth exports, with the result that the market for English broadcloths became saturated, and the Adventurers could no longer sell the cloths piling up in their Antwerp warehouses.

2 This was compounded by the government's clumsy attempt to deflate the currency in the summer of 1551, which damaged the credit of English merchants and led to an increase in the price of English cloth. Nevertheless, the consequences were not catastrophic. Cloth exports fell back for a time, but by the end of the 1550s they had recovered, and remained at a steady level of about 100,000 cloths a year for the rest of Elizabeth's reign.

3 It was the declining status of Antwerp that permanently altered the pattern of English trade. This was due to various events:

- The bankruptcies of both the French and Spanish crowns in 1557, after a long period of war, dealt a blow to the international banking system.

- Religious persecution, followed by the outbreak of the Dutch revolt against Philip II in 1566, shook the city's prosperity.

- In 1576 there occurred the 'Spanish Fury', when unpaid and mutinous Spanish troops sacked Antwerp.

- In 1585 Dutch rebels finished off the remains of the city's trade by blocking the mouth of the Scheldt, Antwerp's outlet to the sea.

4 Long before this final blow, English merchants had been looking for an alternative to Antwerp as a mart for their cloth. They tried Middleburg at the mouth of the Scheldt, and various German ports, including Hamburg and Stade. These had the advantage that they were outside Philip II's jurisdiction, because in 1568 Philip had tried to bring pressure on the English government through a trade embargo (see chapter 22).

New trade routes

Due to these developments certain English merchants, encouraged by the government, and in particular by the far-sighted William Cecil, started looking for new markets for their cloth. Some of these were to involve long and dangerous journeys into unknown areas of the globe.

1 In the Mediterranean a new trade with the independent Moslem kingdom of Morocco developed from the early 1550s, based on the exchange of cloth for sugar. In 1585 a regulated company, the Barbary Company, was set up under the leadership of the Earl of Leicester. However, in spite of the growing demand in England for sugar, Leicester's company failed to make a profit, and trade with Morocco remained fairly small scale.

2 Trade with the Guinea coast also developed in the 1550s. The first black slaves were brought to England in 1555, but the slave trade only took off when John Hawkins started a series of slaving voyages to Spanish America, selling slaves from Guinea to the Spanish settlers. This lucrative enterprise ended sharply when Hawkins' fleet was attacked at St John of Ulua in 1568 (see chapter 22).

3 After about 1570 English merchants also resumed contact with the eastern Mediterranean, as the Turkish sultan was interested in English lead and tin for armaments, as well as grain and fish. The Turkey

Company, incorporated in 1581, prospered, and a permanent English agent was installed at Constantinople. In England, exotic luxuries from Turkey were much in demand; the Countess of Shrewsbury had 32 Turkish carpets at Hardwick Hall by 1601.

4 Because the Hanseatic League had been weakened by war with Russia, it became possible to reduce its special privileges in England, and English merchants were able to penetrate the Baltic and bring back naval stores such as timber and tar. In 1579 the Eastland Company was set up to coordinate their efforts.

5 The Russia, or Muscovy, Company of 1555 came about as a by-product of attempts to find a 'north-east passage' round Asia to Cathay (China). The voyage of Willoughby and Chancellor (1553) failed to find the passage, but Chancellor entered the White Sea and made an overland journey to the court of Ivan the Terrible in Moscow, where he was granted the right to trade throughout Russia. However, this trade was never very substantial; also, efforts to trade with Persia via the Volga and the Caspian Sea were unsuccessful.

6 The most ambitious venture of all was the creation of the East India Company in 1600, in order to rival the Dutch by trading with India and the Far East. Four ships under James Lancaster, who had already made an earlier voyage to India, set out in 1601 to sail to Java via the Cape of Good Hope and India. This enterprise, again, was fairly small scale, but it did make a profit for those who had invested in it.

The new markets compensated to some extent for the decline of Antwerp, but probably English foreign trade did not expand overall. Also, English cloth continued overwhelmingly to be the main export. There was, however, some change in the types of cloth sold. Heavy broadcloths continued to dominate the market, but lighter cloths, more suitable for the Mediterranean and the East, were being produced on an increasing scale. These 'new draperies' came mainly from East Anglia, where many immigrants from France and the Netherlands had settled, fleeing religious persecution at home, and bringing their skills with them.

One must not think in terms of a 'commercial revolution' at this period; the real importance of the new trade routes, as of the new **joint-stock companies**, lay in the future. Nevertheless, the pride in the achievements of his contemporaries of Richard Hakluyt, the Elizabethan scholar who did so much to record and popularise the new exploration and trading ventures, is justified:

KEY TERM:

Joint-stock companies

The Muscovy Company and the East India Company were institutions of a new kind, in which merchants no longer traded as separate individuals, but instead invested in a joint project. Their capital was used to provide both the ships and the goods for the expedition. One advantage of this arrangement was that anyone could contribute who possessed the necessary funds. This meant that the circle of commercial investment was widened. Peers, courtiers, and even Elizabeth herself, invested in these voyages, and shared in the profits. Another advantage was that the risk was equally distributed, and because contributions were limited it was unlikely that failure would lead to individual bankruptcies.

'... it can not be denied, but as in all former ages there have been men full of activity, stirrers abroad, and searchers of the remote parts of the world, so in this most famous and peerless government of her most excellent Majesty, her subjects through the special assistance and blessing of God, in searching the most opposite corners and quarters of the world, and to speak plainly, in compassing the vast globe of the earth more than once, have excelled all the nations and people of the earth.'

Task: essay-writing

'How successful was the Elizabethan government in its economic policies?'

For suggestions about essay-writing look at the end of chapter 10. Points relevant to this question can be found in chapters 28 and 29, as well as this chapter.

Further reading

C. G. A. Clay, *Economic Expansion and Social Change; England 1500–1700*, vol. II (Cambridge University Press, 1984).

Ralph Davies, *English Overseas Trade 1500–1700*, Studies in Economic History (Macmillan, 1973) – a good introduction to the subject.

G. D. Ramsay, *English Overseas Trade during the Centuries of Emergence* (Macmillan, 1957) – still one of the best books on this topic.

31 Literacy and education

Measuring literacy

How many people could read and write in sixteenth-century England? Did the number increase significantly as the century progressed? These questions are surprisingly difficult to answer with any precision. To start with, there are the views of contemporaries, but these differed widely, and in any case they were not necessarily in a better position to judge than a modern historian. Thomas More thought that 'far more than the four parts of all the whole divided into ten could never read English yet', which suggests that up to 60 per cent of the population could read. But More's contemporary, Stephen Gardiner, believed that reading was 'such as few can skill of, and not the hundredth part of the realm'.

In order to try to get behind such anecdotal evidence historians have examined a variety of sources, among which are book production, book ownership, schools, and signatures and marks.

Book production

The argument here is that if more books were being printed this must have been the result of an increasing demand for reading material; also the availability of more books must have stimulated more people to learn to read. There certainly were more books as the century went on – we know this because new titles had to be registered by the Stationers' Company. The snag is that we do not usually know how many copies of a particular work were printed, nor who bought them. It could be, for instance, that the increasing numbers of books were actually read by a small but enthusiastic book-buying public, in which case this tells us nothing about the alleged rise in literacy.

Book ownership

Perhaps this might be a more precise measure of literacy. Probate inventories record the possessions of the deceased, and have survived in large numbers for certain parts of the country. They have been analysed to see how many of them mention books; for instance, only 1 per cent of a collection of sixteenth-century Oxfordshire inventories do so, whereas the figure for Norwich inventories between 1584 and 1638 is 39 per cent. The problem is that inventories were only required for people who had possessions to leave. The poor did not have them, and neither did women – unless they happened to be well-off widows.

Figure 31.1 *A printing workshop, c. 1600*

Another difficulty is that even if someone did own a book this does not prove they could read. This is particularly obvious in the case of the book most often mentioned in inventories, the Bible. A man might own a Bible because his father had left it to him; he might have treasured it without actually being able to read a word. Bibles were sacred objects and were used in many ways – for swearing oaths, to record the birth of children, for warding off evil spirits. There are reports of girls sleeping with a Bible under their pillow and a sixpence inserted in the Book of Ruth so as to dream about their future lover. As David Cressy says, 'the power of the Bible was enormous but did not need literacy to unlock it' (see 'Further reading' section on page 275).

Schools

Again, the connection here is not as clear as it might seem at first sight. There undoubtedly was a major extension of education in the second half of the century, but most of the evidence for this concerns grammar schools. We know far less about the more informal arrangements for teaching young children to read – at home or in the so-called 'petty' schools. Also it was often children from better-off families who went to the new grammar schools, and they may already have possessed basic literacy before they went. So the fact that 136 new grammar schools were founded during Elizabeth's reign does not prove much about the rise of literacy.

Signatures and marks

Easily the best test of literacy is whether someone could sign their name on a document, or whether they had to make a 'mark' instead. Marks ranged from simple scrawls to more elaborate designs, often referring to the writer's craft or trade (see Figure 31.2). Of course, the ability to sign one's name does not prove total literacy, but it is a good indication, given that children were always taught to read before learning how to hold a pen and write. A major advantage for the historian in using this test is that it provides a universal and standard measurement of literacy, so that different parts of the country can be compared, as well as different historical periods. David Cressy has used mainly the records of church courts which contain many signatures/marks – these often have the additional advantage that the profession or craft of the person signing is given. Using this source he has come up with tables which give an accurate idea of how literacy varied as between socio-economic groups, and geographically (see Figure 31.3 for some examples).

Unfortunately the sources for the first half of the Tudor period are too sparse to provide reasonable samples, but Cressy estimates that whereas at Elizabeth's accession male illiteracy was about 80 per cent, and 95 per

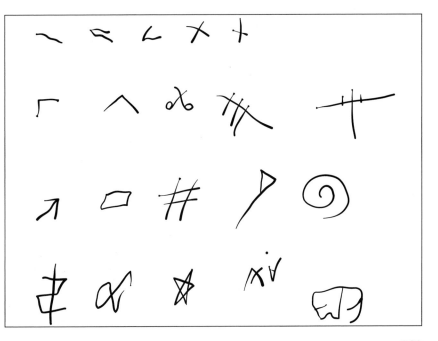

Figure 31.2 *Personal marks made on depositions in the diocese of Norwich, 1580–1620. Row A: simple scrawls and crosses; B: mason, husbandman, tailor, thatcher, woolcomber; C: fletcher, brickmaker, brickmaker, baker, tailor; D: glazier, worsted weaver, mason, merchant, yeoman.*

Figure 31.3 *The ability to read and write varied according to sex, social status, occupation and geographical location, as shown in tables (a) and (b) which are derived from the records of ecclesiastical courts. These dealt with wills, marriage licences and other documents which required either a signature or, in the case of the illiterate, a 'mark'.*

Illiteracy in the Diocese of Durham, 1561–1631

Social group	No. sampled	No. signing with mark
Clergy/Professions	208	5 = 2%
Gentry	252	53 = 21%
Tradesmen/Craftsmen	725	470 = 65%
Yeomen	1326	971 = 73%
Servants	18	14 = 78%
Husbandmen	379	345 = 91%
Labourers	176	172 = 98%
Women	706	690 = 98%

Illiteracy in the Diocese of London: Essex and Hertfordshire 1580–1640

Social group	No. sampled	No. signing with mark
Clergy/Professions	177	0 = 0%
Gentry	161	5 = 3%
Yeomen	319	105 = 33%
Tradesmen/Craftsmen	448	188 = 42%
Husbandmen	461	337 = 73%
Labourers	7	7 = 100%
Women	324	308 = 95%

From David Cressy, Literacy and the Social Order *(CUP, 1980)*

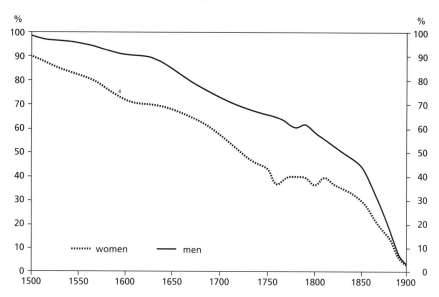

Figure 31.4 *Estimated illiteracy of men and women in England, 1500–1900*

cent for females, at the beginning of the century the figures may have been about 90 and 99 per cent respectively. The rise of literacy in England is a process which has been continuing at a fairly steady rate from that time until now, with women always behind men, until quite recently.

An educational revolution

Most of the formal schooling available in the fifteenth century was associated with the Church, and was geared to the training of priests. This was so with the two universities, Oxford and Cambridge, and with the choir and grammar schools attached to cathedrals. There was also a slow spread of grammar schools catering for the laity, and there must have been many freelance teachers who conducted short-lived schools, although these tended not to leave much trace in the records.

The sixteenth century saw a rapid growth of interest in education, and the founding of many new schools. This educational revolution, as Lawrence Stone describes it, was due to several factors, which included the influence of the Renaissance, the Reformation, and the growth of a state bureaucracy. The following extracts illustrate some of the motives behind the contemporary demand for more education.

1 From *The Boke Named the Governour*, the first treatise on education to be written in English, which went through at least five editions before 1558. Its author, Sir Thomas Elyot, was Henry VIII's ambassador to Charles V.

'Forasmuch as all noble authors do conclude and also common experience proveth that where the governors of realms and cities be found adorned with virtues and do employ their studies and mind to the public weal, as well to the augmentation thereof as to the establishing and long continuance of the same, there a public weal must needs be both honourable and wealthy. To the intent that I will declare how such personages may be prepared I will use the policy of a wise and cunning gardener who, purposing to have in his garden a fine and precious herb, that should be to him and all other repairing thereto, excellently commodious or pleasant, he will first search throughout his garden where he can find the most mellow and fertile earth, and therein will he put the seed of the herb to grow and be nourished ... Semblable [i.e. similar] order will I ensue in the forming the gentle wits of noblemen's children, who from the womb of their mother shall be made propise [i.e. suitable] or apt to the governance of a public weal.'

2 Thomas Cromwell took a keen interest in education, and as Henry VIII's powerful chief minister he was in a position to shape government policy. This is an extract from the Royal Injunctions of 1536 [*i.e.* instructions to the clergy], of which he was the author.

'The parsons, vicars and other curates aforesaid shall diligently admonish the fathers and mothers, masters and governors of youth, being within their cure, to teach or cause to be taught their children and servants, even from their infancy, their pater noster *['Our Father', i.e. the Lord's Prayer], the articles of our faith, and the ten commandments, in their mother tongue ... that the said fathers and mothers, masters and governors do bestow their children and servants, even from their childhood, either to learning or to some other honest exercise, occupation or husbandry, exhorting, counselling, and by all the ways and means they may, as well in their said sermons and collations as other ways, persuading the said fathers, mothers, masters and other governors, being under their cure or charge, diligently to provide and foresee that the said youth be in no manner wise kept or brought up in idleness, lest at any time afterwards they be driven for lack of some mystery [i.e. craft] or occupation to live by, to fall to begging, stealing or some other unthriftiness; forasmuch as we may daily see, through sloth and idleness divers valiant men fall, some to begging and some to theft and murder ...'*

3 John Colet founded the earliest Renaissance grammar school in England, St Paul's, London, in 1509. In this extract from the school statutes he discusses the curriculum.

'*As touching in this school what shall be taught of the masters and learned of the scholars, it passeth my wit to devise and determine in particular, but in general to speak and sum what to say my mind I would they were taught always in good literature both Latin and Greek, and good authors such as have the very Roman eloquence joined with wisdom ... All barbary, all corruption, all Latin adulterate which ignorant blind fools brought into this world and with the same hath distained and poisoned the old Latin speech and the very Roman tongue, which in the time of Tully [Cicero] and Sallust and Virgil and Terence was used ... I say that filthiness and all such abusion which the later blind world brought in, which more rather may be called blotterature than literature, I utterly abanish and exclude out of this school and charge the masters that they teach always that is best.*'

4 The reformer Thomas Becon wanted to enlist schoolmasters in the struggle to achieve a full protestant Reformation. This extract is from a book published in 1559.

'*If the youth of the Christians were brought up from their tender years in the knowledge of God's most holy and blessed word and had their breasts thus furnished with the armours of the holy scriptures against the damnable opinions of the papists and of such other wicked sectaries as the devil hath raised up in this our time, the christian commonwealth should soon have another face both in doctrine and manners. For the alone occasion of all the evils wherewith we are troubled most miserably nowadays, whether we respect learning or life, cometh only of the naughty and wicked education of the youth.*'

Grammar schools

The increase in the number of endowed grammar schools is the most obvious and best-documented feature of the educational revolution of the late sixteenth and early seventeenth centuries. Grammar schools were mainly for teaching Latin, although the syllabus might include other subjects such as Greek or, occasionally, arithmetic. Latin, although not exactly a 'useful' subject, was still seen as the passport to all forms of higher culture and education. For this reason it tended to be the children of 'upwardly mobile' tradesmen, craftsmen and professionals who were sent to the new grammar schools, even though those who endowed them often laid down that they should be free in order to serve the local poor.

We know quite a lot about the organisation of Tudor grammar schools because the school statutes provided by the founders were usually very detailed. At St Paul's, for instance, Colet not only specifies exactly what each class had to learn and what textbooks should be used, but is explicit in other, crucial areas:

> *'To their Urine they shall go thereby to a place appointed and a poor*
> *Child of the School shall see it conveyed away from time to time and have*
> *the avail of the Urine; for other causes, if need be, they shall go to the*
> *waterside.'*

Most grammar schools had at least four classes for the different age-groups. Boys – never girls – usually started school at about the age of eight and stayed for five or six years. In the smaller schools there would have been only one master – sometimes assisted by an usher – who had the seemingly impossible task of attending to four or five classes, all in the same large schoolroom. One way round this was to get some of the older boys to teach the youngest. The noise level can be imagined; as one social historian mildly comments, 'teaching must often have been carried out in an atmosphere unconducive to reflective study'.

Inevitably, discipline was harsh. Tudor schoolmasters seem firmly to have believed that sparing the rod would spoil the child, and canes or bundles of switches were prominent in every classroom, and even figure in some school seals, such as at Louth in Lincolnshire. This is in spite of the fact that educational writers, including Roger Ascham, condemned the too-frequent use of corporal punishment as counter-productive. There was little awareness of children as beings with special needs. To put it in modern terms, the Tudor school was curriculum-centred, not pupil-centred. Evidence of this is the sheer length of teaching time. Annual holidays were short by our standards, and the school day interminably long – often ten hours in summer, starting at six in the morning, and a seven-hour day in winter, starting as soon as it was light, to avoid the expense of candles. Altogether, Tudor schoolboys had a fairly wretched time of it, as Shakespeare recognises, in the famous speech about the seven ages of man, from *As You Like It*:

> *Then the whining schoolboy, with his satchel*
> *And shining morning face, creeping like snail*
> *Unwillingly to school.*

There were other forms of education apart from the grammar school, although they have left fewer traces in the records. Anyone – such as the village priest or someone unable to do physical labour through disability – could set themselves up as a teacher, or start a 'petty' or 'dame' school where young children could learn to read. For the rich, a private tutor might be considered more suitable than the rough-and-tumble of the local school, and such tutors occasionally also taught girls, as in the case of Thomas More's three daughters, or of Elizabeth and Mary Tudor.

Universities

The sources for working out the numbers of students attending Oxford and Cambridge, the only two universities in England, are deficient before the mid-century, but it is clear that numbers went up in the second half of the century. By the 1580s about 900 students a year were admitted to the universities of Oxford and Cambridge, although the figure went down slightly during the less prosperous 1590s. Basically, there were two kinds of university student: those, usually from a poorer background, who aimed at a career in the church, and an increasing number of gentlemen's sons, who went to acquire some cultural polish. The latter often did not work very hard and left before taking a degree, but their increasing presence must have helped eventually to raise the educational standards of the upper classes. Two reforms which affected the universities at this time were the rise of the colleges and the growth of the tutorial system. Students now tended to live in their college, whereas previously they had boarded in town. Also, they now received some individual attention from their tutors instead of merely attending the lectures and disputations.

The London Inns of Court, often collectively described as a third university, were also becoming increasingly fashionable after the mid-century. A gentleman might enrol his son at one of the Inns for a year or two, not so much to acquire legal training – although a smattering of law was always useful in these litigious times – but rather as a kind of finishing school, where he might get to know the city, sow his wild oats and make some influential contacts. Annual admissions at the Inns went up from 100 a year in 1550 to about 250 in 1600.

Conclusion

Political and economic developments, including the growth of bureaucracy, the Reformation, and the increase in wealth, undoubtedly all contributed to a general raising of educational standards in the later part of the sixteenth century. This is easier to demonstrate in regard to formal institutions like the grammar schools and the universities, but it is also certain that there was a general rise in literacy. In fact, England may possibly have been the most literate nation in the world by the early seventeenth century. Nevertheless, well over half of all men, and perhaps 90 per cent of women, still could not sign their name. In the age of Shakespeare and Spenser, the majority of English people were still living, as they always had, in a predominantly oral culture.

Task: working with sources

1 For each of the four extracts printed on pages 271–2, explain in your own words why the author supports more emphasis on education.

2 Read the 'Conclusion' above again. What effect would an increase in literacy in England have on:

   a religious beliefs and behaviour?

   b making the country easier, or harder, to rule?

   c the popularity of plays and poetry?

Further reading

David Cressy, *Literacy and the Social Order: Reading and Writing in Tudor and Stuart England* (Cambridge University Press, 1980) – a pioneering account. See also the same author's edition of documents, *Education in Tudor and Stuart England* (Edward Arnold, 1975).

Rosemary O'Day, *Education and Society, 1500–1800* (Addison Wesley Longman, 1982).

Nicholas Orme, *Education and Society in Medieval and Renaissance England* (Hambledon Press, 1989).

Joan Simon, *Education and Society in Tudor England* (Cambridge University Press, 1966) – remains the standard work on the subject.

32 How did the Elizabethan theatre evolve?

At about the same time that Philip II was planning his invasion of England, Tudor drama entered its golden age. This was the age of Kyd and Marlowe, Shakespeare and Jonson, lasting from the 1580s through to the mid seventeenth century. These playwrights wrote in English for all classes of society, and their plays contained exciting plots and believable characters. All this was new, but it derived from earlier sources – some popular and others more refined and aristocratic.

Antecedents

Miracles and moralities

This was the popular, urban drama of the late middle ages. Miracles were plays which enacted scenes from the Bible; moralities were allegorical productions in which virtues and vices were personified. They were played in annual cycles in towns such as Coventry, Wakefield and York; the players were amateurs, the language often coarse and down-to-earth, and they attracted mass audiences. Inevitably, this tradition was too much associated with the old religion to be allowed to continue by the new Protestant authorities after the Reformation. The last morality cycle in the country, the York plays, was closed down by Edmund Grindal, Archbishop of York, in 1574.

Latin plays

From at least Henry VIII's reign there was a humanist tradition whereby students at the universities and the Inns of Court, as well as grammar schoolboys, put on plays in Latin. When Elizabeth visited Cambridge in 1564 she was regaled by the students of King's College with a three-hour performance of a play by the Roman author, Plautus. The Queen, being fluent in Latin, may have enjoyed this, but it is unlikely that all her accompanying courtiers did.

Masks (or mummings, or disguises)

These were socially exclusive entertainments which took place at court or in the great houses of the aristocracy. Sir Edmund Chambers, authority on the Elizabethan stage, explains how they worked:

> *'The mask is not primarily a drama; it is an episode in an indoor revel of dancing. Masked and otherwise disguised persons come, by convention unexpectedly, into the hall, as a compliment to the hosts or the principal guests. Often they bring them gifts; always they dance before them, and they invite them to join the dance ... This intimacy between performers and spectators differentiates the mask from the drama.'*
>
> E. K. Chambers, *The Elizabethan Stage*, vol. 1 (1965).

See also the illustration of Sir Henry Unton's mask (Figure 32.1).

Figure 32.1 Sir Henry Unton, a well-to-do Elizabethan gentleman, is seated at dinner with his guests while a chamber orchestra plays and masquers in classical garb parade round the room, 1596

The children's companies

In Tudor London there were two famous companies of choirboys who were also trained to give dramatic performances. These were the Children of the Chapel Royal and the boys of St Paul's Cathedral. They acted in sophisticated comedies with witty dialogue, such as those by John Lyly. Their performances were very popular with the Court, although not with puritan pamphleteers, one of whom launched a bitter attack on them in a pamphlet entitled 'The Children of the Chapel Stript and Whipt' (the puritans always wanted to whip somebody!):

> *'Even in her majesty's chapel do these pretty upstart youths profane the Lord's Day by the lascivious writhing of their tender limbs and gorgeous decking of their apparel, in feigning bawdy fables gathered from the idolatrous heathen poets.'*

Early Tudor drama

The first non-religious plays in English date from Henry VII's reign and were performed in the great hall of a lord's house. The earliest of those whose text has survived was Henry Medwall's *Fulgens and Lucre*, a story about a young Roman girl who had to choose between a rich and a poor suitor. It was put on in 1497 at Lambeth Palace under the patronage of Cardinal Morton. Although it contained elements of a morality, there was also a reasonable plot and some realistic characterisation as well as humour. Both the author and the printer of this play were associated with Sir Thomas More, who himself may have written comedies, although none have survived.

Actors' companies

In the last two decades of Elizabeth's reign there evolved out of these varied elements a drama which was original and flexible, and capable of appealing to a wide audience, from the Court and the nobility to the urban poor. One feature of the new drama was the formation of companies of professional actors, regulated under a system of royal licences authorising them to play under the patronage and protection of specific noblemen. The first of these was Leicester's Company, licensed in 1574, followed by companies under the earls of Warwick, Nottingham, Pembroke and others. These companies soon had their own London theatres as bases, but they also acted at command performances in the royal palaces, and they went on provincial tours, so that large numbers of people were able to see them perform.

We know quite a lot about one of these companies, the Lord Admiral's, because it was managed by Edward Alleyn, whose father-in-law, Philip Henslowe, kept a diary that has survived. Alleyn put on, and himself took the title roles in, three highly successful plays by Christopher Marlowe, *The Jew of Malta*, *Tamburlane* and *Dr Faustus*. The most famous of all the companies was 'the Lord Chamberlain's men', which Shakespeare wrote for, and which was managed by Richard Burbage. About a dozen of Shakespeare's plays were performed during Elizabeth's reign, and the Queen herself is supposed to have attended the first night of *A Midsummer Night's Dream* in 1595.

The new theatres

The real breakthrough came with the setting up of new, permanent theatres in London. The first of these, called 'The Theatre', was built by James Burbage (the father of Richard) in 1576, on an open field at Shoreditch outside the City boundary. Previous to this, plays had often been performed on temporary platforms set up in inn yards (see Figure 32.2). The new theatres looked like small Roman amphitheatres; they were round, open to the sky, and capable of holding an audience of about 2,000. For a penny entrance fee spectators could stand in front, or to the side, of the stage, and for a higher fee they could have a seat in one of the galleries. Behind the stage was the tiring room where the actors prepared for their entrances, and above was a roof with a ceiling decorated with stars, known as the 'Heavens'. The hut above the Heavens contained pulleys, so that actors portraying gods could be raised and lowered onto the stage from above. If devils were required they could appear through a trapdoor from 'Hell', the space under the stage.

Elizabethan theatres had no fixed scenery, though there might have been decorated curtains or an arras (such as the one behind which Polonius was hiding when Hamlet ran him through with his sword) at the rear of the stage. The compensation was that the actors were much closer to the audience, and especially to the 'groundlings' – the spectators standing next to the stage – than is possible in a conventional theatre. Modern productions 'in the round' are going back to the kind of stage that the Elizabethans knew, in order to regain that lost intimacy.

By the turn of the century several theatres had been built, mostly on the south side of the Thames, so as to be as far as possible from the juris-

Figure 32.2 *A playhouse, about 1595*

diction of the City of London and its puritan governors. The most famous was the 'Globe', built in 1599 by Richard Burbage and his partners, including Shakespeare. The first 'Globe' was burnt down in 1613 when a cannon exploded during a performance of *Henry VIII*, but it was rebuilt, and lasted until all the theatres were suppressed by the Cromwellians in the 1640s. Theatres came back into fashion after the Restoration, but by now they had become more sophisticated, with proscenium arches, as in most modern theatres. (There is now a modern reconstruction of the 'Globe' in London, built to similar specifications as the original – but using modern technology. The idea is to recreate the atmosphere and ambience of the Elizabethan theatre in the late twentieth century.)

Attacks on the theatre

There had always been opposition to plays and actors, but as the theatre became more popular, so the attacks of its enemies grew increasingly strident. A variety of grounds were alleged for this opposition, some of them practical, others moral or philosophical. The following extracts from contemporary sources illustrate these:

1 From a pamphlet published in 1577 by a puritan minister,
   John Northbrooke.

*'By the long suffering and permitting of these vain plays, it hath stricken
such a blind zeal into the hearts of the people that they shame not to say,
and affirm openly, that plays are as good as sermons, and that they learn
as much or more at a play than they do at God's word preached ... Many
can tarry at a vain play two or three hours, when as they will not abide
scarce one hour at a sermon ... I speak (alas! with grief and sorrow at
heart) against those people that are so fleshly led, to see what reward there
is given to such crocodiles, which devour the pure chastity both of single
and married persons, men and women, when as in their plays you shall
learn all things that appertain to craft, mischief, deceits, and filthiness, etc.*

*'If you will learn how to be false and deceive your husbands, or
husbands their wives, how to play the harlots to obtain one's love, how to
ravish, how to beguile, how to betray, how to flatter, lie, swear, forswear,
how to allure to whoredom, how to murder, how to poison, how to
disobey and rebel against princes ... shall you not learn, then, at such
interludes [i.e. plays] how to practise them? ... Therefore, great reason it
is that women (especially) should absent themselves from such plays.'*

2 From a sermon preached at St Paul's Cross by another
   puritan, Thomas White, in 1578.

*'Look but upon the common plays in London, and see the multitude that
flocketh to them and followeth them. Behold the sumptuous theatre
houses, a continual monument of London's prodigality and folly. But I
understand they are now forbidden because of the plague. I like the policy
well if it hold still, for a disease is but lodged or patched up that is not
cured in the cause, and the cause of the plagues is sin, if you look to it well:
and the cause of sin are plays: therefore the cause of plagues are plays.'*

3 From a letter from the Lord Mayor and Aldermen of the City
   of London to the Privy Council, 1597.

*'To the Lords against Stage-Plays ... Among other inconveniences it is not
the least that they give opportunity to the refuse sort of evil-disposed and
ungodly people that are within and about this city to assemble themselves
and to make their matches for all their lewd and ungodly practices; being
as heretofore we have found by the examination of divers apprentices and*

*other servants who have confessed unto us that the said stage-plays were
the very places of their rendezvous, appointed by them to meet with such
other as were to join with them in their designs and mutinous attempts.*

*'They are the ordinary places for vagrant persons, masterless men,
thieves, horse-stealers, whoremongers, contrivers of treason and other idle
and dangerous persons to meet together and to make their matches to the
great displeasure of Almighty God and the hurt and annoyance of her
Majesty's people; which cannot be prevented nor discovered by the
governors of the city for that they are out of the city's jurisdiction.*

*'They maintain idleness in such persons as have no vocation, and draw
apprentices and other servants from their ordinary works and all sorts of
people from the resort unto sermons and other Christian exercises to the
great hindrance of trades and profanation of religion established by her
Highness within this realm.*

*'In the time of sickness it is found by experience that many, having sores
and yet not heart-sick, take occasion hereby to walk abroad and to
recreate themselves by hearing a play. Whereby others are infected, and
themselves also many things miscarry.'*

Censorship and control

From the end of the fifteenth century there had existed a court func-
tionary called the Master of the Revels, whose task was to organise the
Christmas festivities at Court, including pageants and tournaments. This
official gradually became more important until finally, in a royal patent
dated 1581, he was put in charge of the censorship of all plays, and
empowered:

*'to warn, command and appoint ... all and every player ... either
belonging to any nobleman or otherwise ... to appear before him with all
such plays, tragedies, comedies or shows as they shall have in readiness or
mean to set forth, and them to present and recite before our said Servant
or his sufficient deputy, whom we ordain, appoint and authorise ... to
order or reform ... all such shows, plays ... as shall be thought meet or
unmeet unto himself or his said deputy.'*

The censorship exercised by Edmund Tilney, who was Master of the
Revels during the 1580s, does not seem to have been excessive. It was
directed not against sex or violence, but mainly against criticisms of the
government, or anything that might possibly have led to political unrest.

The Privy Council, under whom the Master of the Revels acted, had an ambivalent attitude towards the theatre. The Councillors recognised that ordinary people were entitled to recreational facilities. Some of them, such as Lord Hunsdon, the Lord Chamberlain, had their own companies of actors. However, they were also influenced by the arguments of the Puritans and the City authorities that the playhouses were a threat to law and order, especially in times of unrest, or plague. In 1597 the Council ordered an end to all performances and the destruction of three play-houses, but soon afterwards they allowed two new ones to be built: Burbage's 'Globe' in Southwark, and Alleyn and Henslowe's 'Fortune' in Finsbury. By the end of the century there were no less than five in operation.

Elizabeth and her bishops totally suppressed the traditional, amateur drama of the miracles and morality plays. However, professional actors took the place of these provincial amateurs, and by the end of the reign the drama was flourishing, with purpose-built theatres, companies under noble protection, and large audiences. Then, under the Stuarts, all theatre companies were put under the direct patronage of the monarch. The theatre now started to lose its popular appeal and to become part of the exclusive culture of the Court, a culture which was to be destroyed by Cromwell and his puritan supporters.

Task: historical interpretation

1 Look at the three extracts on pages 281–2 which attack the theatre. Can you explain the essential difference between the kind of criticisms made in extracts **1** and **2**, and those made in extract **3**?

2 What points might a supporter of the theatre have made in answer to:
   a Northbrooke and White?
   b the mayor and aldermen?

Further reading

Frederick S. Boas, *An Introduction to Tudor Drama* (Oxford University Press, 1933; reprinted 1963).

A. Gurr, *The Shakespearean Stage, 1574–1642* (Cambridge University Press, 2nd edn, 1980).

E. K. Chambers, *The Elizabethan Stage*, 4 vols. (Oxford University Press, 1923; reprinted 1965).

C. Walter Hodges, *The Globe Restored; a Study of the Elizabethan Theatre* (Oxford University Press, 2nd edn, 1968).

Boris Ford (ed.), *The Cambridge Cultural History of Britain*, vol. 3 'Renaissance and Reformation' (Cambridge University Press, 1992) – a good introduction to the subject, with a comprehensive bibliography.

33 What was the role of women in sixteenth-century England?

There is much more interest in women's history today, yet it remains a difficult subject because the historical record of the lives of the vast majority of women is so sparse. At this time women were excluded from all official positions – such as magistrate, juror or churchwarden – and they rarely owned property. Consequently, they tended to appear in official records only when their behaviour deviated from the norm – in other words, if they got into trouble. Even in parish registers, women are hard to trace because they passed from father to husband, changing their names and roles as they went. Also, practically all women were illiterate, so they could not write books or letters about themselves, or keep diaries. Even if they did, they were lucky if the manuscripts were preserved, let alone published. It has been argued that women inhabited a separate culture parallel to, but concealed behind, the better-documented, official, male one. The job of the historian is to try to explore this culture.

A patriarchal society

By the definition in the 'key term', sixteenth-century England was clearly a **patriarchal** society. Men controlled political and economic life; they also wrote the books, preached the sermons, painted the pictures and designed the buildings. The message that women were inferior to men was hammered home in every conceivable way.

KEY TERM:

Patriarchal

A patriarch, according to the dictionary, is a male religious leader, or the father or ruler of a tribe or family – for example, Abraham. However, today the term **'patriarchal'** has been adopted by feminists to describe any society, including our own, in which women are dominated by men. The cultural products of such a society will tend not only to reflect, but also to reinforce, its gender inequality.

The point that men dominated political life is not contradicted by the fact that England was ruled by females during the second half of the century. Mary and Elizabeth were exceptions – biological accidents in the line of royal succession who happened to be female. Elizabeth herself seemed to concur with the doctrine of male superiority when she proclaimed, in her famous Armada speech, 'I know I have the body of a weak and feeble woman, but I have the heart and stomach of a king'.

The usual, male point of view was forcefully put by Thomas Becon when he addressed his God on hearing of the death of the young Edward VI:

> '... in the stead of that virtuous prince thou hast set to rule over us a woman, whom nature hath formed to be in subjection unto man, and whom thou by thine holy apostle [Paul] commandest to keep silence, and not to speak in the congregation. Ah, Lord! to take away the empire from a man, and to give it to a woman, seemeth to be an evident token of thine anger toward us Englishmen.'

Women, while almost invisible politically, nevertheless played a vital role in the world of work, both domestic and public. The distribution of work between the sexes, as described by Mary Prior, has a distinctly modern ring:

> 'The division of labour between the sexes was efficient and inequitable. It depended on the obedience of the woman to the man, as Eve to Adam. Men decided what they would do and left the rest to women. The realm of work was therefore divided into two parts. What man did was definite, well-defined, limited – let us call it A. What the woman did was everything else – non-A. So the realm of work was divided without residue. We might call it the Jack Sprat Principle of the Division of Labour. According to this, if, for instance, a man was a glover, his work was clearly defined, and whatever else had to be done to keep the home fires burning was his wife's duty. If he became ill and could do less and less, then she must do more and more, supervising the apprentices, seeing the orders were fulfilled; or even by some employment, like taking in washing, she must supplement a failing business.'

Mary Prior (ed.), *Women in English Society 1500–1800* (1985).

One class of female who might have been expected to achieve some independence was the well-off widow. It is true that widows often continued their husbands' businesses, but they were not usually fully accepted by the trading community, and could not, for instance, hold office in craft guilds. There were, too, considerable pressures on widows to remarry. A woman heading her own household contradicted the patriarchal theory of the need for male leadership. When a widow died she might have been running a successful business for years, but she was invariably described in her will simply as 'a widow'.

Marriage

Tudor women were expected to marry – although a surprising proportion did not; a survey of Ealing, London, in 1599 found that almost a quarter of women aged between 40 and 70 were still single. If a woman did marry, she and her property immediately passed into the control of her husband, and she had no security against him spending her money or disposing of her movable goods. However, it was possible for a well-to-do father to provide his daughter with a marriage settlement, an income from land, which the husband could not touch except with her consent.

It used to be thought that before the industrial revolution people tended to marry at a much younger age than today, but research using parish registers has shown this to be wrong. The mean age of marriage in Elizabethan and Stuart England was about 26 for women, 27 to 29 for men. The delay was usually because it was necessary for the man to establish himself economically before he could contemplate marriage. Craft apprenticeship often lasted into the mid-twenties, and a young farmer might need to wait until his father died or retired, so that he could take over the farm lease.

What was a sixteenth-century marriage really like? According to Lawrence Stone, in his classic study *The Family, Sex and Marriage in England 1500–1800*, most marriages at this date were fairly low-key affairs in which the emotional ties between husband and wife, and between parents and children, were weak. For the majority, the claims of the 'extended family' – cousins, grandparents, and so on – as well as the claims of the local community, the nation and the church, tended to override those of their immediate family. Stone argues that it was not until the late seventeenth century that the modern 'domesticated nuclear family', with its closer, loving relationships, started to emerge. Before this, husband–wife relations were usually based more on economics than on love.

This thesis may have been true of most upper-class sixteenth-century marriages, in which dynastic and financial interests tended to be uppermost. Marriages for the sons and daughters of noblemen were often arranged for them when they were children because too much was at stake to allow them to marry whomever they felt like. For the landed classes, marriage was an important means of maintaining, or improving, one's status, a method which some fortunate women could also pursue, given that they had a higher life-expectancy than men. The career of **Bess of Hardwick** illustrates what a strong-minded gentlewoman could achieve, given a certain amount of luck.

PROFILE: *Bess of Hardwick*

Elizabeth, Countess of Shrewsbury, or **Bess of Hardwick**, as she is better known, was born in 1518 into an impoverished minor gentry family from Derbyshire. She made her fortune by a series of four marriages, each more lucrative than the one before. Her second husband, Sir William Cavendish, gave her six children and bought her the estate at Chatsworth, where she built her first house. Her fourth husband, George Talbot, Earl of Shrewsbury, elevated her into one of the oldest and richest families in the land, although by 1583 she had quarrelled with him and they were living apart. His death, in 1590, freed her to spend her immense inheritances as she wanted, and she was able to indulge her passion for building. The result was Hardwick Hall, described by Sir Roy Strong as 'the crowning jewel of the age'. Bess of Hardwick died in 1608, a wealthy woman, although two of her ambitions were unfulfilled: that Elizabeth should visit her at Hardwick, and that her granddaughter, Arabella Stuart – whose father had been Darnley's younger brother – should succeed to the English throne.

As regards the rest of Tudor society, other historians think that Stone is unduly pessimistic, for there is much evidence of loving marriages during the century – from popular literature such as ballads, to letters and wills, in many of which the dying husband took pains to provide for his future widow, and expressed his love for her. 'Relations within the early modern family were more loving, caring and "modern" than a number of recent historians have claimed,' argues J. A. Sharpe.

Nevertheless, even in the most affectionate marriages, the husband was still expected to dominate (see Figure 33.2). Take, for instance, the idea often stressed by contemporary commentators that in a truly loving match the two partners become as one. This to us seems to suggest total equality, but here is the opinion of one writer offering advice to newly-weds in 1568: the husband 'by little and little must gently procure that he may also steal away her private will and appetite, so that of two bodies there may be made one only heart'. In other words, the two are to be as one – at the expense of the wife's individuality.

It was not easy to terminate officially a marriage that had broken down. Divorce, or annulment, was extremely rare – one of the main grounds for seeking the annulment of a marriage having been removed in 1540 by a reduction in the Church's prohibited degrees of kinship. Occasionally, the Church allowed separation on grounds of cruelty or adultery, although in both these cases the law was biased in favour of the husband. A wife's

Figure 33.2 *Portraits of a married couple, Mr and Mrs Wakeman, both painted in 1566 by the same artist. Notice how the husband's dominance and the wife's passive submissiveness are conveyed through stance, gesture and clothing.*

adultery was punishable by the loss of her dowry, but there was no such penalty for a husband, and the law allowed a man to beat his wife. Privately-agreed separations, such as that between Bess of Hardwick and George Talbot, were probably common among the upper classes; lower down the scale the commonest way to end an unhappy marriage was simple desertion – walking out of the house was, of course, much easier to do for the man. Over eight and a half per cent of the married women in a survey of the poor of Norwich made in 1570 had been deserted by their husbands.

Sex and babies

Contraception may have been practised but there is, not surprisingly, little evidence, as it was considered sinful by contemporary moralists. There is only one – early seventeenth-century – reference to *coitus inter-ruptus* in the church court records so far investigated, and the first mention of condoms occurs in an early eighteenth-century medical treatise. It is difficult to know how much extra-marital sex took place in sixteenth-century England. Using parish registers, it is possible to work out how many brides were pregnant before they were married, and the proportion seems to have been quite high – about one-fifth. However, this is not evidence of promiscuity – it merely shows that sex between an engaged couple was widely seen as permissible. Abortion may have been fairly frequent, and the killing of unwanted babies, although both of these are difficult for historians to detect. So many babies were still-born anyway, or died shortly after birth, that infanticide would have been very difficult to prove.

One form of 'natural' contraception that certainly was common was breast-feeding. This produces in the nursing mother the hormone, prolactin, which inhibits ovulation. Women generally breast-fed their infants for two to three years, and this made them less likely to conceive during this period. Demographic studies have shown that if the infant died during the first two years the woman was likely to conceive again shortly after its death.

An additional piece of evidence is that the fertility of upper-class women was higher than the rest of the population owing to the fact that they did not usually breast-feed. Instead, they were expected to hand their babies over to 'wet nurses' – there was pressure to do so from husbands and friends. In several parishes within reach of London certain women made a living out of nursing babies from wealthy London families. Here, for example, are four entries from the burial register of Chesham, in Buckinghamshire, over one year (notice that the wet nurses do not even rate names):

> **26.3.1585** *Jane daughter of one Robert White of London nursed first by the wife of Adrian Goodchild and lastly by Ric. Smythes wife.*
>
> **26.4.1585** *A nurse child of one of London nursed by Ric. Twytchells wife.*
>
> **12.5.1585** *John Gallopp a nurse child of London nursed by the wife of Adrian Goodchild.*
>
> **5.9.1585** *Anthony son of John Edwardes of Tetsworth in the county of Oxford and nursed by John Lewys wife, tailor.*

Dorothy McClaren, in Mary Prior (ed.), *Women in English Society 1500–1800* (1985).

So the choice for wives during their child-bearing years was between an infant in the womb or one at the breast. How far this was a conscious choice is uncertain; as J. A. Sharpe wrote: 'this was a society many of whose members were strangely innocent in sexual matters. Sexuality was little discussed other than in very general terms.'

Just as adultery was held to be a more serious offence for a wife than for a husband, so the same double standard held for single women of any class. An unmarried daughter who became pregnant could expect little mercy from her family; if a marriage could not be arranged she would be lucky if she were not put out into the street. For the poor, bastardy was also likely to involve a charge on the parish, and here again, punishment was usually more severe for the woman. The following is an extract from the diary of a Kent Justice of the Peace:

'24 December [1583]. *Mr Dr William Lewyn and I [JPs] took order that Margaret Dutton should be first whipped at Gravesend and then sent to the house of correction for a bastard woman child there born and begotten on her by Robert Cole, as it is thought, whom also we committed till he give sureties to appear at the Easter sessions, for to stand to the order of the bench there, because he refused to perform the order set down against him by my Lord Cobham and Mr Somer.*

'*The same day also he and I took like order for the whipping of Abigail Sherwood for a bastard man-child born by her at Chatham and for her like sending to the house of correction. But as touching the reputed father, we left the decision thereof to the ecclesiastical trial, for that she confessed herself to have been carnally known of many men. The child also was dead so that nothing was to be done in the parish.*'

Conyers Read, *William Lambarde and Local Government* (1962).

The effects of the Reformation

The Reformation changed many aspects of English life. One effect on the position of women was that after the dissolution of the monasteries it was no longer possible to become a nun, which limited the options available. To balance this, however, marriage prospects improved as the clergy no longer had to remain celibate but were permitted to take wives.

It has been argued that the Reformation gave the family a greater importance in religious life, particularly as regards religious instruction and prayer. One duty that fell to wives was the religious instruction of young children, upon which the Protestant reformers laid great stress. More generally, it has been suggested that Protestantism, by asserting the priesthood of all believers, and the significance of individual faith and judgement, may have raised the status of women. People of all classes, and both sexes, were encouraged to read the Bible for themselves.

As against this optimistic picture of women reading the Bible, and teaching their children to read it, however, one has to remember that it could only have applied to a tiny minority. Female literacy among all classes remained extremely low well into the next century. Out of 706 women sampled between 1561 and 1631 from the records of the church courts in the diocese of Durham – admittedly a remote and backward part of the kingdom – 690 (98 per cent) could not sign their own names (see chapter 31).

Opportunities for women to display determination and even heroism arose from the schisms caused by the Reformation. Frequently, within a penalised religious minority it was the women who took the lead – in supporting forbidden beliefs and practices, sheltering outlawed persons, hiding banned books. Early in the century there were many women in the Lollard movement (see chapter 3); others were martyred for their Protestant faith under Henry VIII or Mary. For instance, Anne Askew, the daughter of a Lincolnshire knight, was arrested, interrogated and finally burnt, in 1546, for denying the doctrine of transubstantiation. Women like her broke the contemporary stereotype of females as frail, demure and easily led.

> *'Though some died at the stake alongside their husbands, they were not merely passive victims, guided only by human affection or despair. Rather do they appear as free agents who had trained themselves for the task, embracing the ideas of a biblical Christianity and a "true" church. Their inspiration arose from hearing sermons, from witnessing other martyrdoms, above all from reading – or hearing read – the Bible, and becoming convinced that their salvation depended on their adherence to the cause. Many are shown as activist members of Protestant groups or congregations. Some deprived themselves of food in order to train for the conditions they would meet in prison. Others left their husbands and children, finding employment in strange places or hiding from persecution in "bushes, groves and fields". In their resolute, independent spirit, their rejection of women's conventional submissiveness, they seem a new race of beings in English history.'*
>
> A. G. Dickens, *The English Reformation* (2nd edn, 1989).

Another group of women who broke the stereotype were those female Catholic recusants in Elizabeth's reign, who risked their lives by putting their religion before the demands of the state. In many recusant households it was the wife who provided the religious leadership, while her husband concentrated on maintaining public respectability, often acting as a 'church papist' to avoid the penalties of the 1581 Act (see chapter 27). Sometimes these wives got away with it – on the whole public opinion was against the state intruding into families, or punishing husbands for their wives' behaviour. However, in other cases, especially if it was suspected that priests were being sheltered, the wife was arrested. Because married women technically owned no property, it often proved impractical to fine them, so they were locked up, sometimes for long periods. In 1594, for instance, it was reported that 11 recusant women had died in Ousebridge gaol, York, out of 30 imprisoned

PROFILE: *Margaret Clitheroe*

Margaret Clitheroe was not a gentlewoman but the daughter of a York chandler, and the wife of a butcher. She was a devout Catholic who managed to spend two hours every day in prayer and devotion, as well as attending mass and evensong when possible, although she was daily occupied in the butcher's shop until the evening. When she was arrested and charged with assisting Jesuits and seminary priests it was stated that she had been very active, maintaining three hiding places for priests on the move. She refused to answer these charges in order not to betray the names and whereabouts of priests, and so she was condemned to the barbarous punishment for those who would not plead, which involved being pressed to death by increasingly heavy stones. She died in 1586, aged 30, but she left two sons who went abroad to study for the priesthood and a daughter who became a nun.

there during the previous 30 years. The first woman to die for the Catholic faith in Elizabethan England was **Margaret Clitheroe**.

Task

As has been shown in this chapter, historians disagree about the nature of marriage in sixteenth-century England. Here are two contrasting views:

> *'About all that can be said with confidence on the matter of emotional relationships within the sixteenth and early seventeenth [century] family at all social levels is that there was a general psychological atmosphere of distance, manipulation and deference; that high mortality rates made deep relationships very imprudent; that marriages were arranged by parents and kin for economic and social reasons with minimal consultation of the children; that evidence of close bonding between parents and children is hard, but not impossible, to document; and that evidence of close affection between husband and wife is both ambiguous and rare.'*

Lawrence Stone, *The Family, Sex and Marriage in England 1500–1800* (1979).

> '*Married love clearly existed in practice and was highly valued as an ideal. We cannot say how typical it was ... Surviving correspondence of that time is sufficiently abundant to show that in many marriages expectations were high, emotional demands extensive, mutual involvement deep, and shared interests and sense of humour very important.*'
>
> Ralph Houlbrooke, *The English Family 1450–1700* (1984).

Each member of the class should research evidence of the nature of a marriage, or marriages, from sixteenth-century England. After briefly reporting back, the class should discuss whether the evidence they have assembled supports Stone's or Houlbrooke's views.

Further reading

Ralph A. Houlbrooke, *The English Family 1450–1700* (Addison Wesley Longman, 1984) – the standard work on the topic.

Mary Prior (ed.), *Women in English Society 1500–1800* (Methuen, 1985) – an interesting collection of articles from the feminist point of view.

J. A. Sharpe, *Early Modern England; A Social History 1550–1760* (Edward Arnold, 1987) – has a useful chapter on family life.

Lawrence Stone, *The Family, Sex and Marriage in England 1500–1800* (Penguin, abridged edn, 1979).

34 What was 'the great rebuilding'?

Building under Henry VIII

Before 1547 the Crown was the main inspiration for upper-class building in England. The young Henry VIII's many interests included architecture, where he had a strong desire to impress Europe, and in particular his arch-competitor, Francis I of France. Yet the brilliant promise of Henry's early years, in this field as in others, was not entirely fulfilled. It is true that he acquired many houses, and built, or rebuilt, many more – he owned over 60 by his death. However, of these it seems the only one to show much originality or flair was Nonsuch in Surrey, which was intended to rival Francis I's palace at Fontainebleau. Unfortunately, Nonsuch was demolished in the seventeenth century; our only knowledge of it comes from archaeological research and one or two contemporary illustrations (see Figure 34.1).

Henry VIII was also the main inspiration and driving force for members of the political elite to build their own houses. Due partly to the following factors, the king was often in a position to dictate where and how his courtiers and nobles lived:

1 During the reign several of Henry's most important subjects had their careers cut short by accusations of treason. In 1521 Edward Stafford (Duke of Buckingham) was executed for treason, one of the charges being that he had displayed his own status and power too extravagantly in his rebuilding of Thornbury Castle, which at that time rivalled any house owned by the king. The fall of someone as wealthy as Buckingham meant rich pickings for others, and Henry was able to reward his favourites with Buckingham's estates, on which they raised their own houses. The fall of Wolsey in 1529 was another opportunity to benefit from the spoils of the victim – although in this case Henry kept for himself Wolsey's two largest palaces, Hampton Court and York Place.

2 From the 1530s the king also had the monastic properties at his disposal, to sell or give away to favoured servants. A former monastery, especially if it was in good order and had not been totally dismantled by the monastic commissioners, was a bargain. Several landowners built themselves houses on ex-monastic land; some, such as Thomas Wriothesley at Titchfield, incorporated monastic buildings into their new country houses.

PALATIVM REGIVM IN ANGLIÆ REGNO APPELLATVM NONCIVTZ,
Hoc est nusquam simile.

Figure 34.1 Nonsuch Palace, Surrey: an engraving by Franz Hogenberg, 1582

3 After becoming head of the church Henry made it his policy to reduce the wealth and status of the bishops. This included forcing several of them to give up their great London houses, which also ended up in the hands of courtiers. One example was Edward Seymour, the future Duke of Somerset, who built Somerset House on what had been the Bishop of Chester's property on the Strand.

For these reasons, many of Henry's courtiers found themselves with land on which to build a house fitting their status. Yet again, as with Henry's own projects, there was not much architectural innovation. The comparative peace of the countryside meant that fortified houses were no longer necessary, and it became fashionable to turn one's medieval castle, or fortified manor house, into something more comfortable. War-like trappings – such as battlements and moats – were retained for reasons of prestige, but inside, new domestic ranges appeared, with walls pierced by windows, and the skyline punctuated with chimneys. It was important, however, to avoid the mistakes made by Buckingham and Wolsey, and build on so lavish a scale as to rival the king. In any case, most of the efforts of these early Tudor builders are no longer visible today, having been pulled down or modified by their Elizabethan successors.

Elizabethan 'prodigy' houses

Between Henry's death and 1603 not a single royal palace was built or acquired. Elizabeth was not interested in squandering her scarce resources in this fashion. As Parliament was informed in 1571, she did not require 'gorgeous, sumptuous, superfluous buildings'. Now it was the turn of courtiers and statesmen to make the architectural decisions rather than the monarch. Elizabeth encouraged her subjects to build on a scale which, earlier, would have been considered a threat to the status of the monarchy. Each summer she went on progress to a different part of the country, enjoying the hospitality of the principal houses in the region. If courtiers wished to receive their rewards in the way of offices and patronage they had to be prepared to build on the scale necessary to entertain the Queen in appropriate style, which meant providing for about 150 people for as long as they wanted to stay.

A royal visit was definitely a mixed blessing – the expense was appalling, and so was the risk of Elizabeth disapproving of the accommodation available. As Cecil wrote to Sir Christopher Hatton about their respective houses, 'God send us both long to enjoy her for whom we both meant to exceed our purses in these'. Cecil himself extended his mansion, Theobalds, in Hertfordshire, until it was the largest house in the kingdom. Elizabeth stayed there 13 times – but he made enough to pay for it all. It was different for Hatton, who put himself heavily into debt by building the nearby Holdenby, which then stood for ten years, full of servants, waiting for the royal visit that never came. The house was always a white elephant. It went on Hatton's death to a nephew who could not afford to run it, was sold to James I in 1605, and was finally pulled down during the reign of Charles II.

Huge houses such as these, built more for splendour and prestige than comfort, and with an eye to a royal visit, were known as 'prodigy' houses. Leading examples were Cecil's houses of Theobalds and Burghley, Leicester's at Kenilworth, Hatton's at Holdenby and Kirkby, Sir John Thynne's at Longleat, **Sir Francis Willoughby's** at Wollaton and the Countess of Shrewsbury's at Hardwick. Many of them today, according to Lawrence Stone in *The Crisis of the Aristocracy*, 'still lie heavily about the English countryside like the fossilised bones of the great reptiles of the Carboniferous age'. Some, including Holdenby and Theobalds, were built round courtyards like medieval palaces; others consisted of a single dominating mass, sometimes on an E plan, with a central porch and a wing on either side of the main block.

Architecturally, these great palaces were a mixture of Gothic and classical. As under Henry VIII, there was much conscious copying of the features of medieval castles, such as battlements and towers, or the hammer-beam roof in the hall at Burghley House. This was in keeping with the contemporary spirit of romantic nationalism – the owners of 'prodigy' houses were the devoted knights of Elizabeth, the virgin queen, who had to be protected against a hostile world. The fort-

PROFILE: *Sir Francis Willoughby*

Sir Francis Willoughby was a Nottinghamshire landowner who exploited his inherited estates to the full, by developing coalmining, iron-smelting, and the growing of woad for cloth dyeing. He was a cultivated gentleman who owned a library of some 250 books, including several on architecture, and he was a man obsessed with wealth and status. During the 1570s he invested over £1,000 a year for eight years in building Wollaton Hall on the site of an old manor house. It was intended as a showplace to impress the Queen, and its apartments were designed to be grand enough for a royal visit. To advise him Willoughby employed the well-known architect – although this term had not yet come into fashion – Robert Smythson, the designer of Longleat. Smythson was familiar with the work of continental architects, among them Andrea Palladio (1508–80), and he was prepared to employ classical motifs, varying them to suit English taste. Wollaton, which still survives today (see Figure 34.2), is a romantic and exuberant palace in stone, perched on a hillside, with wide views over the surrounding countryside.

Figure 34.2 Wollaton Hall, Nottinghamshire, built in 1588

ifications were not serious, and the high walls were pierced with numerous windows and surmounted with decorative features. By this time, too, something was known of the rules of classical building. Many gentlemen had in their libraries translations of French or Italian writers on architecture, and they occasionally tried to show their sophistication by embellishing their new homes with classical motifs. However, it was not until much later that the concepts of proportion, harmony and simplicity, which were at the heart of the classical ideal, were properly understood in England.

Within a prodigy house the main rooms usually included:

1 *The hall*   Still a large and decorative room at the main entrance of the house, but its importance had much declined, and it was no longer used for eating or entertainment as it once had been.

2 *The great chamber*   The ceremonial pivot of the house, used for important, formal meals, as well as for music, dancing and dramatic performances. It was usually the most richly decorated room in the house, with tapestries, elegant furniture, heraldic glass in the windows and elaborate plasterwork.

3 *Withdrawing-chamber(s)*   The owner's private sitting, eating and reception rooms, leading off the great chamber. Often the bed-chambers adjoined them.

4 *The long gallery*   Sixteenth-century doctors stressed the need for regular exercise, and long galleries made this possible in all weathers. They were long and comparatively narrow; the one built at Worksop in the 1580s, which was the largest in England at the time, measured 212 by 36 feet [64.6m × 11m]. A second function of the gallery was to hang portraits, which made them into status symbols as well as places of exercise.

5 *Parlours*   All the above rooms were usually on the first or second floors; below them were the ground-floor parlours, which tended to be more informal. Increasingly, there was a trend for the owners of the houses to live and eat in the more private atmosphere of the parlours, and leave the ceremonial rooms for visitors and special occasions.

The great rebuilding

The most widespread architectural changes of the century took place at a lower social level than the 'prodigy' houses. In 1953 W. G. Hoskins wrote an influential article in which he argued that between about 1570 and 1640 a revolution took place in the housing of the greater part of the population. This involved the rebuilding or modernisation of the medieval house, and a remarkable increase in household furnishings and equipment.

What enabled many yeomen and husbandmen to convert their homes, or build new ones, was the rapid rise in food prices during the second half of the century (see chapter 16). Freeholders, and tenant farmers whose rents were fixed and could not be altered, were in a position to mark up large profits owing to the widening gap between their costs and the selling price of their produce in the market (see chapter 29). As William Harrison put it in 1577:

> '*Every man almost is a builder and he that hath bought any small parcel of ground, be it never so little, will not be quiet till he have pulled down the old house (if any were there standing) and set up a new after his own devise.*'

In and before the early sixteenth century the houses of most people below the gentry consisted mainly of a single, dark room, open to the roof, and heated by an open fire in the middle of the floor. By the mid seventeenth century this was no longer so. Houses were now divided into several rooms; there was often an upstairs floor, and living rooms at least were heated by enclosed fireplaces and lit by glazed windows.

The crucial improvement when modernising an existing medieval house was to replace the open hearth with a fireplace and chimney. Having done this it was no longer necessary to leave the house open to the roof so as to let the smoke out, so the main room, or hall-house as it was called, could be horizontally subdivided with an upper floor. Other rooms could also have fireplaces, either from the hall chimney stack or from other chimneys, and it now became possible to sleep upstairs in relative comfort. Whereas in Henry VIII's reign the average house contained three rooms, between 1570 and 1603 it had four or five. Towards the end of Elizabeth's reign a yeoman might have six, seven or eight rooms, a husbandman two or three, rather than the one-room cottages common in 1500.

At about the same date, cheap panes of glass were becoming available for the first time, enabling draught-free lighting of the main rooms. Without smoke everywhere from the hall fire, the house could now be kept much cleaner. It became worthwhile to brighten up the interior walls by hanging painted cloths – the ordinary man's tapestry – and acquiring more furniture, which also could be covered with ornamental textiles.

A greater variety of clothing, bed-linen and domestic utensils, and the substitution of pewter dishes for wooden ones were other features of this period. Evidence for these changes comes mainly from probate inventories, but also from contemporary writers, such as **William Harrison**.

'The ancient manors and houses of our gentlemen are yet, and for the most part, of strong timber, in framing whereof our carpenters have been and are worthily preferred before those of like science among all other nations. Howbeit, such as be lately builded are commonly either of brick or hard stone or both, their rooms large and comely, and houses of office further distant from their lodgings. Those of the nobility are likewise wrought with brick and hard stone, as provision may best be made, but so magnificent and stately as the basest house of a baron doth often match in our days with some honours of princes in old time ...

'The furniture of our houses also exceedeth and is grown in manner even to passing delicacy; and herein I do not speak of the nobility and gentry only but likewise of the lowest sort in most places of our South Country that have anything at all to take to. Certes, in noblemen's houses it is not rare to see abundance of arras, rich hangings of tapestry, silver vessel, and so much other plate as may furnish sundry cupboards, to the sum oftentimes of £1,000 or £2,000 at the least, whereby the value of this and the rest of their stuff doth grow to be almost inestimable. Likewise in the houses of knights, gentlemen, merchantmen, and some other wealthy citizens, it is not geason [uncommon] to behold generally their great provision of tapestry, Turkey work [Turkish tapestry], pewter, brass, fine linen, and thereto costly cupboards of plate, worth £500 or £600 or £1,000, to be deemed by estimation.

'But as herein all these sorts do far exceed their elders and predecessors, and in neatness and curiosity the merchant all other, so in time past the costly furniture stayed there, whereas now it is descended yet lower, even unto the inferior artificers and many farmers, who, by virtue of their old and not their new leases, have for the most part learned also to garnish their cupboards with plate, their joint beds [expensive beds made by joiners] with tapestry and silk hangings, and their tables with carpets and fine napery.'

William Harrison, *The Description of England* (written in 1577, published in 1968).

Probate inventories

An Act of 1529 stated that a detailed inventory of the 'goods, chattels and cattle' of a deceased person must accompany his or her will. These inventories were made, or 'appraised', by reputable neighbours, who went from room to room noting and assessing the value of all movable goods. Thousands of them have survived, and they are a most important source for the social historian, especially for their evidence about smaller houses, about which little else is known. Because there are so many they can be

---

PROFILE: *William Harrison*

William Harrison (1534–93) was the author of *The Description of England*, first published in 1577, which has been called a classic of social observation. He was a well-educated clergyman, with degrees from both Oxford and Cambridge, but chose to spend most of his life as rector of a small, rural parish in Essex. He was interested in everything – not only political institutions and social classes, but also what people ate, their clothing and their houses. Because he was not a man of obvious genius he shows us more than any other similar writer what the average Elizabethan was really like.

---

used to make statistical comparisons between different periods, or different parts of the country. Much of the evidence backing W. G. Hoskins's assertion that the period of the great rebuilding saw a remarkable increase in household possessions comes from inventories. However, they are not always easy to use. There are often local or dialect words whose meaning has been lost, and the appraisers sometimes mis-valued the property. Also, they did not always specify which room they were investigating, so it is dangerous to deduce a house plan from an inventory.

One example of a probate inventory is printed below, to give some idea of the difficulties as well as the merits of this type of source. Some meanings of words are given, and in most other cases it should be possible to make an educated guess. The original spelling has been retained.

Inventory of Richard Marshall, gentleman of Durham, 30 March 1581

In the hall

One irron chemney with a porr [poker], a pair tonges, a irron showell, ij raken croukes and a gerd iron 13s 4d. A kerved cubbord 1l[£1]. A duble counter [dresser], ij fourmes, and a stoull 12s. One letle foldinge table 3s. Two chares and ij stoulls 2s. The hanginges in the hall, and a glase cagge 1s 8d. On the cubords hed, ij basens, ij euers, ij saltes, ij candelstekes 9s 4d. vij platers, iiij putter dyshes, iiij plattes, vj saweers, iiij banketing dyshes, vi podden dyshes 1l. A payre of playinge tabells 1s 8d. A standing cup of selver 26s 8d. Fower selver spones 10s.

In the buttre

An ambre [cupboard] with iij lokes and keys 6s 8d. xv pece of putter, ij saweers, vj old podden desses 11s 8d. Thre red candelstekes and a chaffen dyshe 1s 5d. Two morters of brasse and ij iron pestells 8s. A potell pott, a three-pynt pott, iij quart potes, a pynt pot, a gyll pot, a flour pot, an old salt, a dossen spones, a ten goblet 4s 6d. A box with trenchers and a box for ottmell 1s. Two harden [linen] bordclothes, a towell, iij table napkens 1s 6d. Two grattes and a lantrone [lantern?] 12d.

In the ketchinge and too-fall [lean-to outhouse]

A irron chemney, a rak crouke and a payre poteleps [pothooks]   7s. Fower brass pottes, a skellet, a posnet, an old yetlen [these are all types of cooking pot] and a letell kettle with iij fett   16s. Two frying panes and a droping pane   2s 6d. A bord, a old maskfatt [barrell], iij choppinge knyffes   1s 6d. Fyve skelles [wooden buckets] for water, a fyche basket   2s. A axe, a hatchet, a old belstaf and a walking staf   12d.

In the chamber

A joynd [wooden] bede and a hurll [made of hurdles] bed, ij old mattresses and a credell   11s. A letell irron chemney and a paire tonges   1s. The hanginge about the chamber, ij platters and a bassen   7s.

In the ouder chamber

Thre chestes, and an old cheste   8s.

In the big chamber

A stand bedd with v cortens and a testers [canopy] of gren and red say [fine cloth]   10s. A lettell joyned table and a cownter   5s 6d. A cheste with loke and key   3s 4d. Thre fether bedes, iij bolsters and ix lettell coddes [pillows]   46s 8d. Two oversey bed coveringes, the one lyned with harden   33s 4d. Sexe coverlettes   12s. Nyne queshinges, and iij thrombe [coarse cloth] ones   18s. Sexe paire and one ode lene [linen] shettes   26s 8d. Two old bordclothes and a dossen table napkens   5s 4d. One joyned bedsted without postes   4s. One hurll bedsted, and hanginges in the chamber   2s. Two payr of whit blankettes 1s. Two chares, v tressells, an old hogshed, a great barrell and a dossen bedstaufes   2s.

For his apparrell

One ewe bowe   6s. A old sattayne dublet and a mellen fostean [?] dublet   12s. A blake cloke with sleves 20s. A Spaneche capp of fressadowe [?]   4s. A freese coott [rough, hairy coat]   2s 6d. Two pair hosse [stockings]   3s. Two gownes of brodclothe   20s. A blake brodclothe coott   3s.

In the stable

A horse   40s. Two kyene   53s 4d. One ryding sadle with stiropes and gertes, another sadle without ger, a lod-saddle without geer, and a brydle   3s 4d. A horse rake, a cawell, iij trowes, a old bedsted, a swall of a tre, and sartayn fyer wood   3s. Two iron forkes and a horse comb   8d. vij sekes   4s. . . .

Durham Wills and Inventories, vol. II (1869).

Task

1 a What can be worked out from this inventory about Richard Marshall's standard of living?

b Would we know from his possessions that he was a gentleman?

c Can one say anything about the plan of his house?

2 Richard Marshall came from one of the poorer counties of the realm. Does his inventory nevertheless confirm any of the points made by William Harrison?

3 What does this example illustrate about the difficulties of using inventories as a historical source?

Further reading

John Buxton, *Elizabethan Taste* (Macmillan, 1966).

Boris Ford (ed.), *Sixteenth Century Britain*, vol. 3 of 'The Cambridge Cultural History of Britain' (Cambridge University Press, 1992).

Alice T. Friedman, *House and Household in Elizabethan England* (University of Chicago Press, 1989).

W. G. Hoskins, 'The Rebuilding of Rural England, 1570–1640', in *Past and Present*, no. 4, Nov. 1953 – a pioneering article which set off the debate on rebuilding.

Maurice Howard, *The Early Tudor Country House* (George Philip, 1987) – a valuable study dealing with a topic where the evidence is scanty.

Colin Platt, *The Great Rebuilding of Tudor and Stuart England* (UCL Press, 1994).

35 England in 1603

Population and the rise of London

By the time Queen Elizabeth died, the population of England was some 4 million – twice what it had been at the accession of her grandfather, the first Tudor, Henry VII. This increase was not distributed evenly throughout the kingdom. Many rural areas had seen the number of their inhabitants decline, as arable farming gave way to pasture – though this was the tail end of a process that had started well before 1485. Conversely, towns were swelling in size – above all London, which now had some 225,000 people living in it, with more arriving every year. The Tudor period saw London establish that predominance in English life which it has never lost. Even in such matters as fashion the capital set the tone, and one writer – not, of course, a Londoner – complained that 'no gentleman can be content to have either cap, coat, doublet, hose or shirt made in his country [local area], but they must have their gear from London'.

Physically speaking, London had changed a great deal. In what we now call 'the City' – which, in the Tudor period, was the principal residential area – the wealthy financier Sir Thomas Gresham built a substantial mansion for himself which had an arcaded ground floor. This served as a model for the Royal Exchange which he erected at his own cost in 1568 and presented to the City as a centre for commercial transactions. Further west, between the City proper and Westminster, the 'new men' who had risen to the top of Tudor society had acquired the houses and lands which had formerly belonged to the Church. The Russells, for instance, had obtained possession of the garden of the abbey, or convent, of Westminster, and were shortly to transform it into the prime residential site of Covent Garden. Sir Nicholas Bacon – Lord Keeper of the Great Seal under Elizabeth, and father of Francis Bacon, the distinguished philosopher and historian – lived in York House, which, as its name implies, had previously been the townhouse of the archbishops of York. Further west still, the Crown had taken over Wolsey's mansion of White Hall and turned it into a royal palace.

The Church

While the bishops had had to part with their town houses they had at least retained their positions. The same was not true of the abbots, who disappeared from the scene completely after the accession of Elizabeth and the establishment of a Protestant church. As for the abbeys over which they had once ruled, these were slowly crumbling into picturesque decay, unless they had been transformed into noble mansions. Although the bishops survived they did so with reduced resources, for Elizabeth had no qualms about seizing episcopal property in order to reward her courtiers. While bishops retained their authority within the church they had lost the major role in secular government which they had enjoyed up to and including Wolsey. Until Whitgift was appointed to it in 1589 the Elizabethan Privy Council contained not one bishop – a far cry from Henry VII's days, when the council had been dominated by ecclesiastics.

Poverty

The growth of London was due in no small part to the pressure of poverty. Men and women who could not find employment in the countryside flocked to the towns, particularly the capital. Their plight was a reflection of the widening gap between rich and poor which opened up as the Tudor period was drawing to its close. The increase in population was not accompanied by any significant increase in jobs, and while those who were doing well out of administration, trade or landowning lived in an ever more opulent style, men and women at the bottom end of the social scale struggled to keep their heads above water. When harvest failures sent grain prices soaring, as was the case in the terrible years of the mid 1590s, the poor came close to starvation and were so weakened by hunger that they could not hold out against illness and infection. Both central and local government intervened at such times with emergency measures – commandeering grain to provide minimum rations and stepping up poor relief – but these were just palliatives. They did not alter the underlying inequalities of English society.

Trade and industry

At the end of the Tudor period, as at the beginning, the manufacture of woollen cloth was the single most important English industry. There were very few factories, however. Cloth merchants, or clothiers, rode round the country buying raw wool from the farmers and 'putting it out' to housewives to spin into cloth in their own homes. The finished product would then be collected and despatched to foreign markets. After the mid-century crisis of over-production, Antwerp had recovered its role as the principal distribution centre for English cloth, and the recoinage carried out in the early years of Elizabeth's reign put an end to fluctuations in the value of English currency – so damaging for commerce. However, this era of stability did not last long, for the outbreak of rebellion in the Low Countries in 1572 undermined the position of Antwerp and made the search for alternative outlets more urgent.

One consequence of this was a revival of interest in overseas ventures. The opening up of trade with Russia via the White Sea was one example; Hawkins's transhipment of African slaves to America another (see chapter 30). The Eastland Company built up trade with the Baltic region, while the Levant Company did the same in the Mediterranean. But the most promising development came only at the end of Elizabeth's reign, with the setting up of the East India Company, and by the time this venture started to yield rich rewards the Tudor period was long past. The same was true of attempts to breach the Spanish and Portuguese monopoly of colonisation in the New World. In 1585 Sir Walter Raleigh established a settlement on the island of Roanoke in the area that he named Virginia in honour of his sovereign, the Virgin Queen. It only lasted a brief while, however, for it lacked regular supplies, and further attempts at settlement were hampered by the same basic defect. When Elizabeth died she owned no possessions outside the British Isles – not even Calais, which had been lost under Mary. Keen-eyed observers might have discerned the faint outline of the future British Empire beyond the seas, but this lay well in the future.

So too did the Industrial Revolution. There were advances in industry during Elizabeth's reign, but they were essentially small scale. The production of iron increased, and England became famous for its iron cannon. The extraction of lead was also stepped up, as was the mining of tin, mainly in Cornwall. The principal mining activity was that of coal, centred in the Durham region, from where it was sent to Newcastle for shipment to London and abroad. 'Sea-coals' were already poisoning the London air in Elizabeth's reign, but coal played little or no part in manufacturing. The blast furnaces which opened up expansion in the iron industry, for instance, were fuelled by wood, not coal, and were also dependent upon water power. Hence the industry was located in the woodland regions of Sussex and Kent rather than, as later, the north and midlands.

Government

Although the Wars of the Roses had not wiped out the English aristocracy they had reduced its numbers as well as its influence. This left the way open for country gentry to play a bigger part in the administration of their local areas – for instance, as JPs – and in national affairs, as MPs. During the course of the sixteenth century, however, as new men rose to the top of society – particularly through service to the Crown – a Tudor aristocracy emerged. The Russells became earls of Bedford, the Wriotheleys earls of Southampton, the Dudleys earls of Leicester, and the Paulets marquises of Winchester. Many of these titles were acquired during Edward VI's reign, when first Somerset and then Northumberland were anxious to buy support (see chapter 11). Elizabeth was as careful about the granting of titles as she was about the granting of money, and even William Cecil who served her faithfully throughout the course of his long life was only advanced to the rank of baron – the lowest rung in the aristocratic ladder.

Elizabeth's caution when it came to creating new peers was understandable, for the memory was still fresh of what had happened a century or so earlier, when the great noble houses had come to blows over who should wear the crown. The Queen had no intention of allowing England to slip back once again into the anarchy of the Wars of the Roses, and throughout the greater part of her reign she carefully balanced one interest group or faction against another. But this system broke down in the 1590s. One reason for its collapse was the death of many of the great Elizabethans on whom she had relied for support – Leicester in 1588, Sir Christopher Hatton in 1591, and Burghley (William Cecil) in 1598. Another was the challenge from her young favourite, the Earl of Essex. He chose the military route to fame and covered himself with glory by leading the successful expedition against Cadiz in 1596.

Essex was out for power, determined to fill the vacuum left by the removal of Burghley from the scene. But Burghley's son and political heir, Robert Cecil, was equally determined to maintain his family's hold on power – and the profits that came with it. In the bitter struggle between the two men and their supporters the Queen was the loser, for she could no longer maintain the balance between the factions. Essex's rashness led him into an uprising that cost him his life. The 'Cecilians' were now supreme and the Queen's freedom of action thereby limited.

Fortunately for Elizabeth she did not have much longer to live. Essex was executed in February 1601, and the Queen died at her grandfather's palace at Richmond in Surrey just over two years later. Taken as a whole, her long reign had been outstandingly successful, and was to become more so in retrospect. But the 'Elizabethan system' had broken down by the time she died and she bequeathed to her Stuart successor problems that even she, with all her political skill and courage, would have found difficult to resolve.

Index

Addison Wesley Longman Limited,
Edinburgh Gate, Harlow,
Essex CM20 2JE, England
and Associated Companies throughout the World

First published 1997
© Addison Wesley Longman Limited 1997
Set in 10/13 Meridien Roman
Produced by Longman Singapore Publishers (Pte) Limited
Printed in Singapore

ISBN 0 582 08404 0

Acknowledgements

We are grateful to the following for permission to reproduce photos and other copyright material:

Reproduced by permission of the Baroness Herries, page 73; from the Collection at Blair Castle, Perthshire, page 132; Bodleian Library, Oxford, page 43; Bridgeman Art Library/Private Collection, page 197; The British Library, page 122; by permission of the Syndics of Cambridge University Library, pages 65, 107 above, 142, 164, 182, 196, 201, 262, 280; His Grace the Archbishop of Canterbury, pages 102 above, 228 (photo: Courtauld Institute of Art); The College of Arms, page 123; E.T Archive, pages 28, 105, 209, 295; © The Earl of Rosebury, page 77; Mary Evans Picture Library, page 67; Fotomas Index, pages 127, 246; Getty Images, pages 90 left, 102 below, 130, 223, 268; National Gallery, London, page 119; National Maritime Museum, London, pages 214, 215; National Portrait Gallery, London, pages 8 below, 29, 33, 41, 52, 55, 111, 277, 287; National Trust Photographic Library/J.Whitaker, page 107 below; City of Nottingham, Public Relations, page 297; Public Record Office, pages 9, 203; RCHME © Crown Copyright, page 5; The Royal Collection © Her Majesty the Queen, pages 8 above, 45; by courtesy of The Marquess of Salisbury, pages 163 (photo: National Portrait Gallery), 178; Time Inc, N.Y, pages 56, 90 right; © The Board of Trustees of the Victoria & Albert Museum, page 179; Visual Arts Library, page 80.

We were unable to trace the copyright holders of the following and would be grateful for any information that would enable us to do so, pages 172, 288.

Cover photograph: *Elizabeth I when Princess,* portrait by an unknown artist. The Royal Collection © Her Majesty Queen Elizabeth II.
Series editors: Eric Evans and Christopher Culpin
Publisher: Joan Ward
Editor: Steve Attmore
Designer: Michael Harris
Picture researcher: Louise Edgeworth
Artwork: Tony Richardson

The Publisher's policy is to use paper manufactured from sustainable forests.